THE CONTINUITY OF COTTON

THE CONTINUITY OF COTTON

PLANTER POLITICS IN GEORGIA
1865–1892

Lewis Nicholas Wynne

MERCER

ISBN 0-86554-215-5

The paper used in this publication meets
the minimum requirements of American National Standard
for Information Sciences—Permanence of Paper
for Printed Library Materials, ANSI Z39.48-1984.

Library of Congress Cataloging-in-Publication Data
Wynne, Lewis Nicholas.
The continuity of cotton.
Bibliography: p. 185
Includes index
1. Georgia—Politics and government—1865-1950.
2. Plantation owners—Georgia—Political activity—
History—19th century.   3. Reconstruction—Georgia.
I. Title.
F291.W96   1986   975.7'04   86-12777
ISBN 0-86554-215-5 (alk. paper)

CONTENTS

For Jeanette, Patrick, and Lisa

PREFACE

One of the most intriguing aspects of Southern history in the post-Civil War period is the role played by the antebellum planters who had once dominated the social, political, and economic activities of the region. For men who had shaped the entire context of prewar society, the unsuccessful effort to create a separate nation was financially and psychologically devastating. Emancipation—the cost of failure—struck at the very foundations of planter power, and the millions of dollars in losses it entailed caused severe hardships. For some, the necessity of finding new methods of keeping the plantation system alive was too much, and they quickly succumbed to failure. For others, emancipation was simply another in a long line of challenges that had to be met and mastered.

The central question asked in this study is, "To what extent did antebellum planters, or their descendants, manage to retain their power and influence in the postbellum period?" Were they, as C. Vann Woodward suggests, forced to assume new roles as urban-industrial elites, merged into the mainstream of a national industrialized economy and stripped of their distinctive identity as planters? Or, as Wilbur J. Cash argued, did they adapt to the new conditions of the postwar period and emerge as the major force in Southern society?

The question of continuity of planters is one that has received a great deal of attention from recent scholars such as Jonathan Wiener and Dwight Billings. Much of the theoretical framework for these recent works is derived from the work of earlier scholars like Ulrich Bonnell Phillips and Cash, and their findings are incorporated into this study. Indeed, many older studies provide valuable insights into the postbellum South and offer more recent scholars of the period an unusually rich source of information.

Many people have helped with this project. Numan V. Bartley and Charles Crowe provided valuable insights and comments during the dissertation stage of this project. Peyton McCrary, my colleague at the University of South Alabama, made critical comments and suggestions, and while I didn't respond to all of them, he did force me to rethink some ideas.

Like me, scholars in Georgia history must be especially appreciative of the tremendous staffs at all the public and private libraries in the state. The University of Georgia, the Georgia Institute of Technology, Georgia State University, Emory University, the Atlanta Historical Society Library, and the Georgia Department of Archives and History provided much needed help.

Rose Snow was especially helpful when this project was being written as a dissertation, and she provided many late night conversations about content and style. She was a pillar of support during a difficult period of my life and deserves much of the credit, if any is forthcoming, for this project. Thank you, Rose.

My children, Patrick and Lisa, are important to any project I undertake, and I love them for their loyal support. Jeanette Boughner deserves special mention also. She helped me with the revisions, encouraged me to complete the project, and always had words of encouragement. I appreciate her "belief in me."

Tampa, Florida
June 1985

PROLOGUE

A NEW BEGINNING

On the first Wednesday in October 1865, Georgians went to the polls to elect delegates to a constitutional convention for the second time in five years. Unlike the election in 1861, when the great question had been that of secession, the 1865 campaign elicited little excitement. The men who were chosen as delegates had the onerous and unwanted task of writing a constitution that would acknowledge the outcome of the Civil War. Satisfied with the 1861 document, which had recognized the dominance of the slaveholding oligarchy in the state, these men had no real interest in drastically altering that document; and few saw any real need to enact changes in a government that had seen them through four years of warfare. Of the 297 delegates to the 1865 convention, twenty-three had served in the 1861 convention; and although twenty-two of them had voted against immediate secession, none of them brought an "I told you so" attitude to the 1865 meeting. Another fourteen delegates had been defeated in 1861, when they had campaigned on a platform of cooperation and compromise.[1] They were conservatives: men who had disagreed with their more radical planter friends in 1861 and who now set about the task of salvaging as much as possible from the old order of antebellum society. They were, wrote a correspondent to the Augusta *Daily Constitutionalist*, "men who [were] the exactest types of the solid country representative, clad to some extent in substantial homespun—though no few shine resplendent in northern ready-made clothes—decorous in demeanor, attentive to business, and anxious to get through and go home."[2]

Herschel V. Johnson, former Confederate senator and slaveholder, was elected president of the convention; and he, along with Charles J. Jenkins, another cooperationist, provided the leadership necessary to com-

---

[1]C. Mildred Thompson, *Reconstruction in Georgia: Economic, Social, Political, 1865-1872* (Savannah: Beehive Press, 1972) 134-35. Allen D. Candler, ed., *The Confederate Records of the State of Georgia*, 6 vols. (Atlanta: C. P. Byrd, state printer, 1909-1911) 1:236-40, 252-60. Dan T. Carter, *When the War Was Over: The Failure of Self-Reconstruction in the South, 1865-1867* (Baton Rouge: Louisisna State University Press, 1985) 3-5.

[2]Thompson, *Reconstruction in Georgia*, 134-35.

plete the task.[3] Johnson's major task was to get the convention to agree on three critical issues: nullification of the secession ordinance, confirmation of emancipation, and repudiation of the state's war debt. These issues, all requirements for readmission into the Union, were resolved with varying degrees of acrimony. The Ordinance of Secession was quickly repealed by a unanimous vote and with little discussion, although the convention refused to annul it. Emancipation and debt repudiation were more hotly contested questions, and their resolution was not so easily accomplished.[4]

There is no doubt that the delegates regarded emancipation as a calamity. On 7 November, W. W. Thomas, a delegate from Coweta County, introduced a resolution that acknowledged emancipation "as one of the unavoidable results of the overthrow of the late revolution," which should be accepted as the only alternative to "perpetual military rule, with its consequent evils and burthens [sic] and perhaps total loss of our civil and constitutional rights." While Thomas's resolution admitted the reality of emancipation, it also contained a spirited defense of slavery. Slavery was "consistent with the dictates of humanity and the strictest principles of morality and religion," and it had allowed Negroes to attain "a higher condition of civilization, morality, usefulness and happiness than . . . [they have] under any other circumstances or in any other portion of the globe." Emancipation, while "a great injury to the white race," would also prove to be "a great curse to the black race." The language of the Thomas resolution, conceding nothing in the way of guilt or wrongdoing, was considered too strong, and the convention tabled it.[5]

A much milder, though equally pointed, resolution was adopted. Referring to emancipation as a war measure, the resolution included a statement upholding the right of slaveowners to seek compensation from the federal government.[6] Emancipation was the price demanded by the federal government for readmission to the Union, and it was the price Georgians would have to pay for losing the war. Herschel V. Johnson reminded the delegates that the emancipation of blacks, who had been "so quiet, so circumspect, so well behaved, so subordinate," was not the product of slave efforts. Instead, emancipation was the "necessary result of superiority of

---

[3]Augusta *Daily Constitutionalist,* 29 October 1865.

[4]Joseph H. Parks, *Joseph E. Brown of Georgia* (Baton Rouge: Louisiana State University Press, 1977) 341-45. Haywood J. Pearce, Jr., *Benjamin H. Hill: Secession and Reconstruction* (Chicago: University of Chicago Press, 1928) 140-51. Although not official delegates, Brown and Hill were given seats in the convention, and both men urged quick action on these issues.

[5]*Journal of the Proceedings of the Convention of the People of Georgia Held in Milledgeville in October and November, 1865* (Milledgeville: R. M. Orme and Son, 1865) 191. Hereafter called *Journal of 1865.*

[6]Ibid., 38.

numbers and resources." Georgians, who had been "thrown at a single leap from the highest pinacle [sic] of prosperity down to the most abject and humiliating circumstances of poverty and political impotency," had no other alternative but to accept emancipation with a "kind, magnanimous, [and] just" spirit.[7]

Having reluctantly agreed to emancipation, the convention then turned its attention to the question of repudiating the state's $18 million war debt. In an exchange of telegrams, Provisional Governor James Johnson informed President Andrew Johnson and Secretary of State William Seward that the convention would probably reject repudiation unless forced to approve it by the federal government.[8] President Johnson replied that "the people of Georgia should not hesitate one single moment repudiating every single dollar of debt created for the purpose of aiding the rebellion against the government of the United States." For the president, it was a simple matter: "They who vested their capital in creation of this debt, must meet their fate and take it as one of the inevitable results of the rebellion, though it may seem hard to them."[9] Seward was equally blunt. "The president of the United States," he wired Governor Johnson, "cannot recognize the people of any State as having resumed the relations of loyalty to the Union that admits as legal obligations, contracts or debts created on them to promote the war of rebellion."[10]

Despite the threats of President Johnson and Secretary Seward, the convention was reluctant to renounce the war debt, and it devoted much of its time to discussions of methods to finance the debt without having to resort to taxation. Few of the delegates were willing to accept Andrew Johnson's hard-boiled advice to take repudiation as "one of the inevitable results of the rebellion." Men who had seen their fortunes eroded by the loss of their slaves were in no mood to approve further losses without considering every possible alternative.[11] Nevertheless, the delegates finally realized that repudiation was an absolute condition to Georgia's readmission into the Union, and in a close vote of 135 to 117, they declared the "debts of this State created for the purpose of carrying on the late war against the United States" null and void.[12] A shift of only ten votes would have defeated the measure.

---

[7]Candler, *Confederate Records*, 4:360-61.

[8]Ibid., 145-46, 171-72.

[9]Ibid.

[10]Ibid., 50-51.

[11]Parks, *Brown*, 341-45. Augusta *Constitutionalist*, 20 October, 3 November 1865. Kenneth Coleman, ed., *A History of Georgia* (Athens: University of Georgia Press, 1977) 207-208.

[12]*Journal of 1865*, 135-36, 185-234. Albert Berry Saye, *A Constitutional History of Georgia, 1721-1945* (Athens: University of Georgia Press, 1948) 255-56.

The settlement of the repudiation issue removed the greatest obstacle to writing a new constitution. Although former slaveowners were forced to submit to economic losses occasioned by emancipation and repudiation, the delegates sought to minimize future losses by limiting the expenditures of the state government and by prohibiting internal improvements. In this respect, the new constitution did not differ from that of 1861. Banks were also subjected to the same stringent regulations imposed by the 1861 covenant, and a two-thirds vote of the legislature was required before a bank could suspend specie payment.[13] Although not enacted in fundamental law, resolutions were passed that petitioned the federal government for tax relief for "holders of large real estates, such as lands, which are, from the embarrassed condition of the people, dormant and likely to remain so for some time to come." The delegates also petitioned the federal government to use an 1865 evaluation of land as the basis of taxation, instead of the 1860 figure the government was using.[14]

Except for the provisions concerning emancipation and repudiation, the new constitution closely resembled that of 1861, and power remained in the hands of Black Belt planters who controlled the legislature. In the sections defining the powers of the General Assembly, however, there were some significant changes. In particular, the Assembly was charged with writing laws that recognized the new status of freedmen. Emancipated but not citizens, freedmen were regarded as wards of the state; as such, they were to be protected by "the State against any evil that may arise from their sudden emancipation." To do this, the General Assembly was authorized to make such laws as were necessary to govern court testimony, marital relationships, inheritance, contractual obligations, and "the regulation or prohibition of their immigration into this State from other States of the Union, or elsewhere." Furthermore, the new constitution contained an explicit prohibition against marriages between blacks and whites.[15] Unable to vote or to hold public office, freedmen were to count as "three-fifths" of a person for purposes of determining legislative representation. Although the federal government could force the delegates to accept emancipation, it could not force them to like it. Delegates granted only the minimum rights demanded by the federal authorities.[16]

Delegates to the 1865 convention were not prepared to make radical changes in the *status quo antebellum.* Grudgingly they incorporated the de-

---

[13]*Journal of 1865*, 216-17.

[14]Ibid., 190, 251-52.

[15]Saye, *Constitutional History*, 258. *Journal of 1865*, 216-17.

[16]Six months after the convention had adjourned, the General Assembly had not fulfilled its responsibility to write laws concerning freedmen. Governor Charles J. Jenkins urged the Assembly to write the laws necessary if "we are to get rid of military rule—and of the Freedman's Bureau." Candler, *Confederate Records*, 4: 511.

mands of the federal government into the state constitution, but only after President Johnson made it clear that such action was necessary. The sympathies of the delegates were best expressed in a resolution that petitioned President Johnson for the release of Jefferson Davis, Alexander H. Stephens, and other high Confederate officials imprisoned in various places. "Mr. Davis was not the leader of a feeble and temporary insurrection," read the text of the resolution, "he was the representative of great ideas and the exponent of principles which stirred and consolidated a numerous and intelligent people." Stressing the idea of collective guilt, the resolution continued, "If he is guilty, so are we. We were the principals, he was our agent. Let not the retribution of a mighty nation be visited upon his head; while we, who urged him to his destiny, are suffered to escape. This people was not his dupe."[17] Proud, but not defiant, the delegates were willing, as representatives of the people, to accept the finality of defeat; but none was willing to admit that the Civil War had come about for trivial causes.

The convention concluded its work after thirteen days. Like the delegates to the Secession Convention, those to the 1865 convention sought to preserve as much of the past as possible. No one knew what the ultimate results of the Union victory would be, but the delegates wanted to leave the future to men who were accustomed to ruling. The conservative republic of slaveowners, constructed with such care in 1861, remained intact. Although now "masters without slaves," it was only a matter of time before former slaveowners would be able to reverse the Union victory. Herschel V. Johnson, the president of the convention, articulated their hopes in his farewell address to the delegates.

It is true our labor system has been entirely deranged, disorganized, almost destroyed; and we are now to enter upon the experiment, whether or not, the means of labor which are left to us, the class of people to which we are to look in the future as our laboring class, can be organized into efficient and trustworthy laborers. That may be done, or I hope it can be done if left to ourselves. . . . We understand the character of that class of people, their capacities, their instincts, and the motives which control their conduct. If we cannot succeed in making them trustworthy as laborers, I think it is not saying too much when we affirm that the Federal government need not attempt it. I trust they will not, and that we will have the poor privilege of being let alone, in the future, in reference to this class of our people.[18]

Secure once again in their control of the political system of Georgia, former slaveowners turned their attention to rebuilding their fortunes. If, indeed, the federal authorities granted them "the poor privilege of being

---

[17]*Journal of 1865*, 252-53.

[18]Percy Scott Flippin, *Herschel V. Johnson of Georgia: State Rights Unionist* (Richmond: Dietz Printing Company, 1931) 266-70.

let alone," few doubted their ability to construct a new system of slavery. As Governor Jenkins observed in his annual message to the General Assembly in 1866, "The planting interest in Georgia can never again be what it has been. . . . Whatever the General Assembly can do to encourage this branch of industry, I earnestly urge upon them." After all, he continued, "They are themselves chiefly of this class, and may be supposed to comprehend its wants."[19]

---

[19]Candler, *Confederate Records*, 4:541-83.

CHAPTER 1

OF PLANTERS AND FREEDMEN

The conclusion of the Civil War brought acute economic problems for the majority of Southerners, black and white. Four years of a war-imposed blockade on cotton, total devaluation of Confederate bonds and scrip, the physical destruction wrought by years of battle fought almost exclusively on Southern soil, and the abolition of slavery combined to reduce the Southern economy to shambles. The hope of immediate recovery for the South lay in the exploitation of its most abundant resource, land, and the utilization of this resource to provide the necessities for a destitute population. In addition, land would also have to provide the capital necessary to rebuild the limited manufacturing capabilities of the region. Yet the abundance of fertile land meant nothing unless some system could be improvised to replace slave labor, and some source of ready credit secured to finance the cost of planting operations.

The quest for a replacement for slavery absorbed much of the energy of Southern planters in the immediate postbellum years. Unlike other forms of agriculture in the United States, cotton cultivation experienced no significant technological advances for the first 100 years after the invention of the cotton gin in 1793.[1] Although gins, presses, and textile mills were converted to steam power, cotton cultivation was carried on by a labor intensive system. Cotton was planted, tended, and picked by hand—tasks that demanded the efforts of many workers. Some planters feared that abolition of slavery and the elimination of physical force as a method of controlling agricultural labor would destroy the value of Negroes as

---

[1]Roger L. Ransom and Richard Sutch, *One Kind of Freedom: The Economic Consequences of Emancipation* (Cambridge: Cambridge University Press, 1977) 8-9. Gavin Wright, *The Political Economy of the Cotton South: Households, Markets, and Wealth in the Nineteenth Century* (New York: W. W. Norton, 1978) 165. Jay R. Mandle, *The Roots of Black Poverty: The Southern Plantation Economy after the Civil War* (Durham: Duke University Press, 1978) 52-70.

workers.[2] As a result, some planters sought alternatives to the continued reliance on black laborers.

"I see but one loophole of escape for the South from the 'sea of troubles' roaring around her so fearfully," wrote a correspondent to the Mobile *Register*, "[and] were I a Southerner, my cry 'in season and out of season,' should be [to] invite and attract European immigration."[3] These sentiments, repeated time after time in rural newspapers, reflected a semi-serious desire by landowners to find a suitable replacement for black labor. Immediately after the end of the war, agencies were established in all Southern states to recruit Europeans as agricultural labor; but despite the lavish promises made to potential recruits, immigration campaigns failed to attract significant numbers of workers. Few immigrants were willing to exchange quasi-serfdom in Europe for a similar condition in the American South. Southern violence and racism, widely reported in the news media, and Southern xenophobia worked to deter immigrants from coming south. Low wages, among the lowest in the nation, likewise contributed to the lack of enthusiasm among immigrants for moving south.[4]

Wages paid to farm workers fluctuated with the price of ginned cotton, and the job market offered little, if any, job security to immigrants. Planters were constantly reminded by rural editors to "remember the price of cotton when they go to employ hands for another year, and not pay too big prices."[5] Wages for males ranged from $75.00 to $120.00 per year. Women were paid approximately two-thirds the wages of a male doing the same work. In some cases, rations of meal and fatback were included as supplemental pay or their cost was deducted from the monthly wage.[6] European immigrants were usually offered higher wages than those normally paid to freedmen, and Alan Conway, in his study of postwar Georgia, cites instances of wages as high as fifteen dollars a month being offered to these workers.[7] Even the prospect of slightly higher wages failed to lure large numbers of immigrants to the South. Perhaps the realization that they were to be used as threats to force freedmen back into the fields was sufficient to keep them out of the region. By and large, the efforts to at-

---

[2]Macon *Telegraph*, 19 April 1866. Greenville *Meriwether Vindicator*, 21 February 1873. Willard Range, *A Century of Georgia Agriculture, 1850-1950* (Athens: University of Georgia Press, 1954) 77.

[3]Mobile *Register*, reprinted in the Greenville *Meriwether Vindicator*, 21 February 1873.

[4]Columbus *Daily Sun*, 9 November 1866. Quitman *Banner*, 1 June 1866.

[5]Lexington *Oglethorpe Echo*, 15 December 1876; 12 January 1877; 29 November 1878.

[6]Eastman *Times-Journal*, 22 May 1879.

[7]Alan Conway, *The Reconstruction of Georgia* (Minneapolis: University of Minnesota Press, 1966) 112.

tract Europeans as agricultural workers proved unsatisfactory, and rural support for such schemes petered out by the late 1870s.

Even at the peak of enthusiasm for the immigration movement, not all planters agreed with the policy. The possibility of a future loss of political power, the prospect of economic competition from immigrants-turned-landowners, and a strong streak of nativism caused some planters to denounce immigration bitterly. The *Oglethorpe Echo*, a newspaper that reflected the opinions of planters in the northeast section of the Black Belt, aired the feelings of natives when it attacked immigration as being responsible for a declining moral standard. Immigrants disrupted the established patterns of Southern society, and the *Echo* warned planters against hiring them. "They are not the class of labor the South needs," cautioned the paper's editor, T. Larry Gantt, "and as citizens, they are neither in sympathy with our laws, our religion nor our traditions." Even more important, he warned, "They will organize the negroes to rebellion and strife, inculcate Communism, Nihilism, and other dangerous doctrines, and rend our now peaceful land with dissention and strife."[8]

Not only were immigrants to be feared as carriers of the various "isms," but also, Gantt told his readers, these "off-scourings of Europe" could not compete with freedmen as laborers. Even the best white immigrants were to be considered temporary workers because the lure of cheap western land would prove irresistible and "if we bring them here it is only to benefit the West as soon as they can leave." Gantt concluded his remarks on this question by admonishing his planter readers to remember, "The white laborer does not suit the Southern farmer, and vice versa. CUFFY, with his multitudinous failings, is the best beast of burden we can find."[9] Simply stated, an influx of white Europeans would create undesirable political and social problems, while Negroes could be more easily controlled by existing legal and extralegal means.

When the efforts to entice Europeans to the South failed, a halfhearted attempt was made to recruit Chinese coolies who had been imported to work on the construction of the Central Pacific Railroad. Coolies were considered an ideal alternative to Negro labor since they could be easily segregated and were unlikely to demand political rights. Although few Chinese workers migrated to the South, several experiments with them were conducted by Georgia planters. "We are informed by the Rev[erend] Mr. Knowles of this city," announced the editor of the Greensboro *Herald* in 1869, "that 30 chinamen have been ordered by the citizens of Wilkes to be used in the capacity of farm laborers . . . [and we] hope it may be extended so far as to test the Chinese fairly as a substitute for negro labor."[10]

---

[8]Lexington *Oglethorpe Echo*, 3 June 1881.

[9]Ibid., 3 December 1880; 17 June 1881.

[10]Greensboro *Herald*, 16 September 1869.

Chinese laborers proved as difficult to recruit as had white Europeans. Few Orientals wanted to compete in a labor market saturated with blacks, and fewer still were willing to voluntarily become part of a society with such rigid racial classifications.

The persistence of immigration efforts by white Southerners appeared to represent a sincere attempt by planters to secure substitutes for freedmen in the cotton fields. Appearances, however, are deceiving; and the actual numbers of immigrants, white or yellow, who came south did not justify the enormous publicity the schemes received. Planters, strapped for cash, could not finance large scale immigration operations, but a lack of cash did not prevent them from using the threat of immigrant workers as a means of intimidating freedmen. Newspapers held up the specter of a massive movement of immigrants southward as a warning to the freedman "of the fate [which] awaits him unless he can and will act as the friend of the Southern white." If freedmen failed to become the "honest and faithful field laborers" the planters wanted, their places would be taken by someone else.[11] The freedman, wrote the editor of the Macon *Telegraph*, was "on trial," and he "must do the work and do it well, or he must get out of the way and make room for some one who will prove a more useful member of society." Freedmen were urged to "take this advice to heart, and act upon it now. Next year may be too late."[12]

After the initial upheaval following the Confederate surrender and emancipation, the realization gradually set in among blacks and whites that, despite their temporary reverses, whites still controlled the land and therefore the wealth and power of the South. Although freedmen hoped for a massive redistribution of plantation lands similar to what had taken place on the sea islands of Georgia and South Carolina, few such grants were ever made. The creation of the Freedmen's Bureau in March 1865 and the persistence of rumors about "forty acres and a mule" being awarded to each former slave led to a widespread belief by freedmen that their hopes for land would soon be realized. So strong was this belief among freedmen in Georgia that Brigadier General Davis Tillson, Superintendent of the Bureau in the state, was forced to issue a general order to all agents to use their influence to "convince the freed people that they are utterly mistaken, and that no such distribution will take place at Christmas [1865], or at any time."[13]

---

[11]Columbus *Enquirer-Sun*, reprinted in the Americus *Recorder*, 2 February 1888. Greensboro *Herald*, 16 September 1869.

[12]Macon *Telegraph*, 30 January 1866.

[13]Brigadier General Davis Tillson, Circular 2, 3 October 1865, Reel 34, Records of the Assistant Commissioner for the State of Georgia, Bureau of Refugees, Freedmen, and Abandoned Lands, 1865-1869. Record Group 105, M-798. National Archives. Hereafter referred to as BRFAL.

Despite the Bureau's authority to rent or sell lands abandoned by their owners, the actual number of Georgia plantations disposed of in this manner was very small. While land confiscation proposals received a lot of attention in Congress and in the national press, Radical Republicans who advocated such measures could not secure the necessary legislative support to enact them. Even if the Radicals had been able to push a general confiscation law through Congress, it is doubtful whether they could have overturned an almost certain presidential veto. The failure of the Federal government to provide freedmen with homesteads subjected them to the mercies of planters. Without land, freedmen had little chance of remaining independent in an agricultural South.

On 3 October 1865 General Tillson issued a circular that defined the role of the Bureau in providing aid to freedmen. Under the Tillson plan, those who were offered jobs and who were physically able to work must take the jobs or lose their eligibility for the subsistence rations doled out by the agency. In order to ensure that able-bodied freedmen went back to the fields, Tillson included a prohibition against their congregating in towns and cities. Freedmen who violated this order would be "compelled, if necessary, to go to the country and accept places of labor found by themselves, or for them, by officers and agents of the Bureau."[14] This program of forced employment hastened the restoration of planter control over blacks in the state.

At the same time it banished freedmen to the countryside, the Bureau also instituted a system of labor contracts that ostensibly provided safeguards for blacks employed by planters. Physical punishment and financial mistreatment were prohibited by the contracts, although stringent regulations that called for subservient behavior were included. The Bureau refused to set a specific wage scale or to "allow it to be done by any community or combination of people," and Bureau agents were instructed to "leave labor, like any other commodity, to sell itself in the open market to the highest bidder."[15] While specific wages were not required, agents were informed that certain minimum wages were to be paid in various areas. These amounts were calculated on the ability of planters to produce cotton and on the availability of labor in an area. Planters in the marginally productive lands of the Upper Piedmont were told that a wage of twelve to fifteen dollars a month was reasonable, while planters along the more fertile coast were required to pay a minimum wage of fifteen

---

[14]Ibid.

[15]Ibid. See also William Cohen, "Negro Involuntary Servitude in the South, 1865-1940: A Preliminary Analysis," *Journal of Southern History* 42 (1976): 31-60. Ronald F. Davis, "The U. S. Army and the Origins of Sharecropping in the Natchez District—A Case Study," *Journal of Negro History* 62 (1977): 60-80. Contract dated 1867, Felix Hargrett Typescripts, University of Georgia. Hereafter referred to as HT.

dollars a month. In other areas, wages varied according to local conditions.[16] Complicating the calculation of wages was the inclusion of the cost of rations or "found" in the final computation. Freedmen and planters were required to submit any contractual agreement made between them to an agent of the Bureau for approval. If the agent thought the terms of the contract were too exacting or the wages inadequate, he could void the contract.[17] If planters refused to abide by the judgement of the agent, he could call upon the military to enforce his decision. In practice, agents were often ignored by both planters and freedmen, and the army proved less than capable of dealing with contract violators. In addition to ruling on the fairness of contracts, Bureau agents also had the responsibility of acting as mediators in contractual disputes. Occasionally they ruled on disputes between planters with conflicting claims on the labor of individual freedmen. Cases of peonage, improper treatment, and illegal indentures also fell within the responsibility of Bureau agents, and much of their time was spent investigating and arbitrating such incidents. All in all, the Bureau's efforts to create a uniform system of contracts failed; and planters used a wide variety of formulas to calculate wages, working conditions, and jobs.[18]

A primary reason for the Bureau's failure in this matter was that many of its agents were initially drawn from the local white population. At the request of General Tillson, the Constitution Convention of 1865 authorized the employment of 250 agents to be recruited from the population of native whites. Thus, with the exception of a few regular army officers assigned to temporary duty with the Bureau, the day-to-day functions of the agency were carried out by white Georgians, many of whom were former slaveowners. It is not surprising, therefore, that the agency accomplished little, nor is it surprising that complaints by freedmen against civilian agents began to mount by 1866. General Tillson, in dismissing Agent James H. Fryer from the Bureau, noted that "of more than two hundred citizen agents of this Bureau, this is the first instance where any of them has taken advantage of his position to abuse, torture, and maltreat freedpeople in his jurisdiction."[19] The abuses that prompted Till-

---

[16]Stephen J. DeCanio, *Agriculture in the Postbellum South: The Economics of Production and Supply* (Cambridge: MIT Press, 1974) 51-62.

[17]General Order 10, 10 January 1866; General Order 13, 16 January 1866, Reel 34, BRFAL.

[18]Captain N. Sellers to Captain Eugene Picket, 24 November 1866; W. C. Morrill to General C. C. Sibley, 27 August 1868; Charles R. Holcombe to General C. C. Sibley, 13 June 1867; Jerome Davenport to General C. C. Sibley, 31 January 1867, Reel 15, BRFAL.

[19]Brigadier General Davis Tillson, General Order 48, 15 March 1866, Reel 34, BRFAL.

son's comment, made in mid-March 1866, were to become the rule rather than the exception by the end of that year.

Under strict instructions not to interfere with the actions of local civil authorities, Bureau agents who were so inclined found their ability to protect freedmen limited. Since Georgia experienced little in the way of disruption of civil government, concerned agents were often frustrated by local authorities who sided with planters in virtually all disputes.[20] In March 1868 additional restrictions were placed on agents when they received orders to surrender all judicial functions to state and county courts. Agents could take action only in cases where such action was specifically authorized by the Commissioner for the state. Even this limited authority was ended in August 1868, at the very time Ku Klux Klan terrorism reached its highest level in the state.[21]

The surrender of its judicial and police powers to local authorities in early 1868 ended the effectiveness of the Bureau in Georgia. In 1869 its already diminished powers decreased further, and in 1870 the agency ceased to exist altogether. During the last two years of its operation, the Bureau was reduced to collecting and reporting data on the number and kinds of outrages committed against freedmen. What influence the agency retained among freedmen was quickly dissipated as it sought to persuade Negroes to abandon politics and submit to the economic domination of planters.[22]

Overall, the record of the Freedmen's Bureau in Georgia was not very impressive. Agency politics, ostensibly meant to help freedmen make the adjustment from slavery to freedom, often forced them into situations that allowed ex-slaveowners to reestablish their control over the former slaves. In January 1866, for example, the Bureau adopted a policy that made former masters responsible for the care and feeding of the very young and very old freedmen who remained on the plantations. To help planters defray the costs of such care, the agency allowed them to "bind out" young freedmen through indentures and apprentice agreements. Although the rationale for such a policy was the provision of food and housing for freedmen unable to care for themselves, the result was a rash of kidnappings when some unscrupulous planters took advantage of the policy to ensure a permanent source of labor for their plantations. Bureau agents reported many cases where freedmen sought to reclaim their children only

---

[20]R. D. Claiborne to General Davis Tillson, 10 January 1867. L. Lieberman to General C. C. Sibley, 31 August 1868, Reel 22, BRFAL.

[21]Confidential Circular, 5 March 1868; Circular Letter 4, 3 August 1868, Reel 34, BRFAL.

[22]Circular Letters, 8 and 13 April 1868, Reel 34, BRFAL. Thompson, *Reconstruction in Georgia*, 50-56.

to find out that they had been bound to former masters by local courts.[23] Planters argued that children born to slaves were illegitimate and therefore wards of the court, which could, if it so chose, bind them out as laborers. The question of the legal status of slave children was finally resolved when state legislatures passed laws that acknowledged the legitimacy of slave marriages. Only after these laws were enacted did freedmen gain widespread recognition of their rights as parents.[24] Even then an occasional recalcitrant planter might insist that the children born to slaves were wards of the courts.[25]

Forcing freedmen to work under penalty of imprisonment was another policy adopted by the Bureau that had a deleterious effect. First implemented in occupied Louisiana in 1863, this policy came in response to planters' complaints about a labor shortage and coincided with efforts by the federal army to rid itself of the responsibility for caring for freedmen.[26] By denying able-bodied freedmen rations, the army and later the Bureau hoped to force them into supporting themselves through "gainful employment."[27] Utilizing hastily passed vagrancy laws and the threat of physical punishment, the Bureau collected unemployed freedmen and transported them to areas experiencing labor shortages.[28] In addition, Bureau officials encouraged labor recruiters to visit areas where a labor surplus existed and to recruit freedmen for work on plantations in areas of labor scarcity.[29]

The Bureau's policy of forced labor was applauded by white planters. Unlike Bureau officials who wanted to see freedmen become self-sufficient, planters were concerned only with securing enough workers to make a cotton crop. Motivated by different goals, Bureau agents and planters became unlikely partners in efforts to force freedmen back to the plantations. Neither the Bureau, with its paternalistic approach to solving the freedmen's problems, nor planters, with their concern for reestablishing a profitable plantation economy, cared about the views of the freedmen

[23]Macon *Telegraph*, 3 January 1866.

[24]Louis S. Gerteis, *From Contraband to Freedom: Federal Policy toward Southern Blacks, 1861-1865* (Westport CT: Greenwood Press, 1973) 86.

[25]Davis, "U. S. Army," 73-74. Charles Rauschenberg to General C. C. Sibley, 1 January 1868, Reel 32, BRFAL.

[26]Gerteis, *From Contraband*, 75-91, 101-104.

[27]Colonel H. B. Sprague, General Order 3, 7 December 1865, Reel 34, BRFAL.

[28]Gerteis, *From Contraband*, 83-90. Davis, "U. S. Army," 75-76. Brigadier General Davis Tillson, General Order 40, 3 March 1866, Reel 34, BRFAL.

[29] DeCanio, *Agriculture*, 32-35. James T. Harmon to Captain N. Sellers Hill, nd, Reel 15, BRFAL.

on that matter; and neither consulted them about it.[30] As proof of its effectiveness in dealing with the problem of black unemployment, the Bureau pointed to this program of forcing freedmen back into the cotton fields.[31]

Despite the direct and indirect assistance they received from Bureau agents, planters resented even the meager protection the agency offered to freedmen. Confident that free labor would never be successful without the use of the lash, some planters complained that the agency's prohibition against corporal punishment would make freedmen worthless as laborers. The editor of the Macon *Telegraph* voiced these feelings when he chastised the Bureau for not allowing the use of physical force against freedmen. "Remove restraint from him," he wrote, "[and the Negro] will lapse into thriftless savagism. Voluntary labor on the part of the negro is a myth. He is voluntarily lazy and improvident."[32] Federal officers who commanded the small garrisons stationed in rural areas of the state frequently sympathized with planters and occasionally used troops to intimidate freedmen who objected to the treatment some planters gave them. "Two Federals, in blue uniforms and armed, came out . . . and whipped every Negro man reported to them, and in some cases unmercifully," wrote the Reverend John Jones to Mary Jones in July 1865. "Another party visited Colquitt and punished by suspending by the thumbs. The effect," he concluded, "has been a remarkable quietude and order in all this region."[33] As late as 1881 the editor of the *Oglethorpe Echo* declared that force was necessary to make blacks work, and "Nothing but fear will make him honest, truthful, and industrious, and he is not afraid of anything but the old fashion lash."[34]

Even the Bureau's policy of collecting and distributing workers was attacked by planters and newspaper editors. Once again, the *Telegraph* spoke for planters when it denounced the agents of the Bureau who were

carrying on a gigantic negro-trading enterprise, far more offensive in most of its features than the old slave selling and buying business of the South, and which is a source of enormous profit to the agents who trade and transport the negroes from State to State. The negroes cost nothing; they can be seized anywhere and sent anywhere; the government pays all the bills for food, clothing, and transportation—pays salaries to the negro-labor brokers and traders, while they pocket

---

[30]Charles C. Jones, Jr., to Mary Jones, 28 May 1866, in Robert Manson Myers, ed., *The Children of Pride: A True Story of Georgia and the Civil War* (New Haven: Yale University Press, 1972) 1337-39.

[31]Gerteis, *From Contraband*, 83-90. Ransom and Sutch, *One Kind of Freedom*, 60-64.

[32]Macon *Telegraph*, 19 April 1866.

[33]John Jones to Mary Jones, 26 July 1865, in Myers, *Children*, 1281-83.

[34]Lexington *Oglethorpe Echo*, 4 February 1881. DeCanio, *Agriculture*, 22-30.

from ten to thirty dollars commission on every negro sent from one plantation to another, from one State to another, and have the privilege, because they have the power, of selling a black to-day, and, under any paltry pretense, stealing him to sell to a better paying party to-morrow.[35]

The estimated cost of this activity was twelve million dollars a year, if such an account was true. Interestingly, the editor of the *Telegraph* did not question the rights of planters to buy freedmen, although slavery had been legally abolished for over a year.

While some planters complained about the Bureau's transferring laborers from areas of labor surpluses to areas of labor scarcities, other planters took advantage of this policy to keep wages down. Scarcity of labor often meant that freedmen would not work for the wages initially offered, and planters who encountered this attitude relied on the Bureau to provide labor from other areas of the state.[36] In Georgia apparently there were shortages in some areas, particularly along the coast where freedmen were able to gain temporary control of large tracts of land.[37] Roger Ransom and Richard Sutch argue that real labor shortages often existed and that planters were justified in their complaints against the Bureau.[38]

During its brief tenure, the Freedmen's Bureau contributed much to the development of postwar economic patterns in the South. Despite the frequent abuse heaped upon it by whites, the agency greatly aided the reestablishment of planter control over the Southern economy. However, few significant changes in the condition of freedmen came from Bureau policies and activities. The greatest failure of the Bureau, and of Reconstruction in general, was its failure to carry out a program of land confiscation and redistribution. Without land, freedmen were forced to continue in their roles as subservient agricultural workers. Without land, blacks found themselves ensnared in a complex web of debts, contracts, and economic intimidation.[39] Even the extension of political rights could not compensate for the lack of an economic base from which an independent class of black yeomen farmers could emerge. When its demise came in 1870, the Bureau's positive contributions to the welfare of freedmen had been minimal.[40]

---

[35]Macon *Telegraph*, 10 May 1866.

[36]DeCanio, *Agriculture*, 24-25. Cohen, "Involuntary Servitude," 31-60.

[37]Macon *Telegraph*, 27 February 1866. Mary Jones to Charles C. Jones, Jr., 28 May 1866, in Myers, *Children*, 1339-42.

[38]Ransom and Sutch, *One Kind of Freedom*, 55-56, 67.

[39]Jonathan M. Wiener, "Planter Persistence and Social Change: Alabama, 1850-1870," *Journal of Interdisciplinary History* 7 (1976): 235-60.

[40]See Martin E. Mantell, *Johnson, Grant and the Politics of Reconstruction* (New York: Columbia University Press, 1973).

Its most visible contribution was the inauguration of the contract labor system. Originally introduced to apply only to wage labor, contracts were modified and adapted for use with sharecropping and tenancy. Spelling out hours of work, specific wages, and deductions for time missed, they also defined the expected social behavior of freedmen who were employed by planters.[41] Although contracts supposedly protected both freedmen and planters, the system worked largely to the advantage of the latter since they, unlike freedmen, had experience with contracts, were usually literate, had dealt with legal matters before, and controlled the state government, which enacted contract laws. So complex were these laws in Georgia, the Macon *Telegraph* dedicated the better part of three entire issues to printing them. State legislators apparently made these statutes complicated in order to discourage freedmen from learning and using them.[42]

The contract labor system was quickly abandoned in Georgia following the demise of the Bureau. Among a variety of reasons, white chicanery and the lack of cash were major factors in the system's failure.[43] Unscrupulous planters, protected by legal technicalities, would frequently force laborers to leave plantations immediately after the harvesting of crops but prior to marketing them. Because most contracts contained provisions forbidding workers to leave without the landowners' permission, workers who left—even though forced to do so—forfeited their wages. So widespread was this practice that General Tillson, the Bureau Commissioner for Georgia and certainly no friend of freedmen, issued an order prohibiting it. "Planters, who having planted crops and not needing labor, force freedmen to leave and refuse to pay wages claiming that the freedmen violated the contract," read the order, "are forbidden to discharge workers without payment or consent of [the] Bureau."[44] In 1867 General C. C. Sibley, Tillson's successor, reported to General O. O. Howard, the Bureau's top official, that "difficulties in regard to . . . settlement for wages have multiplied."[45] A month later Sibley again reported that "difficulties arising between the freedmen and whites on settlement for the year's labor continue to multiply. The spirit of oppression is to be found almost everywhere."[46]

---

[41]Parks, *Brown*, 358. Labor contracts in the possession of John Pattillo, Southern Technical Institute, Marietta, Georgia. See also contract, 12 January 1866, HT.

[42]Macon *Telegraph*, 9, 10, and 11 January 1866.

[43]DeCanio, *Agriculture*, 16-56.

[44]General Davis Tillson, circular 8, 17 July 1866, Reel 34, BRFAL.

[45]General C. C. Sibley to General O. O. Howard, Report for October 1867, dated 26 November 1867, Reel 32, BRFAL.

[46]General C. C. Sibley to General O. O. Howard, Report for November 1867, dated 28 December 1867, ibid.

Even planters who wanted to follow the spirit as well as the letter of their contracts frequently found it impossible to do so. The absence of large amounts of cash and the refusal of banks to lend money on land made it virtually impossible for some planters to meet their payroll obligations.[47] Faced with a demand for cash, planters occasionally resorted to issuing private scrip to be redeemed after the year's cotton crop was sold.[48] Crop failures in 1866 and 1867 further reduced the supply of hard money, and even honest planters resigned themselves to not being able to meet their payrolls.

Another reason for the increasing unpopularity of the wage labor system among freedmen was the retention of organizational forms that replicated those of slavery. Planters, accustomed to slave agriculture, wanted to retain the large work gang as the primary method of labor, including the use of overseers and "bosses." All too often, freedmen discovered that the contracts they had made their marks on contained clauses permitting planters to employ overseers who were authorized to use whips "when necessary." When freedmen refused to work under these conditions, planters accused them of being unreliable—a view that was perpetuated by early historians of the period.[49] In their recent study of Southern agriculture, Ransom and Sutch identify dissatisfaction with the gang labor system rather than any inherent personal failings as the cause of the "unreliable habits" of freedmen.[50] Interviews with former slaves conducted under the auspices of the federal government in the 1930s tend to substantiate these conclusions.[51]

Given the difficulties experienced by both freedmen and planters under the wage labor system, it is not surprising that it was largely abandoned by 1868. With the end of the wage system came the breakup of the antebellum pattern of plantation agriculture, although not of the plantation itself. Alternative methods of cotton cultivation were devised to give planters continued control of land and freedmen, methods that also managed to provide freedmen with a semblance of independence. Sharecropping and tenant farming, alternatives to wage labor and forms of

---

[47]Conway, *Reconstruction of Georgia*, 106-20. Mary Jones to Charles C. Jones, Jr., 28 May 1866, in Myers, *Children*, 1339-42.

[48]Ransom and Sutch, *One Kind of Freedom*, 56-80.

[49]Conway, *Reconstruction of Georgia*, 106-20. Thompson, *Reconstruction in Georgia*, 65-68.

[50]Ransom and Sutch, *One Kind of Freedom*, 50-67.

[51]George P. Rawick, ed., *The American Slave: A Composite Autobiography*, vol. 13, Georgia Narratives (Westport CT: Greenwood, 1972). See also Ronald Killion and Charles Waller, eds., *Slavery Time When I Was Chillun Down on Marster's Plantation* (Savannah: Beehive Press, 1975).

cultivation that had existed in nonplantation regions during the antebellum period, were adapted to the new conditions. The disastrous growing seasons of 1866 and 1867 made planters even more willing to adopt either one or the other of these forms since sharecropping and tenantry spread the risks of farming between landowner and laborer.[52]

In the immediate postwar years of 1866 and 1867, some whites regarded the practice of renting land to Negroes with hostility. In some cases, whites who rented their land to blacks suffered ostracism and physical abuse from other whites. When two of her Liberty County neighbors decided to rent their plantations to freedmen, Mary Jones reacted to their decisions with resentment. "I understand," she wrote to her daughter,"Dr. Harris and Mr. Varnadoe will rent their land to the Negroes. The conduct of some of the citizens has been very injurious to the best interest of the community."[53] Although the price of land in some areas dropped from an antebellum high of sixteen to twenty dollars an acre to less than fifty cents an acre in the immediate postwar period, the adamant refusal of most whites to sell to freedmen precluded the establishment of small, individually owned farms by blacks.[54] Even if white landowners had been willing to sell or lease land to freedmen, it is doubtful that many blacks could have found the money needed to begin farming operations. The average cost for the first year of farming a forty acre parcel was between $250 and $500, more than most freedmen (and many whites) could afford. Planters who owned the best agricultural lands in the state before the Civil War had already made the initial investment in equipment and animals; and although they lost some of both as a result of the war, they nevertheless retained enough to continue farming.[55]

The solution to the problem of land and labor in the postwar years was the adoption of tenantry and sharecropping systems. Under the first arrangement, individual families rented small parcels of land from a landowner for a fixed sum or a specified amount of produce. The need for cash was a major drawback to this system, since tenants not only had to pay a cash rent, but also had to furnish their own equipment, seeds, and supplies. For this reason, tenant farming was not as widely practiced as was sharecropping. Few freedmen could afford to become tenants because of the high cost of beginning operations. Planters disliked cash ten-

[52]Mandle, *Roots,* 28-51.

[53]Mary Jones to Mary S. Mallard, 17 November 1865, in Myers, *Children,* 1307-1309.

[54]Thomas J. Pressly and William H. Scofield, eds., *Farm Real Estate Values in the United States by Counties, 1850-1959* (Seattle: University of Washington Press, 1965) 47-49.

[55]Wiener, "Planter Persistence," 242.

antry because tenants were legally considered to be independent farmers and were not subject to the supervision of landowners.[56]

An 1874 Georgia Department of Agriculture survey revealed that most planters approved of the wage labor and sharecropping systems, but few considered tenantry a desirable method of cultivation.[57] Similar results were reported in the *Meriwether Vindicator* in 1875 in an article about the "planters of Burke County [who] recently met at Waynesboro and [who] resolved that of the three classes of labor, the wage system was the best; that the share system *will do if properly supervised*, and that the tenant system should be abandoned." Supervision was the critical element of the sharecropping system as far as planters were concerned, and the right to direct the activities of sharecroppers was recognized by state and local courts as being the prerogative of the landowner.[58] In 1874 the *Oglethorpe Echo* advised planters of a decision by a local justice of the peace specifying that "where a party rented land from another for a part of the crop, the owner of the land had the right to appropriate part of the products of said land before harvesting, as the landlord is part owner in the growing crop." Part ownership conveyed the right of supervision, a right planters eagerly exercised.[59]

Under the sharecropping system, a laborer was given broad supervision by landlords but was usually allowed to set his own pace and to work at the tasks he chose. Although the line between sharecropping and share tenantry was a fine one, the usual distinction made between the two rested on the amount and kind of supplies contributed by the landowner. Under the most common sharecropping arrangement, the landlord furnished land, seeds, fertilizer, animals, tools, and a house. In return he received a fixed share of the crop according to a ratio previously agreed upon. A common arrangement was the fifty-fifty split, although other percentages were sometimes used. Unlike cash tenants, sharecroppers were required to contribute only their labor to the system.

Sharecropping as an efficient system of agriculture has been widely debated by economists and historians, but no common agreement has been reached. In the postwar South, sharecropping served many functions—social and economic. Socially, sharecropping preserved the antebellum class structure. Planters occupied the top rung of rural society, while freedmen were consigned to the lowest level. In many ways, sharecrop-

---

[56]Robert Higgs, *The Transformation of the American Economy, 1865-1914: An Essay in Interpretation* (New York: John Wiley and Sons, 1971) 93-96.

[57]*Georgia Department of Agriculture, Annual Report for the Year 1875* (Atlanta: J. H. Estill, 1876) 87-88.

[58]Greenville *Meriwether Vindicator*, 17 December 1875. Italics mine.

[59]Lexington *Oglethorpe Echo*, 16 October 1874.

ping approximated the old slave system. As an economic system, sharecropping allowed for the maximization of the limited resources of both landowner and laborer. Gradually, sharecropping became the dominant form of agricultural cultivation in the South.[60]

The shift to sharecropping significantly altered the internal structure of the plantation system, although it did not lessen the economic power of planters. One of the most important changes to come as a result of sharecropping was the end of plantation self-sufficiency. According to Ransom and Sutch, plantations were largely self-sustaining in the production of grain and essential foodstuffs until the early 1880s when furnishing merchants became an important part of Southern agriculture. As a condition for extending credit to landowners and sharecroppers, merchants demanded that the sharecropping system be devoted almost exclusively to cotton production.[61] This interpretation has been challenged by cliometricians Gavin Wright and Howard Konreuther. While not debating the larger question of self-sufficiency, they note the end of agricultural diversification in the South in the eighties, but they put the blame on tenants rather than furnishing merchants. According to their analysis, tenants, particularly those with aspirations of becoming landowners, needed to maximize their earnings and therefore concentrated on growing cotton. If there was a villain, Wright and Konreuther suggest it might be the landowner who deliberately limited the size of plots allotted to tenants. In order to get the maximum returns for their efforts, tenants devoted every available acre to cotton production. The ready market for cotton offered the best opportunity for tenants to become independent farmers.[62]

The adoption of sharecropping and the breakup of large plantations also brought more poor whites into cotton production. Unable to compete with slave labor prior to the war and generally occupying land only marginally fit for cotton production, poor whites within the Black Belt had operated on the fringes of the prewar economy, often existing at subsistence levels. Unlike yeoman farmers of the uplands, these poor whites did

---

[60]Robert Higgs, *Competition and Coercion: Blacks in the American Economy, 1865-1914* (Cambridge: Cambridge University Press, 1977) 49, 68, 138-39.

[61]Roger L. Ransom and Richard Sutch, "The 'Lock-in' Mechanism and Overproduction of Cotton in the Post-Bellum South," *Agricultural History* 49 (1975): 405-25. Roger L. Ransom and Richard Sutch, "Debt Peonage in the Cotton South after the Civil War," *Journal of Economic History* 32 (1972): 641-69.

[62]Gavin Wright and Howard Konreuther, "Cotton, Corn and Risk in the Nineteenth Century," *Journal of Economic History* 35 (1975): 526-51. Wright, *Political Economy*, 164-76.

not develop into a strong element of the antebellum economy.[63] With the introduction of sharecropping, men who had been excluded from the mainstream of the cotton economy now found that they could farm the most fertile land in the region, albeit someone else's land. They also found that they could now compete on equal terms with blacks. To many poor whites, sharecropping offered what appeared to be their best opportunity to move into the landowning class of yeoman farmers.[64] Although the dream of becoming independent landowners proved as illusory for poor whites as it did for blacks, many whites who had not been involved in cotton production prior to 1865 became part of the caste of landless farmers competing for the cotton dollar. John D. Hicks, an early scholar of Southern agriculture, noted the increased participation of poor whites and argued that abolition resulted in a return to the "actual equality of conditions for all men seldom met with anywhere except on the frontier, and rarely on so large a scale even there."[65] This assertion probably overstated the situation, but abolition and the adoption of sharecropping did serve to bring more lower-class whites into cotton production.[66] And perhaps the entry of poor whites into the ranks of sharecroppers helped to create an equality of sorts between blacks and whites—the equality of poverty.

According to one historian of Southern agriculture, race was a determining factor in the way contracts between landowners and sharecroppers were written. Recently Robert Higgs and Stephen DeCanio have examined the question of how much of an impact race had on the negotiation of sharecropping contracts, and their studies indicate that little or no discrimination was discernible. Regardless of color, tenants usually received similar contracts. DeCanio found that although white tenants enjoyed an "edge" over black tenants, it was because of their possession of "non-human" factors such as education, animals, and money. All in all, concluded Higgs and DeCanio, black sharecroppers were equal to white ones in abilities and in opportunities.[67]

---

[63]Wright and Konreuther, "Cotton, Corn and Risk," 540-42. Ransom and Sutch, *One Kind of Freedom*, 104-105.

[64]See Steven Hahn, *The Roots of Southern Populism: Yeoman Farmers and the Transformation of the Georgia Upcountry, 1850-1890* (New York: Oxford University Press, 1983).

[65]John D. Hicks, *The Populist Revolt: A History of the Farmers' Alliance and the People's Party* (Minneapolis: University of Minnesota Press, 1931) 37.

[66]Stephen J. DeCanio, "Productivity and Income Distribution in the Post-Bellum South," *Journal of Economic History* 34 (1974): 422-46.

[67]Robert Higgs, "Patterns of Farm Rental in the Georgia Cotton Belt, 1880-1900," *Journal of Economic History* 34 (1974): 468-82. DeCanio, "Productivity and Income," 445.

The data concerning "land tenure according to color of tenants" appear to substantiate their conclusions. An analysis of the census figures for 1900, the first year tenure was identified by color, reveals that black and white sharecroppers were almost equal in number, with blacks having a slight numerical edge. Of the 82,826 farms cultivated by Georgia Negroes, 70,568 were operated on some kind of sharecropping arrangement. Whites operated 63,272 farms under similar arrangements, although the total number of white operated farms (141,865) was almost twice that of farms operated by blacks. While representing a near balance in terms of actual numbers, the percentages of farmers to sharecropping/ tenancy, once again calculated on the basis of race, reveal a different picture. Of all Negroes engaged in farming in Georgia in 1900, 85.2% were either sharecroppers, share tenants, or cash tenants. White sharecropper/ tenants, on the other hand, accounted for only 44.6% of the total number of white farmers in the state. After thirty-five years of freedom, Georgia blacks still found themselves under the thumbs of white planters, and many poor whites found themselves "companions in misery" to the former slaves.[68]

The degree to which sharecropping/tenancy came to dominate Georgia agriculture in the postwar years is evident in the census data for the period (table 1.1). For example, the number of farms in the state increased nearly 86,000 units between 1880 and 1900. Of these, 72,000 were sharecropper/ tenant homesteads; only 14,000 were owner-operated units. This represented a ratio of 5.1 sharecropper/tenant farms for each new landowner.[69]

Sharecropping experienced its greatest period of growth during the first twenty-five years of the postwar era and leveled off during the 1890s. Although census figures are not available for 1870, a logical assumption would be that the decade of the 1870s accounted for the largest number of farm units being converted into sharecropping plots. Of the total number of units given over to sharecropping in the nineteenth century, 57.5% were allocated by 1880. The growth rate for sharecropping was 42.6% for

TABLE 1.1

YEAR	TOTAL FARMS[a]	OWNED	TENANTS[b]	SHARE-CROPPERS[c]	% [= (b + c) ÷ a]
1880	138,626	76,451	18,557	43,618	44.8%
1890	171,071	79,477	29,413	62,181	53.5%
1900	224,691	90,131	58,750	75,810	59.0%

[68]*Twelfth Census,* "Statistics of Agriculture," Table 10 (Washington: U. S. Government Printing Office, n.d.) 68-71.

[69]Compilation of data from tables in 1870, 1880, 1890, and 1900 censuses.

the years between 1880 and 1890, but this dropped to only 21.9% in the last decade of the century. The decline in the expansion rate of share-cropping in the 1890s was accompanied by a 99.7% increase in the number of cash tenants. Furthermore, there was a substantial increase in the number of individuals who owned their land when compared to the number of new owners between 1880 and 1890: 13.4% to 3.9%. The increase in the rate of growth of cash tenantry and land ownership can be explained by two factors. First, land prices in Georgia stabilized during the 1870s and 1880s, but the depressed money market made purchasing land and cash tenantry difficult. The late 1890s brought increasing prosperity for farmers, and although they were not years of plenty, individuals were able to take advantage of the stable cotton market to accumulate enough money to purchase land. The second factor accounting for increased land ownership and cash tenantry was the movement of substantial portions of the rural population to the cities, a condition that made more and better land available to those who remained in the countryside.[70]

The effect of sharecropping/tenancy on farm size is also demonstrated by census data. From 1870 until 1900, the average Georgia farm decreased in size from 188 acres to 117.5 acres, and the total number of farms increased dramatically.[71] Farms between twenty and fifty acres increased in number from 21,971 in 1870 to 73,408 in 1900. A second category of farms, ranging from fifty to one hundred acres, increased by 33,880 units for the same period. The number of farms from 100 to 500 acres increased even more dramatically by a total of 55,610 units. The rapid increase of both large and small farms is consistent with the rise in sharecropping and tenancy. Greater numbers of smaller farms were needed to accommodate the growing numbers of tenants and share-

TABLE 1.2

INCREASES IN FARMS BY SIZE, 1870-1900			
	SIZE IN ACRES		
YEAR	20-50	50-100	100-500
1870	21,971	18,371	17,490
1880	36,524	26,054	53,635
1890	55,287	32,316	59,343
1900	73,408	52,251	73,100
% INCREASE	334%	285%	418%

[70]Pressly and Scofield, *Farm Real Estate Values*, 47-49.

[71]Compilation of data from 1870, 1880, 1890, 1900 censuses.

croppers. Merchants and planters tended to consolidate their holdings as many small farmers fell victim to the vicissitudes of fluctuating cotton markets and the crop lien system.[72]

The contract was the glue that held the sharecropping system together. A holdover from the days of the Freedmen's Bureau, a sharecropping contract might be a long, explicit document that spelled out the obligations of the landlord and tenant in minute detail, or it might be a simple document that merely specified the ratio of the crop division and the kinds of supplies to be furnished by the landlord. Governed by the same system of laws enacted for wage labor contracts, sharecropping contracts provided landlords with the legal means they needed to control their tenants. Although recent cliometric studies of sharecropping argue that discrimination did not occur in the allotment of land or resources, they also acknowledge that it was part of the daily existence of black laborers in the South.[73] Much of the discrimination came as a result of community customs and through the system of state laws. Contract laws were part of this systematic oppression.

Laws prohibiting the employment of laborers already under contract were known as "enticement" laws, and violations were usually deemed misdemeanor offenses. Newspapers frequently carried warnings to landlords not to hire certain laborers because they were " under contract" already. Typical of such notices is the one that appeared in the *Meriwether Vindicator* in early 1873:

NOTICE

Richmond Hall, Col[ored], who was in my employ for the year 1873, having left me without provocation, all persons are hereby notified not to hire him. I will prosecute any one who harbors or hires said Richmond Hall.

B. L. Sims[74]

Although planters who hired contract violators or enticed tenants to leave the employ of another planter could be punished under enticement laws, they were only occasionally enforced. Because of the rural nature of the South and the keen competition for laborers, it is doubtful that many planters were ever charged with violating these laws. Robert Higgs's recent study of black history dismisses enticement laws as being useless. Higgs also dismisses the impact of other laws prohibiting labor recruitment or heavily taxing out of state recruiters as being negligible. Competition for

---

[72]Jonathan M. Wiener, "Planter-Merchant Conflict in Reconstruction Alabama," *Past and Present* 68 (1975): 73-94. Ransom and Sutch, *One Kind of Freedom*, 78-80.

[73]Higgs, *Competition*, 53-55. DeCanio, *Agriculture*, 91-94. Ransom and Sutch, *One Kind of Freedom*, 99.

[74]Greenville *Meriwether Vindicator*, 18 April 1873; 14 August 1874; 12 March 1875. Lexington *Oglethorpe Echo*, 20 July 1877.

labor negated the laws, and it was difficult for one planter to justify prosecuting another when he himself might be equally guilty of breaking the same law.[75] William Cohen places much more importance on enticement laws, but he readily admits that they were generally enforced only during periods of labor scarcity.[76] While rural editors might press for more stringent laws in their columns because "our landowners need protection from each other in the struggle for labor," and although they might urge the General Assembly to "hold any man who employs a laborer under contract to another strictly accountable for all damage his interference" might have caused, effective laws were never passed.[77] Enticement laws did not go to the root of the planters' problem, which was how to find ways to limit the mobility of freedmen. In order to restrict the movement of laborers from plantation to plantation, most Southern states went the other direction and made infractions of contracts criminal offenses punishable by jail terms. In particular, laborers who sought to avoid debts by flight could be prosecuted under the criminal code, which defined flight as *prima facie* evidence of fraudulent intent.[78]

During periods of labor shortages, landowners sometimes resorted to shady methods to secure workers. In Oglethorpe County, the editor of the *Oglethorpe Echo* recommended that the state "make some officer the guardian over these people [Negroes], whose business it shall be to see that they are honestly dealt by and to give them protection." He was asking for the General Assembly to create a state operated Freedmen's Bureau! The *Echo* went on to describe why such protection was necessary:

> A large majority of them are ignorant and uneducated, and are at the mercy of any unscrupulous white man that may employ them. They are often, we regret to say, imposed upon and after years of labor find a bare subsistence and a load of debt their only reward. Their dependent ignorance is too often used by unscrupulous planters to coerce them into making contracts.[79]

Coercion was an integral part of the lot of sharecroppers, white and black, although blacks were more likely to suffer physical abuse.

Peonage was one of the ways in which planters limited the mobility of tenants. Although outlawed by state and federal statutes, the practice was common in the rural South. Defined as compulsory work for the payment of a debt, peonage was difficult to prosecute because of the state laws allowing planters to prosecute croppers who attempted to flee from legiti-

---

[75]Higgs, *Competition*, 72-77.

[76]Cohen, "Involuntary Servitude," 31-60.

[77]Lexington *Oglethorpe Echo*, 13 February 1881.

[78]Oscar Zeichner, "The Legal Status of the Agricultural Laborer in the South," *Political Science Quarterly* 55 (1940): 412-28. DeCanio, *Agriculture*, 32-40.

[79]Lexington *Oglethorpe Echo*, 13 February 1881.

mate debts.[80] Often, however, planters used illegal means to force laborers into peonage. Once again the *Echo* provides an insight into how laborers were manipulated by planters into agreeing to become peons:

> Some negro in the employ of a farmer is detected in a theft. He is arraigned, tried before a justice, and committed to jail. Then the prosecutor, under the guise of a friend, steps up and binds the prisoner and his uncles and cousins and aunts to work for him one or more years, in consideration of the fact that the farmer is to go on the criminal's bond. He then takes a bill-of-sale to the labor of the whole crew, and they return to work for their prosecutor and emancipator, bound to him as before the chains of slavery were severed by *Lincoln's* emancipation proclamation.

Such practices made "justice . . . a matter of bargain and sale," fumed the editor, and he went on to describe the payoffs involved:

> [I]n fact, there are grave doubts about *Sambo* having stolen at all. Through a connivance of the Solicitor-General and the Judge the case is either dropped or a compromise effected by which the owner of the prisoner gives the Solicitor . . . a fixed sum; payable in the fall—the Judge fixing a small fine, instead of imprisonment, that his friend [the Solicitor] might make a collection . . . but this is always after the criminal has been frightened into selling himself.[81]

The alternative to peonage in these circumstances was the chain gang. Georgia, like other Southern states, adopted the practice of leasing its convicts to private corporations or individuals in return for a specified payment. This practice not only saved the state the cost of maintaining a state prison (and the measure was originally adopted after the Civil War for this reason) but it also enriched the public treasury. Convicts worked under the most deplorable conditions and were subjected to brutal punishments by lessees or their employees. The prospect of being sent to the chain gang was usually enough to ensure that laborers complied with the wishes of landowners.[82]

The various legal and extralegal systems of social and economic control of sharecroppers and tenants ensured that planters would emerge from the chaos of emancipation and reconstruction in as strong a position as

---

[80]See Pete Daniel, *The Shadow of Slavery: Peonage in the South, 1901-1969* (Urbana: University of Illinois Press, 1972). Higgs, *Competition,* 72-75, argues that there is a difference between peonage and the retention of laborers for payment of legitimate debt. Profit is the key to understanding peonage, and only where no original debt existed and one is created is peonage profitable.

[81]Lexington *Oglethorpe Echo,* 18 March 1881.

[82]For an overall view of the convict systems in Southern states, see Matthew J. Mancini, "Race, Economics, and the Abandonment of Convict Leasing," *Journal of Negro History* 63 (1978): 339-52. See also A. Elizabeth Taylor, " The Origin and Development of the Convict Lease System in Georgia," *Georgia Historical Quarterly* 26 (1942): 113-28.

they had held prior to the war. The key to the planters' continued dominance was their ownership of the lands best suited for cotton cultivation and, with the brief exception of the late 1860s, their control over the political machinery of the state. Georgia planters quickly established themselves as masters of the state's economy and just as quickly converted their economic control into political hegemony over blacks. They were not able to assert their hegemony over Southern whites so easily, and the years before the turn of the century were a time of running political battles between planters and their white opponents. Gradually, however, planters were able to parlay their dominance over freedmen into an impregnable base of political power.[83]

For the freedmen, emancipation meant "freedom" and little else. Quickly abandoned by erstwhile allies in the North and denied a share of the primary economic resources of the South, freedmen were forced to reach an accommodation with their former masters. Living in a hostile environment, they were compelled to rely on the traditional patterns of exploitation and paternalism that had marked their relationships with planters before the Civil War. Yet while they were being forced into subservient economic and political roles, freedmen contributed to an abortive effort to destroy the political and economic power of the planter class. As antebellum slaveowners had feared an uprising of slaves against the oppression of the slave system, so, too, did postbellum planters feel that, given the opportunity, freedmen would rebel against them.[84]

---

[83]Wiener, "Planter Persistence," 235-60. Harold D. Woodman, *King Cotton and His Retainers: Financing and Marketing the Cotton Crop of the South, 1800-1925* (Lexington: University of Kentucky Press, 1968) 204-24. Roger W. Shugg, "Survival of the Plantation System in Louisiana," *Journal of Southern History* 3 (1937): 311-25.

[84]Mandle, *Roots,* 28-51.

CHAPTER 2

PLANTERS UNDER ATTACK

The desire of white Georgians to be left alone by the federal government at the end of the Civil War was not to be realized. Planters, having maintained their hegemony through the provisions of the Constitution of 1865, sought to further extend their control by electing Alexander H. Stephens and Herschel V. Johnson as United States senators when the first postwar General Assembly met in 1866. Stephens and Johnson, both prominent members of the shortlived government of the Confederacy, had been active in their opposition to secession; but when war came, they had been instrumental in giving substance to the early Confederate nation. Despite their later disillusionment with the Confederacy and their participation in various abortive peace movements toward the end of the war, both men still supported secession as a legal and philosophical concept. Therefore, Stephens and Johnson still symbolized rebellion in many Northern minds and were considered as "unredeemed" as other Southerners who had supported the rebellion until the bitter end.[1]

The election of Stephens and Johnson heightened the antagonisms caused by the refusal of the General Assembly to ratify the Fourteenth Amendment. The legislators, like their colleagues in the Convention of 1865, were unwilling to grant citizenship to freedmen, to penalize further individuals who had served the Confederacy, or, perhaps more important, to renounce claims former slaveowners held for emancipated slaves—all of which were required by the Amendment. The overwhelming vote against ratification in November 1866 demonstrated the strength of the opposition to Negro enfranchisement. The Senate rejected the proposed amendment unanimously, while the House of Representatives followed suit by a vote of 147-2.[2] The refusal of the Assembly to ratify the Amendment accelerated the developing struggle in Congress between the sup-

---

[1]Conway, *Reconstruction of Georgia,* 40-60. Thompson, *Reconstruction in Georgia,* 140-42.

[2]Thompson, *Reconstruction in Georgia,* 150.

porters of the moderate policies of President Andrew Johnson and the militant advocates of a harsher congressional plan.[3]

The congressional elections of 1866 resulted in a severe defeat for Johnson and swung the balance of power to the Radical Republicans. Johnson's veto of the Civil Rights Act of 1866 provided the necessary opening for Radicals, and they moved to take control of Reconstruction. Led by Senator Charles Sumner and Representative Thaddeus Stevens, Congress enacted several pieces of legislation designed to implement what Radicals perceived as a great social revolution made possible by Union victory. In March 1867, the first Reconstruction Act was passed. As a result, the South was divided into five military districts, each under the command of a major general. Commanders were charged with supervising the registration of all males, black and white, in order to elect delegates to state constitutional conventions. These conventions would revise existing constitutions and ratify the Fourteenth Amendment. These were the minimum conditions that had to be met before Congress would recognize any Southern states as being "reconstructed." Although vetoed by Johnson, the Act went into effect when the veto was easily overridden.[4]

The commander of the Third Military District, of which Georgia was a part, was Major General John Pope, who located his headquarters in Atlanta. Pope immediately implemented the Reconstruction Act and subsequent acts passed by Congress. The occupation of the state by federal troops brought a storm of protest from white Georgians. Charles J. Jenkins, who had been elected governor under the Constitution of 1865, carried an official protest to Washington, but he failed to secure the removal of the troops from the state. Unable to prevail upon Congress, he then filed a petition with the Supreme Court seeking an injunction against Pope's enforcement of the Act. The Court's response was to deny any jurisdiction in the matter. The refusal of the Supreme Court to interfere with Congress's plan for reconstruction left Jenkins and Georgia with no alternative but to obey.[5]

Georgia's political situation changed drastically with the imposition of military rule. Prior to the passage of the Reconstruction Act of 1866, there was little political activity in the state as many antebellum leaders concentrated on rebuilding their fortunes. The prospect of continued military rule ended the relative political tranquillity of the state, and many of the old leaders became active once again.

---

[3]Mantell, *Johnson, Grant,* 1-26.

[4]Olive Hall Shadgett, *The Republican Party in Georgia from Reconstruction through 1900* (Athens: University of Georgia Press, 1964) 2.

[5]Elizabeth Studley Nathans, *Losing the Peace: Georgia Republicans and Reconstruction, 1865-1871* (Baton Rouge: Louisiana State University Press, 1969) 39, 94. Thompson, *Reconstruction in Georgia,* 158-59.

White Georgians were divided over the proper response to congressional reconstruction. One faction, led by ex-governor Joseph E. Brown, advocated quick acceptance of the terms dictated by Congress. This course of action was, they argued, the fastest way to gain readmittance into the Union and to end the political disabilities imposed on some Georgians. To bolster their argument, they pointed to Tennessee, which had ratified the Fourteenth Amendment and had been readmitted into the Union. A second group, led by former Confederate senator Benjamin H. Hill, proposed a "hands off" policy and nonparticipation in the election.[6] A third faction was led by Governor Jenkins and sought to reverse the congressional action in the courts. As C. Mildred Thompson described this latter group, "They determined to resist by any lawful means in their power, and if they had no power of resistance whatever, then submission must come by force and not by consent on their part."[7]

Despite vehement opposition from whites, General Pope established an agency to register black and white males in the state. Registrars were appointed; and, as an incentive to maximize enrollments, their salaries were based on a rate of approximately 26¢ per voter registered. Although some of their leaders counseled nonparticipation, white Georgians turned out in impressive numbers to enroll. Leading newspapers in the state urged registration in order to defeat the constitution that would be written by the state convention. Herschel V. Johnson, the president of the 1865 convention, used the Savannah *News* to urge whites to register and to vote against the proposed convention.[8] When the registration period ended, a total of 188,647 Georgians—white and black—had registered; and whites enjoyed a majority of about 2,000.[9]

The first election held under the Reconstruction Act was to decide if the state would call a convention to comply with the requirements imposed by Congress. This election, held over a five day period in late October and early November of 1867, marked the first time freedmen were able to vote. It also was the first opportunity for the Republican party to organize and participate in state elections. The voter turnout was slightly more than fifty-six percent of the total number of registered voters.[10] Of

---

[6]For a look at the different approaches taken by Brown and Hill, see Parks, *Brown*, 350-405, and Pearce, *Hill*. 142-200.

[7]Thompson, *Reconstruction in Georgia*, 158-59.

[8]Savannah *News*, 18 July 1867. Milledgeville *Federal Union*, 26 July 1867. Atlanta *New Era*, 14 May 1867. Augusta *Chronicle and Sentinel*, 19 June, 1 August 1867.

[9]Thompson, *Reconstruction in Georgia*, 169-72. *Journal of the Proceedings of the Constitutional Convention, 1867-1868*, in Candler, *Confederate Records*, 6: 201.

[10]Conway, *Reconstruction of Georgia*, 148. *Journal of 1867-1868*, 201.

the 106,410 ballots cast, 102,283 (96.1%) were in favor of the convention; only 4,127 were opposed.[11]

Although exact figures are unavailable, contemporary sources generally agree that the bulk of the ballots cast came from freedmen. Howell Cobb, a prominent antebellum politician, spoke for many whites when he labeled the election an "infamous farce." Throughout the state, he wrote to his wife, "the white people . . . have staid [sic] away from the polls." Samuel P. Richards, an Atlanta bookstore owner, noted in his diary, "Elections have been in progress throughout Georgia for three days on the *Convention* question and it has been done almost entirely by negro votes." Another Georgian worried about what a convention elected by Negroes and Republicans would mean to planting interests in the state. "If they have control," he wrote, "*Repudiation*—the abolition of poll tax[es]— a general division of lands—[and] the disfranchisement of Rebels will probably follow with laws regulating the price of labor and rent of lands— all to benefit the negro and the poor."[12] The prospect of a convention filled with former slaves, poor whites, and white Republicans filled many more affluent whites with dread. "It makes me feel wolfish every time I think about those *niggers* there pretending to make laws for Georgia white men," scribbled Richards in his diary.[13]

Prior to the first meeting of the convention, a statewide conference of leading "conservatives" was called in Macon. Rather than label the meeting a "Democratic" convocation and possibly rouse all the animosities of the antebellum political rivalries in the state, organizers sought to minimize the differences among whites by simply using the conservative name. Of primary importance to the Macon meeting was the development of some kind of plan to prevent the adoption of a new constitution that might result in a coalition of poor whites, Republicans, and freedmen. If antebellum alignments were any indication of the way postbellum politics would be conducted, the landed class had every reason to be apprehensive. Steven Hahn's recent study on the complicated relationships between regions and classes in Georgia provides insight into the issues and personalities of the antebellum political battles. In Macon, Benjamin H. Hill and Herschel V. Johnson provided the leadership for the conference and made plans to defeat the new constitution when it was submitted for ratification.[14]

The crux of conservative plans to defeat the new constitution was racism. Hoping to exploit the fears of lower-class whites over the possibility

---

[11]Milledgeville *Federal Union*, 5 November 1867.

[12]Howell Cobb to Mary Ann Cobb, 2 November 1867, Howell Cobb Papers. Entry for 31 October 1867, Samuel P. Richards Diary, Atlanta Historical Society. Conway, *Reconstruction of Georgia*, 148-49.

[13]Entry for 21 December 1867, Samuel P. Richards Diary.

[14]Pearce, *Hill*, 161-62. See also Hahn, *Roots of Southern Populism*.

of racial equality as a result of the enfranchisement of freedmen, Benjamin H. Hill, the president of the Macon convention, condemned Negro suffrage in strong language. "Negro supremacy [will] be permanently enthroned in the State of Georgia," he thundered, "[when] seven hundred thousand ignorant negroes who can neither read nor write, who know nothing of the principles of the Constitution or of legislation, agrarians by instinct and taught by political drill-masters that they have injuries to avenge against the white race [are] admitted to the Ballot box."[15] Hill's remarks were echoed by Herschel V. Johnson, who explained the reasons for white opposition to Negro enfranchisement in several letters to the New York *Tribune*. Johnson framed his remarks in terms of his own personal opinions, but he spoke for many Georgians. "I am opposed to Negroes exercising the franchise," he wrote, "not merely because their skin is black, but because I believe that they are too ignorant to use such enfranchisement rightly and well; that it will be fatal to good government."[16] The opinions of Hill and Johnson could not alter the fact that Congress had already settled the issue: Southern states had to agree to black suffrage if they wanted to be readmitted into the Union. The Macon conference would have to find other issues to use.

The Constitutional Convention met in Atlanta on 9 December 1867, after military authorities rejected Milledgeville because hotel operators and boarding house owners in the capital refused to rent accommodations to Negro delegates. General John Pope ordered the convention to meet in Atlanta where delegates would be assured of finding suitable quarters and where the military could protect them from possible intimidation.[17]

The membership of the 1867-1868 convention was decidedly different from that of the two previous conventions. Among the 165 delegates were 35 Negroes, 79 native white Georgians, 99 Republicans, 46 Democrats, and an additional twenty delegates classified as "nominal" Democrats.[18] The average residency in Georgia for all delegates was 32.6 years and ranged from one year to seventy-three years. The average age for native Georgians was 41.3 years with a range from 24 to 66 years.[19] Most of the delegates were men with little or no political experience. Unlike the planters who wrote the Constitutions of 1861 and 1865, the delegates to the new convention were unaccustomed to wearing the mantle of leadership.

The tone of the convention was set by Foster Blodgett, a Republican from Richmond County, who was elected temporary chairman. In his

---

[15]Flippin, *Johnson*, 284-87.

[16]Ibid., 282-84.

[17]Parks, *Brown*, 394.

[18]Nathans, *Losing the Peace*, 56-57. Pearce, *Hill*, 163.

[19]*Journal of 1867-1868*, 1020-27.

opening remarks, he reflected on the conditions that existed in Georgia and expressed regret "that so many of our countrymen, who have grown up under a system which subjected a part of our people to hard and degrading bondage, are slow to comprehend and acknowledge" the fact that the Civil War had established equality as a "great practical as well as theoretical truth." Blodgett's remarks were considered radical by most whites in the state, and the remainder of his speech was ignored. Although in the context of today's society his comments seem tame, they were aimed at winning the support of specific groups within the state. Of particular interest to the yeoman farmers and the urban middle class was his call for state aid for public education and for credit relief measures. In addition, Blodgett asked the convention to aid planters "who lately [had] enjoyed affluence, who had invested their capital in lands, . . . who [had] controlled at the same time the labor that made them yield their most valuable products, [and who] find themselves, today unable to meet the obligations incurred in days of prosperity." Despite the fact that "some have assailed us with taunts and jeers" and some "were the most active in bringing upon the country the troubles from which it is just emerging," Blodgett reminded the delegates that these planters could not "emancipate themselves from their prejudices." Instead of seeking to punish such men, delegates were encouraged to build a new Georgia based on racial harmony and mutual economic interests.[20] Blodgett's speech became the guidelines for the Republican party in the state as it sought to build new political coalitions as a base of permanent strength.

The need for constructing a broad base of support dominated the actions of Republican leaders in the convention. Although the party could count on the unswerving loyalty of freedmen, some of its prominent members realized that the freedmen alone were not enough to build a permanent, viable political party. While the Reconstruction Acts provided the opportunity for temporary ascendancy by Republicans, Georgia had a white majority that would give Democrats control unless the Republicans created a coalition of whites and blacks, businessmen and farmers. The election of a majority of the convention delegates gave the Republicans a much needed first victory, but their success was due to Democratic nonparticipation rather than real political strength. The continued refusal of white Democrats to vote in future elections was unlikely, however, and future Republican control depended on the party's ability to attract whites into their ranks. Thus, Blodgett's opening remarks to the convention delegates set the stage for a series of direct and indirect appeals to potential recruits. Former Whigs in the Black Belt, yeoman farmers in the mountain and wiregrass sections, merchants and industrialists in the towns, and former Unionists became targets of these appeals. The

[20]Ibid., 207-13.

convention offered Republicans an opportunity to demonstrate their intentions in a positive manner.[21]

In contrast to the 1865 convention, which met for only thirteen days, the convention of 1867-68 lasted for almost four months. During this time, Republicans used the floor of the convention hall as a platform to launch a campaign for voter support. Assured of control of the convention and backed by the military and Congress, they conducted an intense assault on the old planter elite. On 18 December 1867, Aaron Alpeoria Bradley, a Negro delegate from Savannah, introduced a resolution calling for the removal of Governor Charles J. Jenkins and the appointment of Rufus B. Bullock, a white delegate from Augusta, as provisional governor. Although the original resolution failed by a close vote (75-78), an amended resolution that asked only for Jenkins's removal and the appointment of an unnamed replacement passed by a 95-59 majority.[22]

Jenkins was removed by the military authorities on 13 January 1868, and General George G. Meade, Pope's successor, appointed a military officer in his place. John H. Jones, the state treasurer, was removed at the same time and was also replaced by an officer from Meade's staff. The reaction of white Georgians to Jenkins's removal was one of complete shock and outrage. Anna Marie Green, a young Milledgeville girl, recorded some of these intense feelings in her diary. "Our country is in a deplorable condition," she wrote. "Men fear a war of races, and indeed it seems impossible for the white men to submit to negro rule. It is certainly a distressing state of affairs when negroes hold conventions in our state and indeed have every right of suffrage and civil power. Men look ominously at one another and wonder what the times will bring forth. Military despotism [is] our only authority."[23]

The major portion of the delegates' time in the convention was spent on deciding issues that were considered essential to the future development of the Republican party. In a marked departure from the *status quo antebellum,* the convention considered questions that were aimed at benefiting the lower classes and not the planting classes. All in all, the major focus of the convention's attention was on devising programs that would break the hegemony

---

[21]Nathans, *Losing the Peace,* 56-78. Conway, *Reconstruction of Georgia,* 149-61.

[22]*Journal of 1867-1868,* 262-64. Joseph P. Reidy, "Aaron A. Bradley: Voice of Black Labor in the Georgia Lowcountry," in Howard N. Rabinowitz, ed., *Southern Black Leaders of the Reconstruction Era* (Urbana: University of Illinois Press, 1982) 281-308. For a very different view of Bradley, see E. Merton Coulter, *Negro Legislators in Georgia during the Reconstruction Period* (Athens: University of Georgia Press, 1968).

[23]Anna Marie Green to Diary, 31 December 1867, in James C. Bonner, ed., *The Journal of a Milledgeville Girl, 1861-1867* (Athens: University of Georgia Press, 1964) 126-27.

of the landowning elite in state politics and provide the Republicans with an appealing and effective platform for the 1868 state elections.

The first of the major issues to come before the convention was the question of providing some form of relief for individuals caught up in an ever increasing burden of debts. The economy of Georgia, depressed as a result of the war, was worsened by two years of alternating excessive rain and drought. Planters, sharecroppers, and yeoman farmers alike found their plight compounded by a depressed international cotton market and by debts contracted during the war. Rufus B. Bullock, a Republican leader from Augusta who aspired to higher office, introduced a resolution into the convention to suspend all levies, foreclosures, and public sales of property attached for debt until a permanent relief measure could be enacted. Bullock's suggestion was quickly accepted by the convention, and a special Committee on Relief was created to draft the necessary permanent legislation. Most of January 1868 was taken up with the debate over debtor relief.[24]

The major conflict over the provision of debt relief for Georgians revolved around the extent to which the convention should go to eliminate debts, what kinds of debts should be included in the list of exemptions, and the period to be covered by the legislation. Although antebellum laws had provided homestead exemptions for "honest" debtors, a majority of the delegates supported a proposal that would abrogate all contracts consummated prior to 1 June 1865. A minority bloc of delegates led by Amos T. Akerman, a prewar politician from Elbert County, supported a mild resolution that asked Congress to rewrite federal bankruptcy laws. Only congressional revision, they argued, could produce laws that would survive court tests of constitutionality.[25]

The debate on relief demonstrated the lengths to which some Republicans were willing to go to gain the favor of poor whites in the state, and, at the same time, it revealed a growing rift within the hierarchy of the fledgling party. Rufus B. Bullock, the spokesman for the prorelief forces and the leader of the so-called "Augusta Ring," headed a group within the party that wanted to concentrate on uniting freedmen, poor whites in the mountain and wiregrass regions, and workers in urban areas into a strong coalition able to defeat the Democrats. Amos T. Akerman, on the other hand, had been a respected politician in the antebellum period, and he identified the best interests of the Republican party with those of the prewar Whig planters. In his vision of the party's future in Georgia, Akerman saw a strong political organization built on planters, town merchants, and

---

[24]*Journal of 1867-1868*, 306-308, 321.

[25]Thompson, *Reconstruction in Georgia*, 178-81. For the views of prominent Democrats, see the Augusta *Chronicle*, 5 April 1868, and the Macon *Telegraph*, 24 March 1868.

the emerging class of industrialists. To Akerman, real Republicanism amounted to a revival of the Whiggish principles of the antebellum era.[26]

After prolonged debate on the question of relief, the convention voted on 5 February to cancel all contractual obligations entered into prior to 1 June 1865, with certain exceptions. The February vote was anticlimactic since a motion to table the relief measure and to substitute Akerman's bankruptcy resolution had been soundly defeated (88-42) on 28 January. The final vote on the measure was essentially the same (82-45). The vote on relief also demonstrated the strength of the "Radical" faction of the Republican party. An analysis of the relief measure balloting reveals that supporters of the proposal were exclusively Republicans, while opponents were either Black Belt Democrats or Moderate Republicans. Just as the vote revealed the direction the party would take, it also revealed the personal strength of Bullock in the party's counsels.[27]

There was no doubt that the relief legislation, while benefiting some planters, was aimed at curtailing their economic power. Contracts made "with the intention and for the purpose of aiding and encouraging rebellion" were declared null and void, as were debts contracted for the purchase and hire of slaves. Only debts owed to corporations, mechanics, and laborers were allowed to stand; and since the small farmers outside the Black Belt and sharecroppers/tenants/laborers had little to do with corporations, only planters would be affected. Thus the Radicals in Georgia went even further in their assault on private property and privilege than did the Radicals in Congress. Relief became a central issue in the debate over ratification when the constitution was submitted to the voters, and it became a divisive issue within the Republican party.[28]

While the convention debated this question, it also approved several petitions to Congress for relief for the planting class. One memorial asked for the repeal of the war tax on cotton, because "the successful culture of cotton is essential to the prosperity of the people and the full development of the material interests of the State." In addition to this appeal, the convention approved a resolution urging Congress to make $30,000,000 in low interest loans available to the "impoverished planters of the South." The money was needed, continued the resolution, because without it the "extent of suffering among the freedmen . . . [would] be appalling to the Christian heart." The money would allow planters to continue cultivating cotton, which would mean jobs for freedmen. The resolution ended with this reminder to Congress: "The 'nation's wards' cannot be better cared for than by thus providing remunerative labor upon that staple with the

---

[26]Nathans, *Losing the Peace*, 60-62.

[27]*Journal of 1867-1868*, 238, 478-82.

[28]Parks, *Brown*, 398-405. Nathans, *Losing the Peace*, 178-79.

production of which they are already familiar, and which yields to them the greatest reward for that service which they are best fitted by their raising to perform." Although the petitions and resolutions were masterful public relations ploys by the Republicans, few planters took them seriously in the face of the convention's other actions.[29]

Certainly the most controversial of these was granting the right of suffrage to freedmen. Required by the Reconstruction Acts to include a provision for universal manhood suffrage in the new constitution as a condition for readmission into the union, the delegates included a section that conformed to the law. The convention's willingness to ratify the Fourteenth Amendment stood in stark contrast to the nearly unanimous refusal of the General Assembly to do so in 1866.

Although the convention quickly approved the enfranchisement of Negroes, the question of auxiliary privileges inherent in the right to vote provoked heated debate. Some delegates who were willing to grant the right of the franchise to freedmen were less willing to concede that blacks were capable or desirable officeholders. Concerned with building support for their party among the poor whites in north and south Georgia, Republican leaders were wary of publicly committing themselves to making the right to hold office synonymous with the right to vote. This question created a ticklish problem for white Republicans, since to deny Negroes the right to hold office would result in the loss of black votes. Caught in a quandary, the Republicans agreed to a compromise that satisfied neither whites nor blacks.

The opening debate on the right to hold office began on 13 February when a resolution was introduced that imposed a seven-year waiting period before any new citizens could hold public office. Under its provisions, virtually all blacks would be barred from holding public office until 1875 at the earliest. A majority of the delegates reacted strongly against this scheme, and the resolution was defeated. Then John Harris, a Republican from Newton County, offered a motion to delete any reference to officeholding in the enfranchisement article. Although the convention adjourned before a vote could be taken, discussion on the proposal was resumed the next day, and the motion was approved by an overwhelming (126-12) vote. Perhaps indicative of the Republican efforts to avoid a possible schism in the party and among the voters and perhaps the result of overnight compromise efforts, twenty-nine of the thirty-two Negro delegates present voted with the majority to strike the officeholding clause.[30]

Elizabeth Studley Nathans suggests that the motion to withdraw any reference to officeholding was carefully orchestrated, perhaps by Joseph E. Brown, who was serving as an unofficial advisor to the Republicans at the convention. By deliberately leaving the question of the right to hold

[29]*Journal of 1867-1868*, 238, 478-82.

[30]Ibid., 594-99.

office unanswered, the Republicans hoped to work both sides of the street, retaining the support of Negroes and white yeoman farmers in extreme north and south Georgia.[31] Regardless of who conceived of the compromise, the decision to leave the issue vague and uncertain was a shrewd one. Democratic editors also saw the fine hand of Joseph E. Brown behind the Republican tactic, and such supposition was not out of line with the general policy of moderation Brown urged on the Republicans.[32]

On 15 February, the entire question was reopened when James D. Waddell, a Democrat from Polk County, introduced a resolution stating that "white men, only, shall be eligible to any office of trust, honor, or profit, or employment, whether municipal, judicial, or political, in this State, and white men, only, shall serve as jurors in the courts." Waddell's proposal was defeated by a large majority, receiving only nineteen votes in its favor.[33]

Having dodged the issue of Negro officeholding, the convention then took steps to protect possible Republican voters from intimidation. Under the suffrage article of the proposed constitution, electors were granted immunity from arrest for a period of "five days before an election, during the election, and two days subsequent thereto." The only exceptions to this general immunity were arrests of individuals who committed treason or a felony or disturbed the peace. An additional section of this article instructed the next General Assembly to enact such laws as were necessary to provide adequate protection for voters.[34] Despite the attempts by Republicans to remove intimidation as a weapon of white Democrats, this section of the constitution proved to be of little value, since it did nothing to alter the realities of Democratic control of police and judicial systems at the local level. As the elections of 1868 proved, such provisions did not take into account the willingness of extralegal groups such as the Ku Klux Klan to break even the most comprehensive laws.[35]

The suffrage provisions also placed some restrictions on the franchise rights of Georgians, black and white. Although Radical Republicans had proposed the proscription of all whites who had participated in the Civil

---

[31]Nathans, *Losing the Peace,* 68-69.

[32]Savannah *Daily News and Herald,* 20 February 1868. Dawson *Journal,* 5 March 1868. Macon *Telegraph,* 24 March 1868. Although not a delegate to the convention, Brown hovered in the background and served as an unofficial advisor to the Republican leadership. His strong ties with the yeomanry of the upcountry gave him special insight into how they would react to Republican policies.

[33]*Journal of 1867-1868,* 611-14. The vote on the Waddell resolution was 103-19.

[34]Ibid., 891-92.

[35]See Allen W. Trelease, *White Terror: The Ku Klux Klan Conspiracy and Southern Reconstruction* (New York; Harper and Row, 1971).

War as rebels, this proposal was quickly defeated; and the franchise was granted to all males in the state who were twenty-one years old, were citizens of the United States, and had resided in a particular county for thirty days prior to an election. Women, lunatics, and criminals were denied the right to vote. Although quite liberal on the surface, the new constitution continued some antebellum restrictions. For example, voters were required to pay an annual poll tax of one dollar before they could cast their ballots. Although not cumulative, such a tax requirement presented a serious obstacle to potential voters from the lower classes. Still another restriction carried over from the previous constitution stipulated that any individual elected to the governorship was required to have been a citizen of the state for a minimum of six years. This provision eliminated the possibility of a Negro's becoming governor before 1876, since the term of office for the state's chief executive was for four years.[36]

One of the most significant accomplishments of the convention was the inclusion of a provision in the new constitution to allow the state to underwrite railroad construction and other internal improvements. Both the Constitutions of 1861 and 1865 had included prohibitions against such expenditures.[37] Republicans, seeking to disrupt the traditional alliance of urban merchants, businessmen, and planters in the Black Belt, saw state aid as one method by which a new political coalition might be created. Certainly, the matter of internal development and aid to railroads had been a favorite issue of antebellum Whigs, and the increased participation of yeoman farmers in extreme north and south Georgia in the state's economy would decrease the influence of planters. If the Republicans could claim credit for stimulating the economic growth of these regions, surely voters would support the Republican party.[38]

The opening debate on the question of internal improvements came when M. C. Smith, a delegate from Thomas County in extreme south Georgia, introduced a resolution asking Congress to lend $100,000 to the South Georgia and Florida Railroad Company because "the people of Southwestern Georgia are deprived of direct railroad communication with the central and northern part of the State." Smith's resolution was approved with little debate, and its ready acceptance signaled the willingness of the convention to consider a general provision for authorizing state aid. The debate on this provision was generally positive, and although the original proposal included a requirement that all state aid grants have the concurrence of a majority of both houses of the General Assembly, this proviso was dropped from the final version that was approved. The only

---

[36]*Journal of 1867-1868*, 891-92.

[37]Candler, *Confederate Records*, 1: 601. *Journal of 1865*, 216-17.

[38]Hahn, *Roots of Southern Populism*, 91-105.

restrictions placed on corporations receiving state aid were that the "whole property of the Company . . . be bound for the security of the State prior to any other debt or lien, except as to laborers" and that they have privately invested funds at least equal to the amount of state aid requested.[39]

The success of the Republicans in getting the state aid measure included in the new constitution was followed closely by another victory for the party. Seeking to strengthen the budding coalition between yeoman farmers and Republicans, William A. Fort, a delegate from Floyd County in northwest Georgia, introduced a proposal that would exempt homesteads from seizure and sale for nonpayment of debts. This proposal differed from the earlier debt relief measure in that it placed a definite limit on the kind and amount of real and personal property that could not be attached and sold. Just as the relief issue brought heated debate, so too did the homestead exemption measure. Moderate Republicans joined with Black Belt Democrats to protest the proposal. Radical Republicans, again seeking to solidify their appeal to the lower classes of the state, backed Democrats from the Mountain and Wiregrass sections who sought an exemption of $4500 in real estate and personal property. After a heated and prolonged debate, during which several counter proposals were offered by both sides, the Radical-Mountain-Wiregrass coalition was able to push through a compromise measure that guaranteed a real estate exemption of $2000 and a personal property exemption of $1000.[40]

The final vote on the homestead exemption package revealed the extent to which Republican efforts to attract votes from Democrats in the extreme sections of the state were succeeding. The homestead measure passed with seventy-eight affirmative votes, ten of which came from Democrats. The homestead exemption, coupled with the relief and internal development measures, gave the Republicans a solid base upon which to build a class-oriented political party in the state. These economic issues had been resolved in such a way that Republicans could take credit for substantially improving the lot of the poorer classes. Certainly, they would be the major themes the Republicans would stress over and over again in the upcoming state elections.

Even the question of Negro suffrage, a potential "fly in the ointment," had been resolved in such a manner that the traditional antipathy of poorer whites toward blacks had been defused somewhat. Contented with their gains among the lower classes, Radical Republicans ignored the possibility of forming a different, potentially more viable, coalition of Moderate Republicans and Black Belt Democrats. On each of the four major issues

---

[39]*Journal of 1867-1868*, 890-92.

[40]Ibid., 241, 261, 656-57, 699-722. Hahn, *Roots of Southern Populism*, 193-203.

before the convention, a small group of conservatives from each party had placed themselves squarely in opposition to the Radicals.[41]

The formation of alliances within the convention was nowhere more vividly illustrated than by the vote on a resolution endorsing the efforts of congressional Radicals to impeach Andrew Johnson. Introduced by J. A. Madden, a Republican delegate from Burke County, the resolution applauded the Radicals for seeking impeachment of Johnson for violating the Tenure of Office Act in dismissing Secretary of War Edwin M. Stanton. Although Johnson's initial policies had been aimed at breaking the power of antebellum planters, he had moderated his stance as Reconstruction proceeded, and many Radicals in Congress now viewed him as being pro-planter. Deliberately setting a trap for Johnson, the Radicals had moved against him when he dismissed Stanton from the Cabinet. Despite the fact that the Georgia convention had no bearing on the impeachment proceedings, the Madden resolution offered an opportunity for groups vying for power to align themselves with the leading powers in the national Republican party. For Democrats, it presented the chance to make a statement on the entire process of Reconstruction.[42]

As soon as the Madden resolution was introduced, R. H. Whiteley, a delegate from Decatur County, moved to table it. His motion was sustained by a combination of conservative Democrats and Moderate Republicans. Among the Republican leadership, Rufus B. Bullock, Foster Blodgett, and John E. Bryant—all prominent Radicals—voted against it. Amos T. Akerman, Nedom L. Angier, and R. H. Whiteley—all Moderates—voted with the Democrats in support of the motion.[43]

An analysis of the vote against the Madden resolution on the basis of length of residency in Georgia is revealing (table 2.1). Delegates who voted to table it were more likely to be either native Georgians, Southern born,

TABLE 2.1

VOTE TO TABLE MADDEN RESOLUTION					
VOTE ON MOTION TO TABLE	AVERAGE RESIDENCY	NATIVE GEORGIANS	SOUTHERNERS	NORTHERNERS	IMMIGRANTS OR UNKNOWN
YES—71	36.7	36	20	11	4
NO—52	26.3	22	15	14	1

[41]Nathans, *Losing the Peace*, 62-64.

[42]*Journal of 1867-1868*, 748-50. Mantell, *Johnson, Grant*, 24-25, 80-81.

[43]*Journal of 1867-1868*, 1020-27. Although white planters did not particularly like Andrew Johnson, they were unwilling to exchange him for an unknown Radical. Moderates in Georgia sided with Democrats on this issue.

or longtime residents of the state than were those who voted for it. Joining with the Democrats-Moderates were some of the more independent Negro delegates. The vote on the Madden resolution indicated that the actions of Radicals in Congress would not be accepted unquestioningly by Georgia Republicans, white or black.[44]

Despite the efforts of Georgia Republicans to write a constitution that would destroy the hegemony of planters, the final document drawn up by the convention did not represent a drastic break with previous constitutions. Minor changes were made in the selection process for judges, the terms of office for the governor and other state executives were extended, and the period of service for state senators increased from two to four years; but essentially the structure of the state government remained the same as it had been previously. In the House of Representatives, the membership had been increased, and the allocation of representatives was altered to reflect the internal redistribution of population that followed the opening of new lands to cotton production.

The new scheme of representation was the "3-2-1" system. Under this plan, the six most populous counties would have three representatives each; the next thirty-one, two each; and the remaining ninety-five, one each.[45] Republicans, counting on the continued support of the newly enfranchised freedmen, viewed this arrangement as one that would give them a majority in all future elections. They found it difficult to comprehend that Negroes would not vote for the party of emancipation; and the support of blacks in the heavily populated rural counties, when coupled with the votes of urban workers and yeoman farmers, appeared to give the Republican Party a lock on state politics in the foreseeable future. As later events proved, however, any such advantage was temporary, and it soon dissipated under economic pressures applied by Democratic landowners and the physical oppression of the Ku Klux Klan.[46]

Just as Republicans viewed reapportionment as beneficial to their party's future, so too did they consider the decision to move the capital to Atlanta. Milledgeville, which had been the capital since 1807, was located in the heart of the Black Belt and linked to the planter class by location, tradition, and economics. Atlanta, the fast developing center of industry and transportation in the state, was located on the fringe of the mountains— a section from which Republicans hoped to draw support. Unlike Milledgeville, which was tied to the prewar South of planters and slaves, Atlanta symbolized the rising expectations of men of the "New South," who largely rejected the old values of the planter class. Finally, Atlanta was the

---

[44]Ibid.

[45]Louis T. Rigdon, II, *Georgia's County Unit System* (Decatur GA: Selective Books, 1961) 16-17.

[46]Nathans, *Losing the Peace*, 68-69.

headquarters of the Third Military District, a last bastion of Republican support should the need arise. For these reasons, the Republican majority in the convention put through a resolution making the question of permanently relocating the capital in Atlanta one of the items to be voted on when the constitution was offered for ratification.[47]

The final action of the convention fixed the date of the ratification election as 20 April 1868. During the same election, voters would also choose a new governor, legislators, and other state officials. The April election was to be the first test of the coalition the Republicans had worked so hard to put together. As much as anything else, the convention had served as a vehicle through which the new party could weld the traditional enemies of the planting class into a cohesive political unit. In creating their coalition, Republicans sought to placate virtually every group within the state from poor whites and Negroes to former Whig planters.

For planters, the outcome of the convention had ominous overtones. Previous constitutions had allowed them, under the "three-fifths" concept, to exercise a disproportionate share of political control, but the enfranchisement of Negroes presented the specter of having the Black Belt become the center of Republican power. In addition, the inclusion of an internal improvements provision in the new constitution threatened to shift the economic center of the state from the Black Belt to other areas opened to settlement by new and state supported railroads. Planters had no illusions about the new constitution and realized that its ratification would pose a serious threat to their continued dominance of the state. A quick response was needed to avert catastrophe.

To counter the concrete Republican programs of reform and economic aid, the Democrats/planters offered a blatant appeal to racism. The Rome *Weekly Courier* launched the Democratic offensive when it explained the meaning of the new constitution to the people of north Georgia:

> It means first and foremost universal negro suffrage and negro equality . . . social and political tyranny . . . miscegenation and all the nameless horrors that follow the forced amalgamation of races . . . robbery and jobbery of every description . . . wholesale lying, speculation, robbery . . . [and] the subjection of a white majority to a negro minority. Are the people prepared to submit to this? Are they ready to become the Slaves of Slaves?[48]

---

[47]Ibid.

[48]Rome *Weekly Courier,* 27 March 1868.

CHAPTER 3

A PERIOD OF TURMOIL

The first test of the alliances established by the Republicans during the convention would come less than six months after that body had adjourned. On 20 April 1868, the new constitution was to be submitted to the voters for ratification or rejection. At the same time, voters were to choose a new governor, members of the General Assembly, and other state officials. Seeking to maintain the political momentum they had generated in the October-November election of convention delegates, Republicans utilized the last week of the convention to select their nominees for state office.

On 22 January, the Republican State Executive Committee called a nominating convention for Atlanta on 19 February. Less than two weeks later, the Committee canceled the convention call and substituted a call for a party caucus made up of delegates to the convention.[1] The caucus, dominated by supporters of Rufus B. Bullock, assumed the role of nominating convention since the "delegates to the Constitutional Convention were elected by an almost unanimous vote of the Republicans of Georgia."[2] This decision represented a shrewd move on the part of Bullock to prevent the selection of more moderate Republicans to an open convention. Bullock supporters, a minority among the white leaders of the party, realized that such a convention would probably be controlled by Moderates and that Bullock would be passed over in the nominations.[3] A caucus of convention delegates, having been courted for months by Bullock and his allies, would select Bullock.

---

[1]Augusta *Daily Constitutionalist*, 24 February 1868. Shadgett, *Republican Party in Georgia*, 5-8.

[2]Atlanta *New Era*, 6 March 1868. Broadside, Henry P. Farrow Collection, University of Georgia. Hereafter referred to as FC.

[3]Note dated 16 August 1883, FC. Initialed H. P. F., the note reads, "The call for a State Convention in 1868 was issued by Committee—when [Foster] Blodgett saw that I would get the nomination over Bullock he withdrew the call and resolved the constitutional convention into a nominating body."

The decision to change from a nominating convention to a party caucus accentuated the growing differences between the Moderates and Radicals of the state party. The latter boldly seized the party machinery and aligned themselves with the Radicals of the national organization. This move, strenuously opposed by the Moderates, placed additional stress on the alliances created in the convention. The identification of Radicals in the state with men like Thaddeus Stevens and Charles Sumner was a liability when it came to attracting white voters to the party. Nevertheless, Radicals were willing to take the chance that the economic reforms enacted by the convention would prove sufficient to overcome the stigma attached to national Republicanism. The backing of congressional Radicals seemed necessary if the state party was to achieve immediate victory.

The caucus met on 7 March, and, carefully stage-managed by Bullock supporters, promptly approved his nomination as the party's candidate for governor by acclamation. Possible opponents—men like Amos T. Akerman, Henry P. Farrow, and Joseph E. Brown—were given no opportunity to organize any resistance. Faced with a *fait accompli*, anti-Bullock Republicans could only protest the steamroller tactics the Radicals had employed. With the gubernatorial nomination out of the way, the caucus quickly agreed on a platform that called for the ratification of the proposed constitution. Having disposed of its major business before lunch, the caucus adjourned until evening.[4]

Bullock's nomination, a masterpiece of political strategy, threatened the fragile unity of the party, and his supporters spent the afternoon pacifying opposition party leaders. The price for party unity was high, and Moderates extracted promises for important patronage positions from Bullock. Akerman received assurance of Radical support for a high federal appointment, while Farrow was promised a position of power in the state administration. Perhaps the most important concessions were those given to Joseph E. Brown, whose influence among the yeoman farmers of the mountains was critical to Republican success. Brown's price for cooperating with Bullock and for actively backing his candidacy was a share in the distribution of state and federal patronage, plus a seat in the United States Senate. Thus, Bullock was forced to undermine his own future leadership by awarding his most powerful rivals the major political offices a Republican victory would bring.[5]

When the caucus reassembled, it was apparent that a compromise had been reached between Bullock and the Moderates. During the course of the evening, Brown, Akerman, and Farrow appeared before the delegates and urged party unity under the Bullock banner. Although outward

[4]Savannah *News*, 11 March 1868. Atlanta *New Era*, 8 March 1868. Augusta *Daily Constitutionalist*, 12 March 1868.

[5]Nathans, *Losing the Peace*, 77-78. Parks, *Brown*, 406-24.

appearances pointed toward a reconciliation, serious conflicts between personalities and philosophies remained and would surface again after the election.[6]

Democratic reaction to Bullock's nomination was mixed. The December meeting of Democratic-Conservative leaders had advocated a policy of ignoring both the new convention and the state elections. Primarily the work of Benjamin H. Hill, this "policy of ignorance" was based on the belief that ratification was impossible if white voters failed to cast their ballots, because ratification required a majority of the registered voters of the state. On 11 March, Congress passed the fourth Reconstruction Act, which specified that ratification could be accomplished by a simple majority of voters casting ballots, regardless of how small a percentage of the total registered voters they comprised. This action by Congress neutralized the Democrats' strategy and forced them into an active role in the April elections.[7]

Like the Republicans, the Democrats were split into a number of factions. Several issues—some left over from antebellum days— plagued the party, including a reluctance on the part of some antebellum Whigs to use the name "Democrat." In order to placate these men, the Democrats tended to use a hyphenated form of their name—Democratic-Conservatives, although eventually the Conservative portion was dropped. At the heart of the dissension within Democratic ranks was the question of the "proper" stance the party should take on Reconstruction. One group, less inflexible in its approach, pushed for participation in the April election. In particular, this group feared that unless Democrats pursued a vigorous course of action in the campaign, the people of north Georgia—traditionally opposed to the large landowners of the Black Belt—would follow Joseph E. Brown into the Republican party, and the Republicans would dominate the state for the next few years by default.[8]

The relief measures written into the new constitution were being claimed by the Republican party as having been originated and passed by them, and these measures represented a powerful lure to mountain whites and a potent weapon to be used against the Democrats. To counter these Republican claims, Democratic leaders issued a general statement attacking Reconstruction in harsh racial tones. The work of a committee of antebellum Democrats and Whigs chaired by Herschel V. Johnson, it described the convention as having been "without parallel in the annals of the world. Representing negroes only, with the exception of a few thousand whites," the statement continued, the convention wanted "to crys-

[6]Conway, *Reconstruction of Georgia*, 163. Jack B. Scroggs, "Southern Reconstruction: A Radical View," *Journal of Southern History* 24 (1958): 407-29.

[7]Nathans, *Losing the Peace*, 80-101.

[8]Isaac W. Avery, *History of the State of Georgia, 1850-1881* (New York: Brown and Derby, 1881) 373-75.

tallize into constitutional form the policy of bringing the State of Georgia under the domain of *negro supremacy.*" White Georgians would do well to remember that "although history furnishes instances of abolition, yet it affords no example of an attempt by military force to elevate the emancipated slave above his recent master, to subordinate the superior to the inferior race, and clothe the latter with the political power of the State. It is the most outrageous policy ever adopted by a Christian people."[9] By concentrating their energies on the issue of race, Democrats sought to heighten racial tensions within the state and to polarize public opinion on the subject. Republican appeals to the economic interests of poor whites could be blunted by Democratic appeals to prejudice.

Although the Democratic party failed to establish a positive program, it did create a State Executive Committee to coordinate the Democratic campaign efforts. By early 1868, a network of Young Men's Democratic Clubs had been formed, and they became the foundation of the party's organization throughout the state. By mid-February, E. G. Cabaniss, the chairman of the Executive Committee, reported that every congressional district in Georgia, except for the Fourth, had organized a district committee to work with the party faithful.[10]

Democratic success at organizing was not followed by success in selecting a gubernatorial candidate to oppose Bullock. Because of the short time between the adjournment of the Constitutional Convention on 7 March and the state elections on 20 April, the Democratic Executive Committee opted to forego the usual nominating convention and to assume the responsibility for naming a gubernatorial candidate. The Committee's choice was Judge Augustus Reese, a former judge of the Ocmulgee Judicial Circuit in central Georgia. Reese had been removed from the bench by Major General Pope when he refused to obey Pope's order to seat Negroes on juries. As a symbol of white opposition to Reconstruction, Reese made an ideal candidate. Less than two weeks after his selection, however, Judge Reese withdrew his nomination when it was discovered that he was ineligible under the provisions of the Fourteenth Amendment. Thus, with less than a month to go before the election, Democrats found themselves without a candidate.[11]

---

[9]Flippin, *Johnson,* 284-87. Milledgeville *Federal Union,* 31 December 1868. Participating in issuing the general statement were Thomas L. Guerry of Brunswick; A. H. Chappell, an antebellum Whig; Warren Akin, Joseph E. Brown's gubernatorial opponent in 1859; and Benjamin H. Hill.

[10]Dawson *Journal,* 20 February 1868. Milledgeville *Federal Union,* 31 December 1867. Savannah *Daily News,* 1 January 1868.

[11]Augusta *Daily Constitutionalist,* 15 March 1868. Milledgeville *Southern Recorder,* 17 March 1868. Atlanta *Intelligencer,* 14 March 1868.

Reese's withdrawal left the nomination open to David Irwin. Like Reese, Irwin had served as a circuit judge in Georgia. In 1855, he had been defeated for reelection to the judgeship of the Blue Ridge Circuit by Joseph E. Brown.[12] When Brown was elected governor in 1857, Irwin regained his old position. Although he had been elected as a delegate to the Constitutional Convention, he had refused to take his seat. Despite the Democratic platform denouncing the proposed constitution, he refused to either endorse or condemn the document in public. Judge Irwin's refusal to comment on the constitution was an apparent ploy to draw support from both Democrats and Moderate Republicans. Fearful of Irwin's appeal to conservative voters, Radicals complained to Major General George G. Meade, Pope's replacement as commander of the Third Military District, that Irwin—like Reese—was ineligible to serve as governor. On 4 April, General Meade ruled in favor of the Republicans, and Irwin became the second Democratic candidate in as many weeks to be forced to withdraw from the canvass. With only a few days remaining before the election, the Democratic Executive Committee had to find yet another candidate.[13]

Before officially naming a third nominee, the Executive Committee sought prior approval of their choice from General Meade. The new candidate was John B. Gordon, one of Georgia's highest ranking Confederate heroes and a battlefield opponent of Meade. Gordon had held no public office before the war, but although a political neophyte, he was immensely popular with white Georgians. Meade's approval of Gordon might have been withheld had he known of Gordon's close association with the rapidly growing Ku Klux Klan.[14] A planter before the war, Gordon was closely tied to the conservative leadership of the Democratic party, and his candidacy provided a clear alternative to Bullock and the Republicans. To vote for Gordon was to vote against the Republicans, against Reconstruction, and, most important, against Negroes. To vote for Gordon was also to vote for a restoration of antebellum leadership.[15]

The selection of Gordon as their candidate gave Democrats a well known and dynamic personality behind whom they could rally, and he forcefully articulated the racist theme of the Democrats. Benjamin H. Hill, the recognized leader of the party, lent his voice to Gordon's cause and canvassed the state seeking support for him. Hill launched a scathing attack on the Republicans and the proposed constitution. Labeling it a "corrupt

---

[12]Parks, *Brown*, 17, 410-11.

[13]Nathans, *Losing the Peace*, 83-85. Shadgett, *Republican Party in Georgia*, 8-9.

[14]Trelease, *White Terror*, 20, 74-79. Although there is no positive proof of Gordon's involvement, most observers described him as the "probable Grand Dragon" of the Georgia Klan.

[15]Atlanta *New Era*, 18 March 1868.

instrument," he charged that it guaranteed social equality, exceeded the requirements of the Reconstruction Acts, and contained the patently unconstitutional relief clause. It was, he insisted, nothing more than a cheap trick to win votes for Republicans.[16] The Constitutional Convention was scored by Hill as being a "nigger-New England conclave," which had merely done the bidding of Joseph E. Brown, that "Beelzebub of the fallen."[17] Other Democrats took up Hill's rhetoric, and frequent references were made in the Democratic press about the "Piebald" convention of Radical usurpers that had produced a constitution reflecting only "hate and malignity."[18]

Democratic handbills were circulated throughout the state stressing the theme of racial equality as the most immediate result of a Republican victory.

White men of Georgia! Read and Reflect! Rescue Georgia!

The issue involved in the election on the 20th of April is whether or not Georgia shall pass into the hands of negroes and Yankee political adventurers! Can Georgians rule Georgia? They can! Then go to the polls and vote the Democratic-Conservative ticket.[19]

Democrats were not the only practitioners of explosive rhetoric during the campaign. Republicans struck back with an equally forceful campaign of stump speakers and handbills. Capitalizing on the traditional animosity of poor whites for the large landowners and planters who led the Democrats, they urged lower-class whites:

Be a man! Let the slave holding aristocracy no longer rule you. Vote for a constitution which educates your children free of charge; relieves the poor debtor from his rich creditor; allows a liberal homestead for your families; and more than all, places you on a level with those who used to boast that for every slave they were entitled to three-fifths of a vote in congressional representation.[20]

Although most Republicans preferred to avoid dealing with the question of Negro rights under the new constitution, Democrats concentrated much of their efforts on exploiting this issue. To deal with this problem, Republicans adopted the stratagem of taking both a pro-Negro and an anti-Negro stand. In areas where Negroes constituted the bulk of Republican support, party workers assured blacks that the suffrage clause in the constitution guaranteed them the right to hold public office, just as the Democrats charged. In north Georgia where Republicans sought the support

---

[16]Pearce, *Hill*, 165-71.

[17]Macon *Telegraph*, 24 March, 8 April 1868.

[18]Milledgeville *Southern Recorder*, 17 March, 14 April 1868. Milledgeville *Federal Union*, 24 March, 7 April 1868. See also entry for 9 February 1868, Samuel P. Richards Diary, Atlanta Historical Society.

[19]Quoted in Thompson, *Reconstruction in Georgia*, 186.

[20]Ibid., 187.

of poor whites who were hostile to Negroes, Joseph E. Brown placated whites by stressing the limited nature of the suffrage clause. The constitution did guarantee blacks the right to vote, he argued, but it did not grant them the right to hold office. Brown's argument was a rephrasing of his earlier speech to the constitutional convention, and, while not an official interpretation of the clause, it was sufficient to reassure many north Georgians that a Republican victory would not mean "black heels on white necks."[21]

In addition to seeking the support of poor whites and Negroes, Republicans actively worked to win the endorsement of businessmen, who were previously allied with Black Belt planters. By stressing the probusiness aspect of the new constitution, Republicans hoped to woo these urban elites away from their traditional allies. During the campaign, the proposed Air Line Railroad provided Republicans with an excellent opportunity to impress businessmen with the sincerity of the party's overtures to the business community. The Air Line, when completed, would link Atlanta with Richmond, Virginia and would greatly expand the markets available to Georgia's merchants and manufacturers. Where the constitution of 1865 had expressly forbidden the use of state funds to aid railroad construction, the new constitution authorized liberal state aid. If Bullock was elected, promised the Republicans, aid for the Air Line would be immediately forthcoming. The Atlanta *New Era,* a strong Bullock newspaper, assured the business community that he was a "warm and firm advocate of the Air Line Railroad."[22] Joseph E. Brown, a staunch proponent of Republican-business cooperation, worked to secure support for the Republican cause. His message was simple and direct: only when Georgia was fully restored to the Union could economic progress and prosperity return to the state. Restoration was possible, he argued, only under a Republican administration.[23]

The election was marred by fraud and by sporadic violence. The Ku Klux Klan made its first appearance in the state during the campaign; and although its impact on the April election was minimal, its activities gave Republicans, black and white, a glimpse of what lay ahead. The harsh rhetoric of the Democrats and the terrorism of the Klan contributed to the most widely publicized incident of violence in the campaign. During the night of 31

---

[21]Nathans, *Losing the Peace,* 90-101.

[22]Atlanta *New Era,* 29 March 1868. The Republican appeal to businessmen was somewhat blunted by the party's advocacy of debtor relief. See C. H. Sutton to John S. Dobbins, 28 March 1868, John S. Dobbins Collection, Emory University. Sutton, a lawyer trying to collect debts owed Dobbins, wrote him concerning the impact of the relief measure, "The Constitution will be ratified and the Ordinance sustained however wrong it may be."

[23]Parks, *Brown,* 350-72.

March, masked men entered the bedroom of George W. Ashburn and shot him to death. Ashburn, a white Radical from Columbus and a delegate to the constitutional convention, was a leading member of the Bullock clique. Locally, he had a reputation of cohabiting with black females.[24] Although the mayor of Columbus offered a reward for the capture of the murderers, General Meade was dissatisfied with his efforts and placed the city under martial law. Within a week after the murder, ten men—including two city policemen and a Union soldier—were accused of the crime and arrested by the military. Incarcerated in Atlanta while awaiting trial, the men instantly became heroes of the Democratic cause.[25]

The involvement of the Klan in the Ashburn murder was never proven, and the accused men were released without ever having to face a trial. The quick action of General Meade served Republican interests well. The imposition of martial law in Columbus was a reminder to white Georgians that Reconstruction would end only when Congress decided to end it and until then, the United States Army would protect Republicans.[26] For Democrats, however, the Ashburn murder and the imposition of martial law had an even greater benefit. These events demonstrated that the military could only react to violence, not prevent it. As a result of the ineffectiveness of Meade and his troops in dealing with the Ashburn murder, Klan recruitment received a shot in the arm.

The results of the four days of balloting in April demonstrated how successful Republicans had been in their efforts to forge new coalitions in the state. The constitution was approved by a majority of almost 18,000 (88,172 to 70,200) votes, and the Republicans managed to elect a majority in the General Assembly. In the gubernatorial election, Bullock's margin of victory (83,527 to 76,356) was considerably less, but he managed to carry ninety-three of Georgia's 132 counties. In the counties of north Georgia, the relief and homestead features of the constitution, coupled with the personal popularity of Joseph E. Brown, were successful in attracting the votes of poor whites and yeoman farmers. The majority of Republican votes came from Negroes in the Black Belt, however, and these votes provided the margin Bullock needed to win (table 3.1). Only in the Wiregrass counties did the hoped for support fail to materialize for Republicans. This region had fewer small farmers and Negroes, and, consequently, provided less of a potential base of Republican support. All in all, the tradi-

---

[24]Louise Biles Hill, *Joseph E. Brown and the Confederacy* (Westport CT: Greenwood Press, 1939) 284-86. Conway, *Reconstruction of Georgia*, 158-61.

[25]Atlanta *Constitution*, 3 June 1868. Nathans, *Losing the Peace*, 97-99.

[26]Trelease, *White Terror*, 73-79. George C. Rable, *But There Was No Peace: The Role of Violence in the Politics of Reconstruction* (Athens: University of Georgia Press, 1984) 71.

tional dominance of Black Belt planters appeared to have been smashed by the aggressive campaign of the Republicans.[27]

Although the Republican victory in April was decisive, the coalition that had made success possible began to disintegrate immediately. First, the much publicized relief measures were rejected by Congress when the new constitution was submitted for its approval. Under the provision of the Omnibus Bill, approved by Congress on 28 June, Georgia was readmitted to the Union, but the relief section of the constitution was to be repealed by the General Assembly.[28] The refusal of Congress to sustain the relief provisions lent credence to Democratic charges made during the campaign that relief was a "fraud and a cheat" that the Republicans would never honor.[29]

The suffrage question, so carefully handled by Republican speakers in the election, surfaced immediately after the new General Assembly met. During the campaign, Joseph E. Brown, speaking for the Republicans, had promised white Georgians that Negroes would not be eligible to hold office under the new constitution. Despite his claim, twenty-eight Negroes had been elected to the Assembly and took their seats when the legislature met in July. Within a few days after the Assembly had convened, Milton A. Candler, a white Democratic senator, introduced a resolution calling for an investigation of the situation. Throughout the summer, both houses of the General Assembly debated the question of whether Negroes had the right to hold office, and in early September, the black senators and representatives were expelled from the legislature. Democrats in the General Assembly were joined by Moderate Republicans in this action, although expulsion of the Negroes resulted in a Democratic majority when Democratic opponents were given their seats.[30]

A court challenge to expulsion resulted in a reversal of the Assembly's action. Under the leadership of Chief Justice Joseph E. Brown, the Geor-

TABLE 3.1

PERCENTAGE OF FAVORABLE VOTES CAST IN 1868 ELECTION BY REGIONS			
	NORTH GA	BLACK BELT	WIREGRASS
FOR CONSTITUTION	23.2%	72.6%	4.2%
FOR BULLOCK	21.3%	75.0%	3.7%

[27]*Annual Report of the Comptroller General of Georgia, 1868.*

[28]Parks, *Brown,* 420-22. Joseph E. Brown to Schuyler Colfax, 9 June 1868; Joseph E. Brown to Reuben E. Fenton, 11 June 1868, HT.

[29]Milledgeville *Southern Recorder,* 17 March 1868. Atlanta *Constitution,* 29 June 1868. Macon *Telegraph,* 24 March 1868.

[30]Thompson, *Reconstruction in Georgia,* 193-99.

gia Supreme Court ruled that both the federal and state constitutions recognized the right to hold office as being inherent in the right of citizenship.[31] This interpretation directly contradicted the speeches given by Brown during the gubernatorial campaign, and the decision of the court alienated many of the poorer whites in north Georgia who had voted for Bullock.[32]

A third factor in the disintegration of the Republican coalition was the vicious internecine struggle between Radical and Moderate Republicans. To placate Moderates opposed to his nomination in 1868, Bullock had promised them the lion's share of available patronage jobs. When he won the election, Bullock was forced to redeem his pledges to them, and many of his staunchest supporters found themselves denied a share of the political spoils. His failure to reward such powerful Radicals as John H. Caldwell and John E. Bryant created a potent anti-Bullock faction within the Radical camp. Freed from their commitment to the governor, these men frequently crossed party lines to join with Democrats in frustrating Bullock. Not only did the anti-Bullock Radicals attack the governor, they also conducted an ongoing struggle with Moderates in the General Assembly. Dissension among the Republicans enabled Democrats to exercise greater leadership in the legislature than their numbers would normally have allowed.[33]

There were, of course, other reasons for the dissolution of the April coalition, and none were more important than the activities of the Ku Klux Klan. The Klan made its first appearance in Georgia in March 1868. From then until the congressional elections in November, its campaign of violence and intimidation had a telling effect on the stability of the Republican party. Acknowledged by white leaders to be an essential tool in curtailing Republican influence and power, the Klan spread rapidly throughout the state, usually with the blessings and connivance of the "best people." While rhetoric might fail to convince poor whites and blacks to abandon the Republican party, violence could be persuasive.[34]

Agents of the Freedmen's Bureau, now full-time federal army officers, noted a dramatic increase in the number of violent incidents involving blacks and whites. In plantation counties, the areas of greatest Republican strength, the assaults more than quadrupled the number of similar incidents recorded in 1867. During the course of that year, for example, sixteen freedmen had been killed and forty-seven injured. In 1868, following the enfranchisement of freedmen and the Republican success in state

---

[31]Parks, *Brown*, 436-37.

[32]Macon *Telegraph*, 18 and 20 June 1869.

[33]Nathans, *Losing the Peace*, 102-26.

[34]Rable, *But There Was No Peace*, 144-62.

elections, seventy-five freedmen were murdered and 203 injured. Of these incidents, thirty-six murders were listed as being caused by Ku Klux Klan activities or were credited to "political differences." Thirty-three other murders were described as resulting from "unknown" or "other" causes, vague terms that could have masked political reasons. Of the 203 assaults with injuries, eighty-two were directly attributed to politics, while an additional 101 fell into the category of "unknown" or "other." For these acts of violence, state and federal officials arrested only thirty-seven persons in 1867 and convicted only one individual. Despite a fourfold increase in violence in 1868, only thirty-five arrests were made, with only two convictions.[35] Certainly these figures dramatically reinforced the message white Georgians were sending to freedmen and their allies: in Georgia, it was an almost guaranteed certainty that any act of violence against freedmen would go unpunished.

TABLE 3.2

CAUSES OF VIOLENCE AGAINST FREEDMEN BY WHITES, 1867				
CAUSE	KILLED	INJURED	ARRESTS	CONVICTIONS
UNKNOWN	16	44	34	1
LABOR		3		
TOTALS	16	47	34	1

TABLE 3.3

OUTRAGES (MURDERS AND ASSAULTS) AGAINST FREEDMEN, 1868				
CAUSE	KILLED	INJURED	ARRESTS	CONVICTIONS
aUNKNOWN	23	76	15	1
LABOR	5	20	7	
bPOLITICS	29	51		
cKU KLUX KLAN	7	31	3	
dOTHER	11	25	10	1
TOTALS	75	203	35	2

aIncludes categories listed as "personal" or "unprovoked."
bIncludes category listed as "riots."
cIncludes incidents carried out by "white men dressed in sheets."
dIncludes categories listed as "insolence," "disrespect," "disobedience," or "stealing."

[35]Compilation of Field Reports, Reel 32, BRFAL.

Throughout the spring and summer of 1868, Democratic papers and party spokesmen warned of impending large scale riots in the state. The Milledgeville *Federal Union* noted the riot that had occurred in New Orleans in 1867, and the editor predicted several such riots would sweep Georgia before the presidential election in November. The blame for any such riots that might take place was assigned to the Republicans beforehand, since their "political salvation depends on it, and they have determined to have one, come what may."[36] The Athens *Southern Watchman* echoed this opinion in an editorial that concluded, "It is evident from the number and character of the disturbances of the public peace by negroes in different sections of the State, that bad white men are at the bottom of it and [are] hounding these ignorant people on."[37]

While Democratic editors in Georgia might feign ignorance of Klan violence, observers outside the state were keenly aware of what was happening. W. G. LeDuc, a Northerner, wrote to his friend, James P. Hambleton of Macon, about the impact Klan activities were having on public opinion in his region. "Such men as Wade Hampton, [Howell] Cobb, & [Robert] Toombs—N. B. Forrest—are doing your people more harm than you know, and if you suffer them to provoke another war with the North, God have mercy on your souls."[38] As Numan V. Bartley has written, "Being an active Republican required great personal courage."[39]

Rumors of blacks arming themselves to meet Klan violence with counterforce spread throughout the state and persisted the whole summer. On 31 August, the state Senate adopted a resolution requesting Governor Bullock to issue a proclamation outlawing "violent and unlawful assemblages." On 3 September, the House of Representatives concurred with the Senate and sent the governor a similar resolution. On 4 September, Bullock complied with the wishes of the General Assembly and issued a proclamation prohibiting armed assemblies of any kind, exempting only troops of the federal army. This action lent credence to the rumors circulating that the Union League and the Equal Rights Association, two Republican financed organizations that provided grassroots support for the party, had purchased and stored arms for secret Negro militia groups to use on election day.[40]

---

[36]Quoted in Theodore B. FitzSimons, Jr., "The Camilla Riot," *Georgia Historical Quarterly* 35 (1951): 116-25.

[37]Ibid.

[38]W. G. LeDuc to Dr. James Pinkney Hambleton, 3 September 1868, James Pinkney Hambleton Collection, Emory University.

[39]Numan V. Bartley, *The Creation of Modern Georgia* (Athens: University of Georgia Press, 1983) 63.

[40]FitzSimons, "Camilla Riot," 116-25.

In early September, handbills announcing a Republican meeting to be held in Camilla on 19 September were circulated in southwestern Georgia. The purpose of the meeting was to generate black support for N. P. Pierce, a candidate for Congress, and for John Murphy, a candidate for presidential elector. Groups of Negroes from Albany and surrounding areas gathered on the outskirts of Camilla on the designated day and prepared to march through the town behind a fife and drum corps. In Camilla, angry whites, forewarned of the march by a white named Robert Cochran, lined the streets. As the Republican parade approached the town, they were stopped by Sheriff Munford J. Poore, who asked them to turn around and to abandon their plans for a march. Noting that some of the Negroes carried weapons, Poore tried to persuade them to lay aside their arms. For the white Republicans, any backing down in the face of white opposition would have been politically disastrous, and they urged their followers to ignore the sheriff's warning and advice. When the marchers continued their movement toward Camilla, the sheriff left them and hurried into town to organize a posse to deal with the mob.[41]

As the paraders entered Camilla, they were confronted by a drunken white man, James Johns, who ordered the band to stop playing and the column of men to leave the area. When the Republicans refused to obey him, Johns pulled a pistol and fired into the crowd. Certain that a trap had been laid for them, the marchers returned the fire. In the ensuing melee, twelve Negroes were killed, thirty were wounded, and two disappeared.[42]

Although whites in Camilla blamed the entire affair on the Negro marchers, reports filed by the Mitchell County Freedmen's Bureau agent, Charles Rauschenberg, told of Negroes being hunted down with dogs and horses throughout the night and the following day. The whites in Camilla, he charged, "did not hesitate but seemed to exult in following the example of James Johns . . . firing into the assemblage of the colored people [and] in routing and chasing the unarmed and unresisting fugitives and shooting them down, while running for their lives, and sometimes even after having been wounded, overtaken and after having surrendered themselves to their mercy."[43]

Quickly seized by the Republicans as a campaign issue that would demonstrate how racist and violent the Democrats were, the Camilla affray received extensive coverage in the state Republican press. Nationally, the Camilla riot was used by the Republicans to justify the continued enactment and enforcement of additional reconstruction legislation. Despite the efforts of the Republicans to use the Camilla incident to the party's ad-

---

[41]Charles Rauschenberg to General C. C. Sibley, Reports of Murders and Assaults to Freedmen, 1 January to 31 October 1868, Reel 32, BRFAL.

[42]Ibid.

[43]Ibid.

vantage, their continued exposure of the riot had a boomerang effect since they could not report any arrests or convictions of whites. Instead of working against the Democrats, the Camilla shootings confirmed their effectiveness in controlling local affairs and in negating the power of Republicans. As in the Ashburn murder case, the message was clear. No Republican government, state or national, could protect blacks against the deliberate violence of white Democrats. As Rauschenberg concluded in his report to his superiors in the Bureau, "The colored people from about and South of Camilla dare not come here, and even the few white people who depreciate [*sic*] this state of affairs are afraid to speak about these things *for fear of secret revenge being taken on their person or property.*"[44] Republicans who had benefited from the wholesale support of freedmen in the spring elections now found this support slipping away as the party's inability to protect its members became more and more evident.

Faced with a hostile General Assembly, Bullock was unable to deal with the increased level of violence against Negroes and white Republicans. Federal troops stationed in Georgia were ineffective because of their small numbers, and Moderate leaders opposed Bullock's efforts to persuade Congress to send more.[45] Without additional military support, the governor could only issue unenforceable proclamations and offer rewards. The April election had given Republicans control of the state government, but local governments were left in the hands of Democrats who were sympathetic to and frequently provided the leadership for the Klan.

The November presidential election provided further proof of the impotency of the Republican party and the effectiveness of Democratic violence. Ulysses S. Grant received only thirty-two percent of the votes cast in Georgia, a significant decrease from the fifty-two percent Bullock had gotten in April. Of the ninety-three counties that had given Bullock a majority in April, thirty-eight went into the Democratic column in November, despite Negro majorities in twenty-seven of them.[46] Republicans lost support in every area of the state with the single exception of the Wiregrass, where the party managed to increase its vote slightly. Klan activity, internal squabbles, and the failure of Congress and the Georgia Supreme Court to uphold promises made in April contributed significantly to the decline.[47]

The dismal showing of the party in the November election marked the beginning of attempts by Georgia Radicals to secure the remission of the

---

[44]Ibid.

[45]*House of Representatives: Miscellaneous Documents*, 40th Congress, 3rd Session, No. 52 (Washington: Government Printing Office, 1869). Henry K. McKay to Henry P. Farrow, 7 April 1869, FC.

[46]Thompson, *Reconstruction in Georgia*, 188.

[47]Shadgett, *Republican Party in Georgia*, 14-15. Parks, *Brown*, 430.

state to congressional control. To convince Congress of the need for such extreme action, Bullock journeyed to Washington to present the Radical case. White Democrats in Georgia, he argued, had made a mockery of Reconstruction, and the small number of votes given to Grant in November was proof that Georgia Democrats were as unreconstructed in 1868 as they had been in 1865. According to Bullock, the goals of congressional Reconstruction could be achieved only when Georgia was once again remanded to full military control. Such control was needed, he pleaded, in order to restore Republicans to positions that had been stolen from them through violence and intimidation.[48]

Moderates among the Republican leadership in Georgia opposed Bullock's efforts, and Amos T. Akerman and Henry P. Farrow followed him to Washington to urge Congress to ignore the governor's entreaties. Both men carried with them letters from other prominent Moderates urging caution and moderation.[49] Joseph E. Brown, now Chief Justice of the Georgia Supreme Court, lent his voice to those opposed to remission. In a reply to a questionnaire sent to him by Congressman Nelson Tift of Albany, Brown gave a lengthy discussion of his views on the subject. Bullock's request represented the fears of the Radicals that they would soon lose control of the state government, he wrote, rather than any serious attempt to solve Georgia's critical problems. The real need of the state was not remission or more reconstruction, but laws that would alleviate the causes of discontent—laws that would stimulate industry, provide for the development of the state's resources, and create a permanent system of public education. When such laws were passed, he concluded, Congress could count on a Georgia in harmony with the rest of the nation.[50]

Confronted with two conflicting arguments from prominent Republicans, Congress deferred action on Bullock's request until December 1869. During the interlude, Brown and other Moderates worked to build a new Republican coalition in the state. In a letter to Bullock in December 1868, Brown urged him to adopt a more conciliatory attitude toward conservative Democrats and to work for a union of conservatives in both parties. In Brown's estimation, the Democrats had as many organizational problems as did the Republicans, and by appealing to men of "wealth and intelligence," the Republicans would be able to exploit the weaknesses of their rivals. The Democrats were divided into two distinct and separate wings, he assured Bullock, and the Republicans needed to reach an agreement with the more moderate wing. This group, led by Alexander H. and Linton Stephens, readily accepted Reconstruction as a *fait accompli* and

---

[48]*House of Representatives: Miscellaneous Documents,* No. 52.

[49]Ibid.

[50]Ibid.

wanted to get about the business of economic recovery immediately. The second wing, or the "crazy wing," was led by Robert Toombs and Benjamin H. Hill and still opposed Reconstruction without offering much in the way of a constructive alternative. Only irresponsible acts by Radical Republicans and a mutual opposition to Negro suffrage bound the two wings together, and if Georgia Republicans were willing to make some concessions to the Stephens group, the party could recoup the November losses by splitting the Democrats. As for the "crazy wing" of the Democratic party, Brown advised Bullock to ignore it since "we have no terms to offer them and no wish to coalesce with them."[51]

Although Brown's advice to Bullock went unheeded, he continued to try to convince the governor that remission of the state to military control would be a fatal error for the party. In addition to the letters he sent to Bullock, Brown also worked to convince other party leaders that cooperation with conservative Democrats was the only hope of saving the party in the state. To Joshua Hill, Republican Senator-elect, he wrote a letter urging him to use his influence in the Senate to defeat any attempt to remand the state to military control. The turmoil created by a third reconstruction would cause the people of Georgia to lose "all patience and become desperate under the belief that we are never to have stability."[52] In May 1869, Brown wrote to President Grant and sounded the same theme. Despite the success of the Democrats in defeating Grant in Georgia, the party was "made up of antagonistic elements" that could be manipulated into supporting the president if he made skillful use of his patronage powers.[53] What Brown envisioned was a new political party in the state—one that would represent the interests of wealthy men under the Republican banner.[54]

Brown's initial efforts failed. Bullock and the Radicals, seeking to solve their immediate political problems by congressional action, were unwilling to make concessions and pursued their call for a reimposition of military rule. This policy, considered suicidal by Moderates, produced an open split in the Republican hierarchy. In March 1869, Bullock supporters forced John E. Bryant, a Moderate member of the State Executive Committee, to resign. The rough handling of Bryant alienated the Moderates, and they backed his unsuccessful bid to unseat Bullock's candidate for Speaker of the House when the General Assembly convened the following January. All hope for compromise within the party had ended when

---

[51]Joseph E. Brown to Rufus B. Bullock, 3 December 1868, HT.

[52]Joseph E. Brown to Joshua Hill, 7 December 1868. Cora Brown McLeod Collection. University of Georgia. Hereafter referred to as MC.

[53]Joseph E. Brown to President Ulysses S. Grant, 10 May 1869, MC.

[54]Parks, *Brown*, 437-38.

Bryant was displaced, and the gulf between Moderates and Radicals widened as the party struggled through the next eighteen months.[55]

In mid-1869, Moderates and Radicals clashed again over accusations of financial wrongdoing made against Governor Bullock. In January 1869, Nedom L. Angier, state treasurer and anti-Bullock Republican, had publicly accused the governor of misusing state funds and of fraudulently funneling public funds into business projects of his friend and confidant, Hannibal I. Kimball.[56] Although a friendly state Senate investigated the charges and cleared Bullock of any wrongdoing, the rumors persisted. In response to Angier's accusations, Governor Bullock tried, without success, to have him impeached—an action that gave substance to the stories of corruption. Democratic newspapers capitalized on this rift among the Republicans and took up the cry against Bullock. Soon charges of bribery, mismanagement, theft, and corruption against his administration became the standard fare of these papers.[57]

What little unity the Republicans possessed after the presidential election of 1868 disappeared as the conflicts between Moderates and Radicals escalated. Even the probusiness coalition advocated by Brown and Bryant seemed unlikely because few men wanted to cooperate with a "corrupt" Republican party. In December 1869, Bullock gained a temporary triumph when Congress again placed the state under military rule. The existing state government was declared to be provisional, and the ousted Negro legislators were again seated in the General Assembly.[58] However, even the backing of the military meant only a momentary reprieve for Bullock, and by the end of 1870, he was forced to realize that the days of Republican control were at an end. State elections in December 1870, delayed a full two months by Republican chicanery, gave Democrats control of the elective offices of the state.

This victory was as much a product of Republican failures as it was of Democratic successes. Given the opportunity to build a viable party based on positive programs, Republicans had involved themselves in senseless squabbles for personal power and had allowed their initial support to dwindle to almost nothing. Backed by the most powerful army in the world, they had failed to protect their supporters in the face of increasing Dem-

---

[55]Augusta *Chronicle and Sentinel,* 2 March 1869. Nathans, *Losing the Peace,* 158-59.

[56]Willard Range, "Hannibal I. Kimball," *Georgia Historical Quarterly* 29 (1945): 47-70. Edward M. Mitchell, "H. I. Kimball: His Career and Defense," *Atlanta Historical Bulletin* 3 (1938): 249-83.

[57]Columbus *Daily Sun,* 2 and 23 February; 2 March 1869. Athens *Southern Banner,* 18 February 1870. Rome *Weekly Courier,* 28 July 1871.

[58]Nathans, *Losing the Peace,* 182-91. Milledgeville *Southern Recorder,* 19 July 1870. Atlanta *Constitution,* 18 July 1870.

ocratic violence. The Republicans had been further damaged by their reliance on Congress to maintain their tenuous grip on the state's political
machinery. This course of action, taken against the advice of Joseph E.
Brown and Henry P. Farrow, tended to substantiate Democratic accusations that the objective of the party was to force racial equality on white
Georgians. Economic programs that might have offered a foundation for
future party growth became secondary concerns as Republicans allowed
Democrats to convert every political contest into a struggle between blacks
and whites.[59]

It is ironic that Bullock and the Radicals attempted to heal the rift within
the party only after their defeat in the December elections. The coalition
of conservative businessmen, proposed by Brown in 1868, became a reality in December 1870 when the Bullock-dominated General Assembly
agreed to lease the state-owned Western and Atlantic Railroad to a corporation controlled by leading Democrats and Republicans. But, as Elizabeth S. Nathans has pointed out, for Bullock it was "too little, too late."[60]

---

[59]Milledgeville *Federal Union*, 3 January 1871. Conway, *Reconstruction of Georgia*,
198-201.

[60]Nathans, *Losing the Peace*, 206-12.

CHAPTER 4

A NEW DEPARTURE

The ease with which the Democrats won the December 1870 elections did not reflect the chaos that swept through the party's ranks a few days before the balloting. On 8 December, the party was thrown into confusion when Benjamin H. Hill, the most vocal critic of Republican rule in the state, published an open letter advising the people of Georgia to accept congressional Reconstruction.[1] Hill's letter stunned white Georgians who had followed his advice through three years of stout resistance to Reconstruction. His "Notes on the Situation" was regarded as the official platform of the Democratic party, and his leadership in the Macon Convention had made Hill the dominant force in the party.[2] Throughout the entire period of Republican control of the state government, Hill had railed against other Georgians who counseled conciliation and, in particular, he had attacked the activities of Joseph E. Brown as being "treason." Thus his letter advocating acceptance of Reconstruction represented a reversal of his previous position and, coming at the very moment of defeat for the Republican party, appeared to be nothing less than capitulation to the Bullock Radicals.

In defense of his new position, Hill argued that ratification of the Fourteenth and Fifteenth Amendments was an accomplished fact that nothing could change. Although he labeled the ratification process a "usurpation" of the normal constitutional process, he nevertheless urged Georgians to acquiesce, since even "usurpation the most glaring, succeeding becomes law." The sophistry of Hill's arguments failed to convince white Georgians, and the last paragraph of his letter added to their consternation. Discussing the upcoming elections, Hill reminded Democrats, "It is of secondary importance whom else you choose for your General Assembly; but it is of first importance that you choose honest men." Such a statement from the recognized leader of the Democracy was rank heresy, and the concluding sentence was certain proof that Hill had taken leave of his senses. "A black man who cannot be bought," he wrote, "is better than a

---

[1]Augusta *Chronicle and Sentinel*, 11 December 1870. Savannah *Morning News*, 14 December 1870. Augusta *Constitutionalist*, 17 December 1870. Pearce, *Hill*, 201-15.

[2]Augusta *Chronicle and Sentinel*, 10 June through 1 August 1867.

white man who can and a Republican who cannot be bought is better than a Democrat who can."[3]

Reaction to Hill's letter was swift and bitter. The LaGrange *Reporter* attacked him for attempting to disrupt "the harmony of opposition to Radicalism," while the Milledgeville *Federal Union* lambasted him for having "embarked on board the Radical ship."[4] Isaac W. Avery of the Atlanta *Constitution* saw the fine hand of Joseph E. Brown behind Hill's conversion to Radicalism. The man who had once been labeled the "Beelzebub of the fallen" by Hill was now pronounced a "moderate" since Hill had "leaped clear over the head of the Chief Justice, and landed some mile or two beyond the 're-construction' and 'accept the situation' platform."[5] Another editor saw Hill's action as an effort to "start a new party in Georgia . . . alike antagonistic to extreme Radicalism and Bourbon Democracy."[6] Certainly his new stance was in line with the ideas of Brown, and it was easy to believe that "Joe Brown and Ben Hill [were] cheek and jowl, politically."[7]

Republicans exploited the confusion among Democrats by publishing their own versions of Hill's apparent defection. Typical of these efforts to sow even more disorder and doubts among their rivals was the comment of the Atlanta *New Era*, the recognized voice of the Republicans in the state. "Mr. Hill is now to all intents and purposes with the Union Republican party of Georgia," wrote the paper's editor, "[and] he can be nowhere else since he is not a Democrat any more than he was in 1850 and 1860."[8]

Although confusing to the Democrats, Hill's defection did not prevent a Democratic rout of the Republicans in the December elections, but it did create a vacuum in the leadership of the party. Without Hill, the Democrats had no recognized spokesman nor a concerted plan of action. With the death of Howell Cobb in 1868 and the disfranchisement of Hershel V. Johnson and Robert Toombs, Hill had served as the acknowledged leader of the party. His apparent capitulation to Republicans meant that Democrats would no longer seek his counsel, and, without his unifying influence, the party organization would be left to flounder. Alexander H. Stephens, the one remaining Democrat with enough stature to take Hill's place, was hampered by ill health and refused to assume the mantle of

---

[3]Ibid., 11 December 1870.

[4]LaGrange *Reporter*, 23 December 1870. Milledgeville *Federal Union*, quoted in Nathans, *Losing the Peace*, 203.

[5]Macon *Telegraph*, 8 April 1868. Atlanta *Constitution*, 28 December 1870.

[6]Griffin *Star*, quoted in Nathans, *Losing the Peace*, 203.

[7]Atlanta *Constitution*, 28 December 1870.

[8]Atlanta *New Era*, reprinted in the Atlanta *Constitution*, 17 December 1870. See also Savannah *Morning News*, 19 December 1870. Savannah *Daily Republican*, 13 December 1870.

leadership. At the very moment they were achieving their greatest success, Democrats found themselves leaderless and confused.

Despite the accusations of the press, Hill had not joined the Republican party. Instead, he, like Joseph E. Brown, recognized that political stability was essential to the full recovery of the state's economy. With the defeat of the Radicals in the December elections assured, Hill decided to accept the overtures of Moderate Republicans to form a new, probusiness party in the state. Although a postwar Democrat, he had been the unsuccessful gubernatorial candidate of the Whig/American party in 1857; and although a successful planter, he had maintained close connections with the business community through his legal practice. All in all, Hill was the prototype of the business oriented and conservative Democrat who was to emerge in the 1870s. Once dismissed by Joe Brown as that "poor political maniac," Hill now resolved his differences with Brown in an effort to create a new political coalition in the state.[9]

The immediate cause of this reconciliation was a decision by the General Assembly to allow Governor Bullock to lease the state-owned Western and Atlantic Railroad to private businessmen. The railroad was the single greatest source of patronage for the governor, but mismanagement by his appointed supervisor, Foster Blodgett, had elicited numerous attacks on the Bullock administration.[10] In an attempt to salvage his political career and to save the Republican party in the state, Bullock gave in to pressure by other Republicans, notably Joseph E. Brown, to use the railroad as a means by which a coalition of conservative Democrats and Republicans could be forged—a coalition that might enable him to remain in power a while longer. In a series of complicated and highly questionable maneuvers, the lease was awarded to a corporation including both Brown and Hill, as well as other prominent men from both parties. Bullock was to have an interest in the corporation— or so it appeared—through the inclusion of W. B. Dinsmore, a close personal friend, on the board of directors.[11]

The leasing of the Western and Atlantic to the Brown-Hill corporation was the first step in the creation of this new alliance. Certainly nothing was more indicative of the power of business to overcome political conflicts than the union of Brown and Hill, two bitter antebellum and postwar rivals, in a profit making venture. Political differences were not to interfere with the pursuit of profits, and the Western and Atlantic lease

---

[9]Parks, *Brown*, 426.

[10]Thompson, *Reconstruction in Georgia*, 218-34. Conway, *Reconstruction of Georgia*, 190-97.

[11]Atlanta *Constitution*, 28 December 1870. Augusta *Chronicle and Sentinel*, 4 January 1871. Savannah *Morning News*, 31 December 1870. Augusta *Daily Constitutionalist*, 8, 13 January 1871.

symbolized the "New Departure" of some Georgia politicians from the bitterness of Reconstruction.

The formation of a probusiness alliance between prominent Republicans and Democrats touched off several years of intense political struggles in Georgia. Planters, accustomed to exercising social, political, and economic control of the state, now saw their dominance threatened by this coalition. In tune with the course of industrialism sweeping the United States, the New Departure movement seemed more in keeping with the forces of modernism than did the reliance on agriculture. The critical issue in these struggles was not the process of industrialization, since planters accepted the inevitability of that happening, but was, instead, the question of who would control the scope and direction of industrial development. Indeed, many planters were advocates of industrialization as witnessed by their funding of various industries prior to the Civil War, the strength of the Whig party in the South during the same period, and the use of state funds for building railroads and other transportation facilities. The fusion of some Republicans and Democrats into a probusiness "party" struck at the very heart of the issue of who would dominate the state in the future. If Brown, Hill, and their supporters were allowed to proceed unchallenged and unstopped, Georgia would soon become a state where industry exercised hegemony and where the economic needs of planters would take a backseat.

For planters, the critical need was to find the means to reassert their political dominance of the state so as to ensure the passage of laws that would preserve and protect their preeminence. Unable to stop the gradual movement toward urbanization and industrialization—and, indeed, unopposed to some industrial growth—planters hoped to gain control of the machinery to guide the speed and direction of the process through political action. As long as conservative planters controlled the balance of power in state politics, business-industrialization could proceed unhampered, and yet be subordinated to the needs of agriculture. In many ways paralleling events in Japan and Germany, this "Prussian Road" approach—the regulation of the growth of industry by an agricultural elite—appeared to be the only hope Georgia planters had of remaining a potent force in the affairs of the state. The practices of the antebellum period, similar to the "Prussian Road," were to be perpetuated. Failure to gain and keep control of the political machinery of the state would mean an end of the planting class as an important force in Southern society.[12]

---

[12]Jonathan M. Wiener, *Social Origins of the New South: Alabama, 1860-1885* (Baton Rouge: Louisiana State University Press, 1978) 3-5, 226-27. For an extended discussion of the "Prussian Road," see Barrington Moore, Jr., *Social Origins of Dictatorship and Democracy: Lord and Peasant in the Making of the Modern World* (Boston: Beacon Press, 1966). See also Eugene D. Genovese, *Roll, Jordan, Roll: The World the Slaves Made* (New York: Vintage Books, 1976) and his *In Red and Black: Marxian Explorations in Southern and Afro-American History* (New York: Vintage Books, 1971).

The probusiness factions were aided in their efforts to extend their dominance over the state by members of a new class of businessmen, the country furnishing merchant. This group, which had emerged with the widespread development of tenancy and sharecropping, filled the void left by antebellum factors who were unable to satisfy the credit needs of planters, croppers, and tenants, and became the primary source of essential farm supplies in the South. Planters found themselves operating in a national economy controlled by bankers and industrialists, and the policies of deflation and currency constriction pursued by these financiers worked against them.[13] Unable to convert their assets into cash and unable to secure loans on land from traditional banking sources, planters and their tenants turned to furnishing merchants, with their limited stocks of goods and exorbitant markups, for the credit they so desperately needed.

During the Civil War, large quantities of "fiat" money, or greenbacks, were issued to fund the Northern war effort. When the war ended, financiers who controlled the largest portion of the greenbacks in circulation demanded that the Federal government redeem them in gold. A compliant Congress responded to their pressures and in 1875 passed the Resumption Act, which provided for the redemption of all greenbacks beginning on 1 January 1879. The Resumption Act of 1875 resulted in the creation of a deflationary spiral that made money expensive to borrow and extremely hard to find. For planters who operated on credit, deflation increased the value of their fixed debts, reduced the value of their annual production, and made repayment difficult.[14]

Greenbacks originally issued to pay war expenses were initially intended for Northern use only, and the supply was limited by law. The population explosion that followed the readmission of the ex-Confederate states into the Union reduced the per capita amount of money available. The National Banking Act of 1864 allocated the supply of national bank notes (redeemable in greenbacks) on the basis of population and existing banks. Northern states, with their large urban populations and superior banking facilities, received the lion's share; while Southern states, primarily rural and with limited banking facilities, were forced to make do with what was left. The National Banking Act also prohibited the creation of national banks in cities of less than 6000 persons. This restriction retarded the postwar development of the South, since as late as 1880, only ten percent of the region's population lived in towns of 2500 or more.

---

[13]Robert P. Sharkey, *Money, Class, and Party: An Economic Study of the Civil War and Reconstruction* (Baltimore: Johns Hopkins Press, 1959), traces the actions of Congress on the money question and details the way that votes on money matters reflected class conflicts.

[14]Howard R. Smith, *Economic History of the United States* (New York: Ronald Press, 1955) 339-50.

There were only fifty-five cities of 4000 or more residents in 1880, and three states had only one city of more than 6000. The sparseness of the Southern population meant that few new banks would be created, and the few that did manage to meet the stringent requirements of the National Banking Act were located away from the centers of agriculture.[15]

By 1895, the entire South had only 417 national banks, one-half of which were in Texas. Banks chartered by states or owned by private companies were almost as hard to find, and as late as 1895, 123 of Georgia's 137 counties had no banking facilities at all.[16] Even when private and state banks did operate in rural areas, their services were of little use to either planters or tenants, since most of them were reluctant to lend money on real estate. Falling prices and widespread availability made land undesirable collateral, and sharecroppers and tenants seldom had real property with which to secure a mortgage.[17] National banks were prohibited by law from making large numbers of loans secured by real estate.

The monetary needs of the agricultural community of the United States were in direct opposition to the interests of the industrial sector, and farmers could count on little relief from a national government dominated by industrialists.[18] Men who owned the bulk of outstanding government bonds and who would reap enormous profits when the paper investments were redeemed in gold specie controlled Congress. In 1873, Congress once again responded to the interests of financiers and passed an act that left the silver dollar off the list of coins to be minted. This act and the abandonment of the silver standard by several European countries placed a severe drain on the gold resources of the United States, and gold prices climbed to all-time highs as a result. Vast new discoveries of silver in the American West created a glut on the world market, and silver prices plummeted. Each increase in the price of gold decreased the amount of bullion available to Americans, as speculators hoarded the supply in anticipation of further rises in price. As the gold supply contracted, its scarcity drove the value of the dollar upward. Between 1865 and 1890,

---

[15]Ransom and Sutch, "Debt Peonage," 647. Woodman, *King Cotton*, 319-33, cites figures illustrating the rural nature of Southern society. In 1870, the South was 87.8 percent rural, and this figure had decreased to only 82 percent by 1900.

[16]Hicks, *Populist Revolt*, 40.

[17]James L. Roark, *Masters without Slaves: Southern Planters in the Civil War and Reconstruction* (New York: W. W. Norton, 1977) 148. Wiener, *Social Origins*, 77. Woodman, *King Cotton*, 324-25. Ransom and Sutch, "Debt Peonage," 645.

[18]William Warren Rogers, *The One-Gallused Rebellion: Agrarianism in Alabama, 1865-1896* (Baton Rouge: Louisiana State University Press, 1970) 14-15.

the United States' reliance on the gold standard resulted in an astounding 82.7 percent rate of appreciation for the dollar.[19]

What all of this meant for members of the agricultural community was a reduction in the availability of credit, a corresponding loss of value for harvested crops, and an increase in the value of existing debts. Farmers were forced to take a larger percentage of their crops to pay these debts, many of which had been carried over from the prewar period. The problem of deflation was complicated by a drop in the wholesale price index, a phenomenon that accompanied the growing efficiency of American industry. Planters, yeoman farmers, sharecroppers, and tenants were faced with a market that absorbed more and more of their produce and returned less and less money to them. Caught in an economic squeeze created by forces they did not understand, farmers of all classes responded by increasing production in order to offset lost income.

Increased production aggravated the economic difficulties faced by farmers, and the laws of supply and demand worked to lower prices paid for commodities. Cotton prices were dictated by market conditions in Liverpool, England, and were also affected by crops from Egypt, Brazil, and India. A bumper crop in any one of these countries spelled disaster for American growers. Already hampered by domestic monetary problems, farmers in the United States had to contend with an international market that was becoming more and more competitive. As other countries improved their productive capacity, the demand for American cotton fell off. With supplies constantly increasing and demand decreasing, the prices paid for American cotton dropped continuously throughout the postwar period.[20]

As prices declined, Southern cotton growers attempted to compensate for their reduced income by once again increasing production. In order

TABLE 4.1

PERCENTAGE OF DEBT INCREASE DUE TO APPRECIATING DOLLAR	
5-YEAR PERIODS	% OF INCREASE
1865-1869	35.2%
1870-1874	19.7%
1875-1879	4.5%
1880-1884	11.7%
1885-1890	11.6%

[19]Alex Mathews Arnett, *The Populist Movement in Georgia: A View of the Agrarian Crusade in the Light of Solid South Politics* (New York: Columbia University Press, 1922) 68.

[20]Gavin Wright, "Cotton Competition and the Post-Bellum Recovery of the American South," *Journal of Economic History* 34 (September 1974) 610-35.

to raise the productivity of existing cotton land and to cultivate marginal land heretofore neglected, growers turned more and more to the use of fertilizers. Estimates of the cost of fertilizers per year ranged from twelve to thirty-three percent of the value of the annual crop, but despite the high cost, growers continued to rely on them to increase production. As John D. Hicks pointed out, fertilizers were necessary because without them an acre of land "would not produce over one-eighth or one-tenth of a bale."[21] Figures for the period 1875 to 1879 give stark evidence to the increasing reliance of Georgia farmers on fertilizers. In this half decade, the amount of fertilizer inspected and sold in Georgia increased by 114 percent.[22]

In addition to the fluctuations of the cotton market and the rising price of fertilizer, such variables as drought, insects, and other natural catastrophes adversely affected the returns growers received on their crops. In 1866 and 1867, for example, a scarcity of rain the first year and an overabundance of it the next destroyed a large portion of the crop. Even in years when weather and insect damage was minimal, cotton growers found themselves confronted with other problems. In 1881 and 1882, the market price of cotton actually fell below the cost of production. The Greensboro *Herald* graphically described the plight of cotton producers:

> Oh yes, farmers, cotton is king. . . . Meat at ten cents cash, corn going up gradually, cotton down; but the farmer don't need such trifles: Cotton is just the thing of course: men, women and children and horses and mules can eat cotton and grow fat on it. Put in more cotton farmers, four or five cents a pound now, who knows but what it will open next fall at three cents! Plant more cotton—plant all cotton and get rich.[23]

TABLE 4.2	
GUANO SALES IN GEORGIA 1875-1879	
YEAR	TONS SOLD
1875	55,316
1876	75,833
1877	98,478
1878	85,049
1879	118,583

[21]Hicks, *Populist Revolt*, 46-47.

[22]Lexington *Oglethorpe Echo*, 25 March 1881.

[23]Greensboro *Herald*, 5 May 1881. The editor listed the price of cotton at 4¼¢ a pound. The U.S. Census Bureau figure for 1881 was 10.66¢ a pound. This discrepancy can be explained by the fact that the *Herald* editor was quoting the actual daily price while the Bureau's figure represented a yearly average.

Diversification, advocated by almost every public figure and news medium, was pressed on cotton growers as the only alternative to their problems. Newspaper editors importuned growers to double "their grain crop for every rise that takes place in the cotton market" and promised that such a policy would bring cotton producers wealth and prosperity. After all, wrote the editor of the *Meriwether Vindicator*, "We don't know any man who has gone to pot since the war through planting too much corn, but we know a few who have travelled that road through an overdose of cotton."[24] Concentration on cotton production meant a market that was unpredictable and unstable. Large scale speculation in cotton futures contributed to the market's instability, and speculators, like most of the other factors affecting cotton markets, were beyond the control of growers.[25]

Facing a constant uphill battle to make even a small profit, cotton growers often felt they were being manipulated by sinister international forces that defied control or regulation. The *Oglethorpe Echo* took a poke at these forces and at the stupidity of growers in an 1877 editorial:

> From time immemorial, it has been the custom of those who control the cotton market to permit a rise in price of the staple about the season farmers are preparing for another crop. This is done with a view to delude the planter into putting in another heavy crop, and, strange to say, the trick works like a charm. These dupes "take the bate" every time, and each fall, when the crop is harvested, they find themselves high and dry. This increase in price never occurs until the cotton has passed from the hands of the producer, and hence the only gainers by the transaction are the buyers.[26]

Even the national government appeared to consciously work against the planter. From the end of the Civil War until well into the twentieth century, the Federal government displayed an apparent callousness toward farmers by enacting high protective tariffs that aided industry and further reduced the economic power of agriculture. The imposition of such tariffs, justified on the grounds that they were essential to the development of American industries, served to raise the prices of necessary farm supplies. The *Carroll County Free Press* demonstrated the impact of the tariff on farmers in an 1884 editorial and published a chart to back up its assertion that the tariff was unfair to them.[27]

Arguments that tariffs were necessary to protect industrial growth had little impact on the attitudes of farmers. Accustomed to thinking of themselves

---

[24]Lexington *Oglethorpe Echo*, 26 January 1877. Greenville *Meriwether Vindicator*, 23 January 1873.

[25]Woodman, *King Cotton*, 269-94. Woodman discusses the impact of communications and transportation on speculation as a profession after the Civil War.

[26]Lexington *Oglethorpe Echo*, 26 January 1877.

[27]Carrolton *Carroll County Free Press*, 2 May 1884.

as the mainstay of the American economy, they felt left out of a postwar system that measured wealth in machines and finished goods, instead of bushels of wheat, pounds of tobacco, or bales of cotton.[28] The simple reality of life was that after three hundred years of dominating the nation's economy, moral values, and politics, farmers were now a political and economic minority whose needs were secondary to those of the entrepreneur and whose social values were not readily adaptable to a modern industrial society.[29]

In Georgia and the rest of the cotton South, the period between 1865 and 1900 was a time in which planters and farmers attempted to regain and maintain their control over the economy, and, most important, to shape industrialization to fit the antebellum patterns of development. Before such a Herculean task could be accomplished, however, it was necessary to reestablish the prewar patterns of agriculture. Planters in particular sought to rebuild the plantation system that had afforded them a secure perch from which they could dominate the South.[30]

To achieve their goals, the planters needed a ready source of money or credit with which to begin the arduous work of rebuilding, but because of the "tight" money situation on the national level, they found it practically nonexistent at the local level. The absence of cash made it necessary to find sources of credit to finance the resumption of agricultural operations. "We want credit," announced the *Oglethorpe Echo*, "[because] many

TABLE 4.3

TARIFF RATES FOR 1884	
ARTICLE	% TARIFF DUTY
Sugar	40
Iron and Hardware	60
Salt	80
Boots and Shoes	20
Cotton Goods	45
Blankets	100
Lumber	20
Knives and Forks	45

[28]Wiener, *Social Origins*, and Roark, *Masters*, offer illuminating pictures of the psychological impact Confederate defeat had on the planter elite and of the persistent and successful attempts they made to regain their hegemony regionally. Nationally, planters were not successful in reestablishing their prewar power.

[29]Genovese, *Roll, Jordan, Roll*, 661-65.

[30]Wiener, *Social Origins*, 186-221. Genovese, *In Red and Black*, 391-418.

planters report they cannot go on without help."[31] In the years after the end of the war, this cry for help was raised over and over again.

The need for working capital, either in cash or credit, led to many innovations in the Southern business community to supply the demand. To a small degree, the prewar factor system was revived immediately after the war, but it failed to answer the monetary demands of the postwar sharecropping and tenant systems. Gradually, factors were replaced by country merchants who assumed the responsibilities of supplying planters, sharecroppers, and tenants. Often financed by Northern capital and frequently tied to large supply houses through credit arrangements, country merchants—or furnishing merchants as they were more frequently called—embodied all of the evils of the postwar agricultural systems.[32]

In order to secure supplies for themselves and for their tenants, planters turned increasingly to furnishing merchants. Supplies were needed at the beginning of each planting season, but money to pay for them would not be forthcoming until the crops were marketed. Thus, furnishing merchants, willing to advance supplies on credit, became more and more essential to Southern agriculture. Engaged in a business with enormous risks, such as defalcation by tenants and planters, adverse weather conditions, falling market prices, or any of a number of other catastrophes, furnishing merchants sought to ensure their success by passing these risks on to their customers in the form of higher prices, carrying charges, and interest. Roger Ransom and Richard Sutch have indicated that the furnishing merchants' control of local credit allowed them to impose an overall interest rate of 59.4 percent, excluding the normal price markups. Furthermore, the merchants' small volume of trade—an average of approximately $5000 per year—resulted in the establishment of territorial monopolies. The small volume of business was not sufficient to attract competition from larger merchants and even reduced competition from other small merchants.[33] Utilizing financial profiles collected and published by the R. G. Dun Company, Ransom and Sutch have pieced together the most comprehensive picture available of the financial activities of furnishing merchants.

Protected by territorial monopolies, merchants generally served approximately seventy to eighty families within a five-to-eight-mile radius of their stores. Prices charged by merchants were exceedingly high, often as much as 300 percent above the normal cash prices. In an essay for the Georgia State Agricultural Society in 1878, J. N. Montgomery of Madison County gave the following prices: the cash price for corn was seventy-five cents a bushel, while the credit price was $1.25; the cash price for bacon

---

[31]Lexington *Oglethorpe Echo*, 11 February 1875.

[32]Woodman, *King Cotton*, 295-314.

[33]Ransom and Sutch, *One Kind of Freedom*, 126-48. Ransom and Sutch, "Lock-In," 405-25.

was 8½ cents a pound, while the credit price ranged from fourteen to twenty cents a pound.[34] In 1885, the Atlanta *Constitution* charged that farmers paid from 100 to 200 percent interest on everything they bought on credit. This interest was charged after the initial tripling or quadrupling of prices had been done. In 1889, the *Constitution* revised its figures downward, but even then the amount of interest charged on credit prices was in excess of seventy-five percent.[35] The Greensboro *Herald* reported that interest rates of fifty to sixty percent were common in Greene County in 1885. The *Oglethorpe Echo* warned its readers against paying off their indebtedness with "75 cents a bushel of corn" and then purchasing the same corn back at $1.50 in the summer.[36]

The Georgia Department of Agriculture cited the following interest rates as being typical of those charged by furnishing merchants in 1887:

> The reports show that farmers throughout the State who have been compelled to purchase bacon and corn have paid the following prices: Bacon, average cash price, 8.9 cents; average time price, payable November lst, 11.6

TABLE 4.4

AVERAGE INTEREST RATES CHARGED BY GEORGIA FURNISHING MERCHANTS, 1881-1889	
YEAR	ANNUAL RATE
1881	51.7%
1882	44.2%
1883	63.9%
1884	53.3%
1885	64.9%
1886	74.6%
1887	70.6%
1888	48.1%
1889	63.6%
Average Rate	59.4%

---

[34]*Transactions of the Georgia State Agricultural Society from August, 1876, to February, 1878* (Atlanta: James P. Harrington and Company, 1878) 406.

[35]Atlanta *Constitution*, 3 March 1885; 10 January 1889.

[36]Greensboro *Herald*, 23 January 1885. Lexington *Oglethorpe Echo*, 3 November 1876. Also Thomas D. Clark, "The Furnishing and Supply System in Southern Agriculture since 1865," *Journal of Southern History* 12 (1946): 24-44.

cents. Corn, average cash price, 72 cents [a bushel]; average time price payable November 1st, 98 [cents a bushel]. Assuming the average time of indulgence at four months, it appears that farmers have been required to pay 30 percent advance on cash prices for bacon for the four months time, which is equivalent to 90 percent per annum, or $7\frac{1}{2}$ percent per month. The percentage paid on the purchases of corn was even higher, amounting to 36 percent for four months, which is 108 percent per annum, or 9 percent a month.[37]

The high prices charged by furnishing merchants were justified as being necessary because of the high risks involved in extending credit. "It is not altogether the merchants' fault that such prices are demanded," concluded the report. "The risk on such sales is exceptionally hazardous, and the seller must charge such a percentage as will save him from a loss at the hands of those who fail to pay, or pay at the end of expensive litigation."[38] The Department of Agriculture's explanation was reiterated in the *Oglethorpe Echo* by "Hardshell." "The high prices charged by merchants and factors for goods or money is caused, in a great measure, by that class of persons who borrow and buy recklessly relying on their skill in dodging to pay it; and the consequence has been that honest men were forced to pay the same charges to get advances—paying from 25 to 100 percent to get advances." The penalty for defaulters, continued Hardshell, should be "imprisonment for debt, particularly when there is the slightest evidence of fraud."[39]

The risk factor was an important consideration in the calculation of credit prices charged by merchants, and the difficulty they had in collecting debts is reflected in numerous newspaper advertisements, which were both cajoling and threatening. Typical was one appearing in the *Meriwether Vindicator* in 1874:

> COME and see what your accounts are for 1872-73 and settle forthwith. I am in need of the money and MUST have it. Come forward like HONEST men and avoid UNPLEASANTNESS.[40]

Editors, who drew their advertising support from merchants, lent their influence to attempts to collect outstanding debts. The *Vindicator's* editor, in an editorial entitled "Duty of the Hour," appealed to debtors to "pay their debts promptly." Although the cost in resources might be high, "honor is kept untarnished." The editor then went on to admonish debtors, "If your promise is out to pay, and the holder of that promise demands its fulfillment, comply with his demand, but trade less on your credit in the future."[41] In an econ-

---

[37]*Supplemental Report, 1887, Georgia Department of Agriculture* 13 (Atlanta: Constitution Book and Job Office, 1887) 141.

[38]Ibid.

[39]Lexington *Oglethorpe Echo*, 15 December 1876.

[40]Greenville *Meriwether Vindicator*, 16 January 1874.

[41]Ibid., 17 October 1873.

omy that operated primarily on credit, the most obvious penalty for not paying debts or "squaring up" was the loss of future credit.

The very nature of the furnishing/credit system placed a tremendous amount of power in the hands of those who extended credit or loaned money. The high rate of illiteracy among sharecroppers and tenants made fraud easy; some merchants and landlords, who kept the only records of purchases, altered their ledgers to further increase their profits.[42] C. Vann Woodward described the conditions that faced a tenant seeking credit as being such that he was forced to accept "a loan of an unstipulated amount, at a rate of interest to be determined by the creditor."[43] The degree to which dishonesty prevailed among furnishing merchants cannot be ascertained, but occasional humorous references to the shady practices of some are to be found in regional newspapers.[44]

A large number of customers at country stores were black, while merchants were almost always white. For black tenants and sharecroppers, the potential for merchant dishonesty was much greater, and blacks who challenged these merchants invited violent retribution. Allen W. Trelease's study of Klan activities in the South shows that violence was frequently economically motivated and that it often resulted from minor violations of the Southern social code. In some cases, blacks were killed for simply failing to say "sir" to a white man or for failing to tip their hats to whites. Given this kind of oppression, arguing with a white merchant was sure to bring swift reprisals.[45]

One of the most controversial practices of furnishing merchants was that of requiring customers to sign crop liens as security for credit accounts. Although the complicated methods used to compute prices and interest rates afforded them a comfortable margin for profit, merchants sought to further reduce their business risks by forcing customers to pledge all or a portion of their unharvested crops as collateral. Crop liens provided the

[42]Lawrence Goodwyn, *Democratic Promise: The Populist Movement in America* (New York: Oxford University Press, 1976) 26-31.

[43]C. Vann Woodward, *Origins of the New South, 1877-1913* (Baton Rouge: Louisiana State University Press, 1951) 180.

[44]Mandle, *Roots*, 50. Mandle demonstrates this kind of newspaper humor by quoting a story in vogue during the 1870s. A tenant brought five bales of cotton to a merchant to whom he owed money. The merchant, after some "owl-eyed" figuring, announced that the value of the cotton matched the amount owed by the tenant. The tenant then mentioned that he had one more bale of cotton he had not brought in because it wouldn't fit on his wagon. "Shucks," said the merchant, "why didn't you tell me this before? Now, I'll just have to figure it over to make it come out even."

[45]Trelease, *White Terror*, 74-79. See also Thomas D. Clark, *Pills, Petticoats and Plows: The Southern Country Store* (Indianapolis: Bobbs-Merrill, 1944).

best guarantee of payment of debts, and few merchants were willing to extend credit without first securing them.

The widespread use of crop liens gave merchants increased importance in the agricultural sector of the Southern economy. According to some authorities, this system brought about "a revolution in land titles" and a demise in the planter class in the South. In the opinion of these scholars, the introduction and use of crop liens gave the merchants the means by which they gradually took over the large landholdings of planters and replaced them as the dominant force in Southern agriculture. Without a doubt, some merchants became landowners through the foreclosure process, and some used their store operations as a springboard to becoming large planters. However, while there was some progression from the merchant class to the planter class, it is doubtful that this movement was significant. Instead of being displaced by them, planters conducted a fierce political and economic campaign that eventually forced most of the independent furnishing merchants out of the Black Belt. The functions of furnishing merchants were then assumed by planters, who thereby strengthened their own overall power.[46]

The right to control the activities of sharecroppers and tenants was critical in the conflict between planters and merchants. Possession of a crop lien, argued merchants, made them partners in the unharvested cotton crop, and as such they were entitled to a direct voice in the supervision of croppers and tenants. In order to have some means of evaluating and protecting their investments, merchants often hired men to check on the working habits and crops of credit customers. If a tenant failed to work diligently or to plant his land in cotton, his merchant might demand immediate payment of his store account or refuse to extend him additional credit.[47] In some cases, merchants attempted to dictate the number of days a week a sharecropper/tenant was expected to work. "Many of the merchants down this branch entered into a combination last spring, not to sell any white or colored man supplies on time who would not pledge himself to work the full six days of the week," reported the *Oglethorpe Echo* in 1876. Merchants who undertook direct supervision of credit customers faced considerable opposition from planters, who regarded such action as an assault on their prerogatives.[48]

Another point of contention between planters and merchants was the large profits merchants made from their accounts. These profits were, in a sense, losses for planters, because merchants took a share of the crop before it was sold. A shrewd merchant could withhold his cotton until the market price

---

[46]Woodward, *Origins*, 179. Wiener, *Social Origins;* Roark, *Masters;* and Ransom and Sutch, *One Kind of Freedom* offer new insights into the question of planter persistence.

[47]Mandle, *Roots,* 39-51. Woodward, *Origins,* 179-86.

[48]Lexington *Oglethorpe Echo*, 10 November 1876.

went up, which it usually did soon after farmers picked and sold theirs. Unlike the grower, who was forced to sell in a glutted market, the merchant could wait until the market stabilized and overall supplies were down before selling. In order to retain as much of the profits as possible, planters began to establish their own stores and to furnish supplies to their tenants.[49] To offset the initial advantages possessed by merchants, planters turned to politics.

The political machinery of antebellum Georgia had always been responsive to the interests of planters first, and this pattern continued in the immediate postwar years. In 1866, for example, the General Assembly passed a law that severely limited the ability of furnishing merchants to negotiate crop liens with croppers and tenants. Under its provisions, only landlords could assign liens on growing crops, and because of this limitation, merchants were forced to negotiate through planters.[50] Although this law relieved merchants of the responsibility of supervising tenants, it also restricted the scope of their credit arrangements and took away much of the freedom they had enjoyed in dealing with customers. While it is impossible to determine the extent to which this law reduced the profits of merchants, it is certain that they did not welcome the interference of planters in their business arrangements. Planters occasionally used their power to approve liens to force merchants into treating tenants and sharecroppers more leniently.[51] Such an exercise of power was, according to some scholars, psychologically rewarding to planters, since it maintained the facade of antebellum paternalism. Tenants, black and white, who had to seek the approval of the landowner before establishing credit accounts, could not escape the fact that planters still controlled the allocation of supplies, just as they had done during slavery.[52]

The 1866 law hastened the consolidation of merchant and planter classes. Planters, seeking to reduce the power of merchants, utilized their own resources to establish plantation stores to supply their tenants. By becoming planter-merchants, they retained control of all facets of their agricultural operations; they reduced the growing importance of merchants; and, most important, they increased their own profits. Merchants, eager to eliminate the interference of planters and to climb the ladder of social respectability, became planters as they put their profits into acquiring more and more land. In the older Black Belt, planters tended to become mer-

---

[49]Woodward, *Origins,* 183-85. Judson Clements Ward, Jr., "Georgia under the Bourbon Democrats, 1872-1890" (Ph.D. diss., University of North Carolina, 1947) 290-99.

[50]*Acts of the General Assembly of Georgia, 1866* (Milledgeville: State Printer, 1866) 141.

[51]Clark, "Furnishing and Supply," 30.

[52]Wiener, *Social Origins,* 77-108. Mandle, *Roots,* 47-50. Ransom and Sutch, *One Kind of Freedom,* 89-105.

chants more frequently than merchants became planters. Indeed, the rate of "planter persistence" was much greater than earlier historians of Southern agriculture first realized.[53] As a result of the successful efforts of planters to assume the functions of merchants, the latter were forced to seek more favorable circumstances in the newly opened sections of the Black Belt in southwest Georgia and in the peripheral areas of marginal cultivation in northern sections of the state and in the Wiregrass.

In addition to the 1866 lien law, planters sought other laws to aid them in their struggle against powerful merchants. In 1868, the Constitutional Convention, called to satisfy the demands of Congress, wrote a provision into the new constitution that granted a $3000 homestead exemption to landowners. Although publicized as a relief measure for the poor and publicly opposed by some planters, the homestead exemption provided planters a means by which they could protect themselves against foreclosure. Simply by putting some of their land in the names of wives and children, planters were able to multiply the number of legal exemptions they were entitled to, and merchants were helpless in their attempts to collect debts.[54] Alabama merchants, faced with the same kinds of restrictions, fled the Black Belt for newer cotton lands in that state, and many Georgia merchants followed a similar pattern of movement.[55]

The conflict between furnishing merchants and planters was not soon resolved. In 1873, merchants, politically attuned with the New Departure movement, were able to take advantage of the disorganization in the Democratic party and get a compliant General Assembly to repeal the 1866 law giving planters preemptive rights on liens. The legislature substituted a new law for the old one, allowing merchants to deal directly with tenants and to bypass planters altogether. In addition, the new law extended the types of transactions a lien could be secured on and included the use of crop liens as collateral for cash advances.[56] The 1873 Assembly's action shifted the advantage to the merchants temporarily, but planters struck back swiftly.

Utilizing the Georgia State Grange as a vehicle for organizing resistance, they petitioned a new General Assembly to repeal the 1873 law. The new law, went their argument, was detrimental to cotton growing because it would lead to overproduction as furnishing merchants attempted to in-

---

[53]Dwight B. Billings, Jr., *Planters and the Making of a "New South": Class, Politics, and Development in North Carolina, 1865-1900* (Chapel Hill: University of North Carolina Press, 1979), offers an interesting study of planters in one Southern state.

[54]Atlanta *Constitution*, 11, 27 February 1875. Savannah *Morning News*, 4 February 1875. Columbus *Enquirer Sun*, 23 July 1883.

[55]Ransom and Sutch, *One Kind of Freedom*, 146-48. Wiener, *Social Origins*, 83-93.

[56]*Acts of the General Assembly of Georgia, 1873* (Atlanta: Constitution Job Printing Office, 1873) 42-47. Arnett, *Populist Movement*, 52-54. Greenville *Meriwether Vindicator*, 14 March 1873.

crease their profits by demanding larger crops. Furthermore, planters would be reluctant to put their land into production if they could not supervise the activities of tenants.[57] This argument was self-serving, since planters were themselves guilty of encouraging overproduction because they, like the merchants, profited on increased crops.

A second argument against the 1873 law was the specter of increased debts for tenants. Planters argued that by giving merchants a free hand to strike bargains directly with illiterate tenants, the Assembly was responsible for the creation of a permanent debtor class that would become "like the organ grinder's monkey—with a chain around their ankles, dancing and collecting funds for their owner."[58] Only the unselfish and benevolent intercession of planters prevented merchants from taking every cent of the tenants' income. The pressure brought by the Grange and the threat of more direct political action by planters induced the 1874 General Assembly to undo the damage and replace the 1873 law with its predecessor. Once again, the advantage swung back to the planters as they regained the right to approve all credit arrangements between merchants and tenants.[59]

The 1873 General Assembly also repealed an earlier law that limited the legal rate of interest to seven percent on most transactions and defined usury as interest rates exceeding ten percent.[60] The Atlanta Constitution, an active supporter of rapid industrialization financed by Northern capital, had led a statewide campaign to do away with usury laws and to let the forces of the marketplace set prevailing interest rates.[61] Reacting to pressure from the New South press, the Assembly enacted a new usury law allowing borrowers and lenders to agree to any interest rate they wanted and to have that rate enforced by the courts. As a backhanded gesture to planters, unspecified rates were limited to seven percent.[62] Since the new law encouraged investments in industry and curtailed the amount of credit available to agriculture, planters immediately attacked it through

---

[57]Atlanta *Constitution*, 22 January 1874. Greensboro *Herald*, 29 January 1874. Prominent members of the Georgia Grange included John B. Gordon, Alfred H. Colquitt, William J. Northern, and Leonidas F. Livingston. These men represented planter interests in the Grange and the later Farmers' Alliance.

[58]Greenville *Meriwether Vindicator*, 14 March 1873.

[59]Ibid., 15 August 1873. Ward, "Georgia under the Bourbon Democrats," 290-91.

[60]*Acts of the General Assembly of Georgia, 1871* (Atlanta: New Era Printing Company, 1871) 75.

[61]Atlanta *Constitution*, 23, 25 January 1873; 18, 19 December 1874; 3, 9 February 1875.

[62]*Acts of the General Assembly of Georgia, 1873* (Atlanta: Constitution Job Printing Office, 1875) 105-106. Greenville *Meriwether Vindicator*, 15 August 1873.

the rural press and through the state's planter organization, the Georgia Agricultural Society.[63]

In 1873, the annual meeting of the Agricultural Society passed a resolution demanding the repeal of the "open interest law" and the substitution of the previous law in its place. "As the farmer is the Atlas who carries this great country upon his shoulders," wrote the editor of the *Meriwether Vindicator*, "he has an undoubted right to reform the monstrous evils that have crept into our municipal, State and national governments. And, if he must turn politician awhile to cleanse the great Augean stable of political corruption, we say let him do so."[64] Once again, the planters were able to bring sufficient pressure on legislators to get action in the 1874 General Assembly.

In the 1874 session, a bill to limit interest rates was introduced, and although tabled, it almost passed on a close vote. The next year, the General Assembly repealed the 1873 vote and substituted a planter approved measure in its place. Under the 1875 law, interest rates were limited to seven percent, although rates of twelve percent were recognized in some transactions. If an individual was convicted of violating these limitations, the law provided that he was to lose both the legal and illegal interest collected.[65] The passage of the new law was a victory for planters, since it limited interest rates and kept the money available for agriculture from being invested in higher profit making industrial ventures. The law did little to help sharecroppers and tenants, however, since it placed no restrictions on the hidden interest charges merchants and some planters imposed on credit accounts. Nevertheless, the limitations set by this law represented a significant victory for Georgia planters because it made investments in agriculture as attractive as those in potential new commercial/industrial enterprises.[66]

The conflicts over crop liens and interest rates were instrumental in uniting planters politically. Although they had been the dominant influence in state politics before the Civil War and immediately after it, the Constitution of 1868 had undermined their power by granting the franchise to all males, black and white. The defection of Benjamin H. Hill in 1870 to the probusiness group had left the planter class disorganized and in chaos. The General Assembly of 1873-1874 demonstrated the potency of the new alliance of merchants and the increasingly vocal supporters of industrialization, while planters seemed to be losing their ability to control the state's political machinery. The absence of a strong leader behind whom the planters could unite had made shambles of their traditional

---

[63]Greenville *Meriwether Vindicator*, 15 August 1873.

[64]Ibid.

[65]*Acts of the General Assembly of Georgia, 1875* (Atlanta: Constitution Job Printing Office, 1875) 105-106.

[66]Wiener, *Social Origins*, 83-93. Ransom and Sutch, *One Kind of Freedom*, 146-48.

powers. The ease with which new laws concerning crop liens and interest rates had passed the Assembly, and the difficult time planters had in getting those laws repealed, gave them ample reason to be apprehensive about their economic and political future. Recognizing their diminishing importance in the national economy and realizing also that time would lessen their importance in the state, planters set about regaining their political power.[67] Centering their attack on the 1868 constitution, they demanded a state convention to write a new document. Robert Toombs—malcontent, unreconstructed Confederate, and spokesman for the antebellum planters—emerged from a self-imposed political exile to lead the movement for a new convention. Keying his attack on the 1868 constitution as being the work of "niggers and thieves," he made numerous speeches on the subject in 1874, 1875, and 1876.[68]

The turmoil generated by Toombs and other planters was soon carried into the legislature. By 1875, planters were able to force the convention issue to a vote in the Assembly, and, although unsuccessful, supporters of the convention call came close to securing the necessary majority. The General Assembly of 1876 again voted the question down by a narrow margin, but the next session approved a referendum on the question. Governor Alfred H. Colquitt set 12 June 1877 as the date for the balloting, and both supporters and opponents went to work to ensure victory for their sides.[69]

The results of the referendum are particularly revealing about the conflict between planters and merchants. Traditional interpretations have emphasized the fact that the convention call was approved by a vote of 48,329 to 39,099 and that the majority of the votes in favor of the convention came from the Black Belt.[70] It is true that the Black Belt, as the center of planter power, did provide most of the votes for the convention, but it is also true that most of the votes against the convention also came from Black Belt counties. As Jonathan Wiener has observed about politics in Alabama, planters tended to dominate the older antebellum Black Belt counties in the postwar period; while merchants, forced to seek more lucrative markets by proscriptive legislation, exercised more influence in the

---

[67]Nathans, *Losing the Peace*, 202-77. Parks, *Brown*, 443-85.

[68]Atlanta *Constitution*, 15,21, 28 January 1874; 26 January, 11, 12 February 1875.

[69]*Journal of the House of Representatives, 1875* (Atlanta: Constitution Job Printing Office, 1875) 102, 201, 453.

[70]William P. Brandon, "Calling the Georgia Constitutional Convention of 1877," *Georgia Historical Quarterly* 17 (1933): 189-204. Bond Almand, "The Convention of 1877: The Making and Adoption of a New Constitution," *Georgia Bar Journal* 7 (1945): 419-31.

newer areas of the Black Belt.[71] Certainly the returns in the convention referendum appear to bear out this contention.

The introduction of commercial fertilizers opened many new Georgia counties to cotton cultivation after the war, and the generous application of guano soon brought these peripheral counties into the mainstream of cotton production. Emancipation freed the necessary labor, and poor whites, previously saddled with marginal land, found that fertilizer made their holdings productive. Two areas of rapid growth developed. To the north, the counties at the base of the foothills that had produced mostly grains prior to the war became cotton producers, and, to the south, the Black Belt was quickly extended along the Flint and Chattahoochee River valleys. The heavy use of guano by farmers in the Wiregrass added more land to the total cotton acreage.[72] Through their control of the sources of credit, merchants in these areas quickly became merchant-planters and evolved into the "second branch" of the postwar agricultural elites.[73]

An analysis of the June 1877 election returns reveals the extent to which the newer elites (merchant-planters) opposed the power of planters in the older sections of the Black Belt. In the sixty-six Black Belt counties, the convention question was defeated by a narrow three-vote margin. The principal opposition to the proposed convention came from counties immediately adjacent to the borders of Alabama and Florida that had only recently been opened to cotton production on a large scale [See Map 1]. These counties accounted for 62.7 percent of the 39,099 votes cast against the convention call.[74]

The older Black Belt counties, on the other hand, supplied 50.7 percent of the votes in favor of a convention; but had it not been for the large votes of the antebellum cotton marketing centers of Macon, Augusta, Columbus, and Savannah, the referendum would have lost in this area by the considerable margin of 4,733 votes. Prewar ties to old Black Belt trading partners and a strong anti-Atlanta bias were enough to swing these counties to support the convention call. Atlanta, the only other urban center in the state, had no such ties, and it rejected the proposed convention by 236 votes. Had Macon and the other urban areas followed Atlanta's lead, the margin of defeat in the Black Belt would have been much greater.[75]

---

[71]Wiener, *Social Origins*, 92-108.

[72]Ransom and Sutch, *One Kind of Freedom*, 104-105. Wright, *The Political Economy of the Cotton South*, 158-80.

[73]Wiener, *Social Origins*, 93.

[74]*Comptroller General's Report, 1877*, 82-86.

[75]Ibid.

MAP 1

BLACK BELT COUNTIES OPPOSING
1877 CONSTITUTIONAL CONVENTION

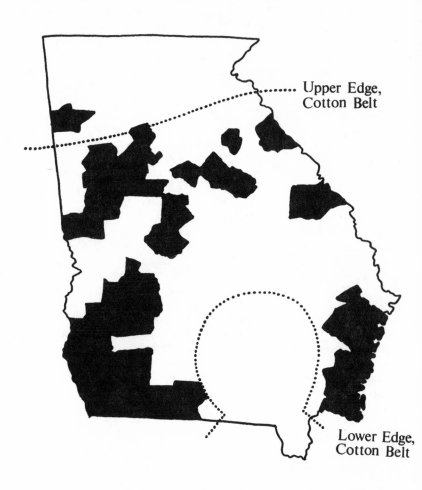

Upper Edge,
Cotton Belt

Lower Edge,
Cotton Belt

Further evidence of the antagonism between merchants and planters is found in the vote of counties on the northern fringe of the Black Belt. Those immediately surrounding Atlanta, which were also new cotton counties, rejected the convention by significant margins. Tied to the city through commerce, residents of these counties identified themselves with the New South. Finally, the last source of opposition to the convention came from the mountain counties, which were historically opposed to planters of the older Black Belt.[76]

There is no denying that the older counties of the Black Belt furnished the majority of the votes in favor of the constitutional convention. What is more important, however, is the degree to which opposition developed within the newer Black Belt counties to what was obviously a scheme to restore political control of the state to prewar planters. Thirty-one of the Black Belt counties rejected the proposal: an obvious indication that the nature of agriculture was changing and that many individuals within the Black Belt no longer depended entirely on agriculture as their major source of income.[77]

When the delegates met in Atlanta on 11 July 1877, few of Georgia's veteran political observers could predict the convention's outcome. Changes in the fundamental law of the state were to be expected, but how drastic these changes would be was unknown. Although the closeness of

TABLE 4.5

VOTES CAST IN BLACK BELT COUNTIES IN JUNE 1877		
NUMBER OF COUNTIES WITH BLACK MAJORITY	FOR CONVENTION	AGAINST CONVENTION
66[a]	24,506	24,509
62[b]	19,773	22,595
66[c]	21,687	27,328
PERCENT OF TOTAL VOTES CAST IN STATE		
NUMBER OF COUNTIES WITH BLACK MAJORITY	FOR CONVENTION	AGAINST CONVENTION
66[a]	50.7%	62.7%
62[b]	45.4%	60.7%
66[c]	47.6%	65.2%

[a] Counties having Negro majority, according to 1880 census.
[b] Excluding urban counties (Bibb, Chatham, Richmond, Muscogee) within Black Belt.
[c] Reversing votes for and against the Convention in urban counties in Black Belt.

[76]Ibid.

[77]Ward, "Georgia under the Bourbon Democrats," 228.

the referendum appeared to dictate moderation, many Georgians remembered the 1861 convention that had taken the state out of the Union despite a much closer vote. Industrialists, merchants, and some politicians were satisfied with the progress the state was making toward industrialization and economic diversification; therefore, they were apprehensive about radical alterations in the state government. A cursory examination of the ideologies of the convention delegates gave credence to these apprehensions because most of them were identified as having considerable planting interests. Although the membership included many professionals—lawyers, physicians, ministers, merchants, and railroad men—almost all of them were described in hyphenated terms such as lawyer-planter or planter-physician.[78] How these men would vote on specific questions regarding economics was a mystery, and Georgians waited to see how the new constitution would take shape.

TABLE 4.6

VOTING BY BLACK BELT COUNTIES AS A FUNCTION OF DATE OF CREATION				
VOTES AGAINST CONVENTION	NUMBER	CREATED BEFORE 1825	CREATED AFTER 1825	CREATED AFTER 1850
50-100%	31	15	16	16
40-49.9%	10	2	8	3
0-39.9%	25	18	7	4*
TOTAL	66	35	31	22
* Includes McDuffie County, created in 1871				

---

[78]Atlanta *Constitution*, 1-12 July 1877.

CHAPTER 5

THE NEW SOUTH
VERSUS THE OLD SOUTH

The struggle between merchant-planters in the newer areas of the Black Belt and those established families in the older areas of the region was aggravated by the emergence of a new political-economic philosophy dedicated to the furtherance of business and industry. This "New Departure" or "New South" movement drew its leadership from a variety of unlikely sources. From the ranks of antebellum planters came men like Benjamin H. Hill and Joseph E. Brown, representatives of the Whig-Democratic coalition that had dominated state politics in the 1850s. From the immediate postwar period came men like Evan P. Howell and, later, Henry Woodfin Grady. They were members of a new generation of political figures who were too young to have had any influence in the antebellum period, but who now loudly and persistently articulated the cause of industrialization in speeches and newspaper editorials. From the Republican party came men like John E. Bryant, Hannibal I. Kimball, and Amos T. Akerman—men who subscribed to the idea that the proper function of government was to aid business.[1] From the ranks of the Democratic party emerged Alfred H. Colquitt, John B. Gordon, and Hill. These men, clad in the raiment of Confederate heroes, brought with them respectability and the possibility of tying the old and new together.

The men of the New South urged Southerners to forget the past and to concentrate on developing the future—a future of factories, railroads, and business. The Civil War had demonstrated the superiority of an industrial state over an agricultural one; and, they argued, if the South was to become an integral part of the nation's economy, it had to give up its reliance on agriculture and join the rest of the country in the industrial

---

[1]Nathans, *Losing the Peace*, 95, 206-12, 224-27.

revolution.[2] The emphasis placed on the future and the seeming denial of the past summed up the general attitude of the New South men: the past, with its unrealistic commitment to cotton and slaves, was gone; the future belonged to a new generation pledged to progress and industrialization. "Manufacturing is the only secret to prosperity in the South," editorialized the Americus *Recorder*, a paper that represented the probusiness interests of newer planters in southwest Georgia. "We have the raw materials in this section in abundance, and whenever we manufacture them we will multiply our wealth ten-fold."[3] For the men of the New South, industrial wealth would command an influence and respect that the old agricultural society could never achieve.

Young or old, Republican, Whig, or Democrat, the New South men were united in their desire to bring the South into the mainstream of the national economy.[4] It is difficult to find a name that adequately describes the advocates of the New South, though the term "New Departure" was frequently applied to them; but so was the name "Bourbon," although its more accepted application was to the planters who resisted industrialization.[5] Because of the confusing use of terms like Bourbon, New Departure, and New South, it is far easier to identify *who* the men who made up the movement were than to place a label on them. They were, according to the editor of the *Recorder*, "the best elements" of the South and included "the *principal* businessmen, lawyers, physicians, teachers, clergymen, merchants, and farmers" who, in keeping with the practices of industry, gave "*efficiency* to the moral activities and discipline of the local communities."[6] Joseph E. Brown described them as the men of "intelligence and wealth" in the state who "always control tenants and laborers."[7] The measure of success for such men was, in the words of Wilbur J. Cash,

---

[2]Paul M. Gaston, *The New South Creed: A Study in Southern Mythmaking* (New York: Alfred A. Knopf, 1970) 1-8. Harold D. Woodman, ed., *The Legacy of the American Civil War* (New York: John Wiley and Sons, 1973). Thomas C. Cochran, "Did the Civil War Retard Industrialization?" *Mississippi Valley Historical Review* 48 (1961): 197-210.

[3]Americus *Recorder*, 13 July 1888.

[4]Woodward, *Origins*, 23-50. Thomas B. Alexander, "Persistent Whiggery in the Confederate South, 1860-1877," *Journal of Southern History* 27 (1961): 305-29. See also Carl V. Harris, "Right or Left Fork? The Section-Party Alignments of Southern Democrats in Congress, 1873-1897," *Journal of Southern History* 42 (1976): 471-506.

[5]Americus *Recorder*, 12 February 1882. Macon *Telegraph*, 5 January 1889. Parks, *Brown*, 526-30. Brown described opponents of his 1880 candidacy for the U. S. Senate as "a few Bourbons who can never accept the situation."

[6]Americus *Recorder*, 12 February 1882.

[7]Joseph E. Brown to Rufus B. Bullock, 3 December 1868, HT.

how well they managed to break "with the physical order of the past" and to give up "the old purely agricultural way of life."[8]

The twin themes of the New South were industrialization and reconciliation. In 1871, Benjamin H. Hill spelled out the general outlines of the New South program when he addressed the University of Georgia Alumni Society in Athens. After reviewing the effects of slavery on the Southern economy, Hill went on to describe a new and different South of the future. In his vision, the South gave up its attachment to cotton, accepted and practiced diversified agriculture, utilized its vast natural resources, and developed its manufacturing potential to the fullest. Such a South was possible, he insisted, if Southerners would only commit themselves to a modern system of education and to the adoption of new ideas. When the South made these commitments, he promised, it would soon "surpass all other [regions] in population and power." It would "honor labor, and make the callings of the miner, the manufacturer, the metallurgist, the machinist, the agriculturalist, and the mechanic, as learned and as honorable as are the professions of law, medicine, and theology."[9] Although Hill's speech was viewed as further evidence of his capitulation to Republicanism, he articulated the essential elements of the New South Philosophy, which subsequent writers and orators merely enlarged to fit particular circumstances.

In order for the South to become industrialized, two important requirements had to be met. First, it had to attract outside capital in sufficient quantities to establish factories to exploit the region's natural resources. This quest for capital led New South boosters to resort to a wide variety of schemes, all of which were duly publicized in newspapers friendly to the cause.[10] Statistics, fiction, fairs, speeches, editorials, and even sermons were routinely employed as a means of spreading the gospel of industrialization.[11] The message was simple and direct: investment in the South meant a safe, sure, and high rate of profit.

The second requirement to be met before industrial success could come to the South was to attract white immigrants into the area in order to have a permanent class of factory workers. Although the presence of freedmen ensured an ample supply of manual labor, it was generally conceded that Negroes were not adaptable to factory work and were to be left in the fields

---

[8]Wilbur J. Cash, *The Mind of the South* (New York: Vintage Books, 1941) 184.

[9]Pearce, *Hill*, 239-44. See E. Merton Coulter, "The New South: Benjamin H. Hill's Speech before the Alumni Society of the University of Georgia, 1871," *Georgia Historical Quarterly* 57 (1973): 179-99.

[10]Atlanta *Constitution*, 7 July 1881; 30 August 1882; 12 July 1886. Macon *Telegraph*, 3, 31 July and 15 August 1887.

[11]Richard L. Wilson, "Sam Jones: An Apostle of the New South," *Georgia Historical Quarterly* 57 (1973): 459-74. Jones, an evangelist, claimed to have made $700,000 by preaching the ideals of the New South.

as sharecroppers and tenants. "Men of experience in agriculture and business" became the targets of New South recruiters who sought a balance to Southerners, who were "not cramped by excessive early schooling." The combination of Southern vitality and Northern practicality was thought to be a magic elixir that would transform the South overnight.[12]

Although planters had given consideration to white immigration into the region in the immediate postwar period, their efforts had been geared to securing docile replacements for slaves and not toward importing competing farmers. The New South campaign, with its emphasis on attracting industrial workers and small truck farmers, brought vehement planter opposition. A massive influx of white factory workers would, they felt, result in a lessening of control over Negroes and a further erosion of planter political power.[13] They feared that a large white laboring class, located in cities and not tied to the agricultural economy, would result in a permanent shift of power to industrialists.

For the New South efforts to attract capital and laborers to the region to succeed, it was necessary to convince the rest of the nation that Reconstruction had been a success. Of particular importance was the need to demonstrate the South's acceptance of the finality of abolition and its rejection of the old slaveholding order. "The men of brains and influence all know slavery is abolished and that it can never be restored," wrote the editor of the Americus *Recorder* in 1882, "[and] in truth they do not want it restored."[14] "It is not uncommon," echoed the Macon *Telegraph*, "to hear Southern businessmen say that the abolition of slavery was the richest blessings to the South."[15] The Galveston, Texas, *News* reported in 1887 that "with few exceptions the leaders who most directed the thought and policy of the South during the era extending from 1861 to 1865 were the readiest, when the star of the Confederacy went down, to accept the situation and yield the points for which, on their part, the war had been waged."[16] The *Recorder* affirmed this statement with the pronouncement that "the great men of war times are, as a rule, among the most liberal and progressive leaders of the whole South."[17]

---

[12]Americus *Recorder*, 3 December 1880; 26 February 1882.

[13]Lexington *Oglethorpe Echo*, 3 December 1880. An advocate of immigration during Reconstruction, the *Echo*, a firm supporter of planter interests, backed away from its earlier stand and worked against immigration during the 1880s.

[14]Americus *Recorder*, 26 February 1882.

[15]Macon *Telegraph*, 4 July 1887.

[16]Galveston (Texas) *News*, reprinted in the Macon *Telegraph*, 8 July 1887.

[17]Americus *Recorder*, 3 January 1882. William B. Hesseltine, *Confederate Leaders in the New South* (Baton Rouge: Louisiana State University Press, 1950) 16.

Despite the assertions of prominent New South leaders concerning the acceptance of abolition, many orators and writers felt it necessary to give additional assurances that Southern blacks were treated fairly. The acknowledged spokesman for the movement was Henry W. Grady, the editor of the Atlanta *Constitution* and a flamboyant orator, whose most famous speech was delivered in Boston in 1889. Ignoring the Ku Klux Klan outrages of the 1860s and 1870s and the day-to-day realities of the chain gang and peonage, Grady enunciated the New South program of white supremacy and benevolent paternalism:

> [W]e treat the negro fairly, measuring to him justice in the fullness the strong should give to the weak, and leading him in the steadfast ways of citizenship that he may no longer be the prey of the unscrupulous and the sport of the thoughtless. We open to him every pursuit in which he can prosper, and seek to broaden his training and capacity. We seek to hold his confidence and friendship, and to pin him to the soil with ownership, that he may catch in the fire of his own hearthstone that sense of responsibility the shiftless can never know.[18]

Racist by today's standards, Grady's tranquil picture of race relations apparently satisfied the North. As long as blacks assumed the "proper" roles as agricultural laborers, Grady continued, harmony between the races would prevail. Only interference from "outsiders" could upset the peaceful balance. "The negro can never control the South," he warned, "and it would be well if partisans in the North would understand this." Instead of constantly harping on the plight of Southern blacks, the North should "remove the outside pressure [and] leave the South to deal with the situation as it exists, and there will be no limit to the kindness and friendliness with which the negro will be treated and advanced."[19] The keys to a permanent solution to the "race problem" in the New South were white political dominance and segregation.[20] Until a satisfactory solution was found, the policy, official and unofficial, of the New South was to treat Negroes with paternalistic patience and a firm hand.[21] Industrialization was to be the exclusive domain of whites; there was no place for blacks.

After limiting the involvement of Negroes to agriculture, the apostles of the New South were nonetheless quick to claim them as an essential part of the South's march toward prosperity. As Paul Gaston has observed, efforts to establish proof of extensive material progress for blacks ranged from "the ridiculous to the sublime." Statistics, the favorite tool of New

---

[18]Mills B. Lane, ed., *The New South: Writings and Speeches of Henry Grady* (Savannah: Beehive Press, 1971) 102.

[19]Ibid., 100. Atlanta *Constitution*, 3 January 1889.

[20]Lane, *The New South*, 139-43.

[21]Eastman *Times-Journal*, 8 November 1883.

South speakers, were manipulated to prove that the economic advance of Negroes since emancipation had been continuous and rewarding.[22] Conveniently for New South publicists, hard data was scarce, and few individuals were skilled enough as statisticians to dispute the myriad of charts and figures used to support white claims of black progress. Ownership of land, the primary indicator of Negro economic progress, was frequently referred to by New South advocates as proof of their claims. In reality, blacks frequently encountered white hostility in their efforts to acquire land. By 1890, only 13,623 Negroes in Georgia had managed to secure title to land.[23] Even though the total number of acres owned and the number of owners increased dramatically in the last two decades of the 1800s, most of the title acquisitions appear to have come through inheritance since the average farm size is reduced by almost thirty percent.

Similar claims were made about the educational progress of Negroes and were equally dubious. In his last public address before his death in 1889, Grady told a Boston audience that "despite the doubts of many wise men if education helps," Negroes received almost $500,000 annually from the state to fund their separate school systems. While some of this allocation came from taxes assessed on the $10 million worth of property owned by Negroes, the bulk of the funds came from taxes paid by whites on property valued at $368 million. Although Grady implied an equal split of tax monies between whites and blacks, the Georgia General Assembly never allocated state funds for education on an equal racial basis.[24]

The progress of Negroes was a favorite subject of New South orators and writers, but the exorbitant claims about material and educational advances were less impressive when viewed in the context of day-to-day reality. A recent study by Richard J. Hopkins illustrates the difficulties faced

TABLE 5.1

LAND OWNERSHIP BY NEGROES IN GEORGIA			
YEAR	ACREAGE [TOTAL]	NUMBER OF OWNERS	AVERAGE SIZE OF FARMS [ACRES]
1874	338,769	2,974	113.9
1880	586,664	5,968	98.3
1890	927,234	13,623	68.1

[22]Gaston, *New South Creed*, 80-116. Ray C. Rensi, "The Gospel according to Sam Jones," *Georgia Historical Quarterly* 60 (1976): 251-63.

[23]Robert P. Brooks, *The Agrarian Revolution in Georgia, 1865-1912* (Madison: University of Wisconsin, 1914) 435.

[24]Lane, *The New South*, 94-96.

by Southern blacks. Generally excluded from factory jobs, they were relegated to menial tasks in cities and to sharecropping, tenantry, or wage-labor in rural areas. Hopkins's study, which deals with the occupational mobility of blacks in Atlanta between 1870 and 1896, found that Negroes faced a static employment situation, while native whites and white immigrants enjoyed an upward mobility rate of fifty-seven percent from manual to nonmanual jobs. Similarly, the movement of both native born and foreign born whites from blue collar to white collar jobs ranged from thirteen to twenty-three percent, while blacks experienced no movement at all. New South rhetoric notwithstanding, entry level tended to determine the top positions blacks could achieve in industry. Freedom from slavery did not mean freedom from discrimination.[25]

In addition to economic discrimination, Georgia Negroes also faced political repression. With the loss of state elections in 1870, Republicans were forced into a minor role in state politics; and with the decline of Republican power, Georgia blacks were deprived of the opportunity to play a positive political role. The United States Supreme Court decision of 1883 striking down most of the provisions of the Civil Rights Acts of 1866 and 1875 further reduced black political importance and returned full control of Southern politics to whites. Although still voters, Negroes played a subordinate role in state politics until nearly all were disfranchised between 1900 and 1908.[26] The abandonment of Negroes by the national Republican party forced them into a tenuous dependent relationship with planters and merchants.[27] Physical violence, economic coercion, and social proscription had solved the race "problem" to the satisfaction of Southern whites, and New South leaders salved the conscience of Northerners by assuring them that the Southern solution guaranteed Negroes progress and prosperity.[28]

Having fully explained the plight of Southern Negroes away, New South men waited expectantly for an influx of Northern capital. "The sooner the Northern capitalist understands he can do more with his money by investing it in the South than in letting it lie idle in the banks or losing it on Wall Street," wrote the editor of the Americus *Recorder*, "the better for him and the better for the South."[29] This sentiment, repeated by other New

---

[25]Richard J. Hopkins, "Occupational and Geographic Mobility in Atlanta, 1870-1896," *Journal of Southern History* 24 (1968): 206-207. Higgs, *Competition and Coercion*, 80-83, disputes the Hopkins thesis and calls such explanations "myths."

[26]Mandle, *Roots*, 107-15. Stanley P. Hirshson, *Farewell to the Bloody Shirt: Northern Republicans and the Southern Negro, 1877-1913* (Bloomington: Indiana University Press, 1962) 102-105.

[27]Lawrence Grossman, *The Democratic Party and the Negro: Northern and National Politics, 1868-1892* (Urbana: University of Illinois Press, 1976) 156-72.

[28]Trelease, *White Terror*, 226-45.

[29]Americus *Recorder*, 22 March 1885.

South papers in Georgia, became a litany recited by hundreds of Chambers of Commerce, Boards of Trade, and Bureaus of Immigration in small towns throughout the state.[30] Every town, village, whistlestop, and crossroads wanted to become the next New York or Pittsburgh.

The center of the New South movement in Georgia was Atlanta. A small town before the Civil War and largely destroyed by Sherman in 1864, Atlanta had recovered quickly. In 1868, it became the temporary capital of the state when the Republicans gained control of the governmental machinery. By 1880, Atlanta's population of 49,137 persons outstripped its nearest rival, Savannah, by nearly five thousand inhabitants. The city's recovery symbolized the New South ideal of an urban and industrialized society arising from the ashes of the war. Property values in the Fulton County-Atlanta area experienced the greatest increase in the state during the postwar period. In 1860, an acre of undeveloped land sold for an average price of eight dollars, while a similar acre brought $68 in 1890.[31] Atlanta's growth was based on its transportation facilities, since the city lacked most of the natural resources needed for manufacturing. The terminus of five major interstate railroads, it was also an important way station on the through routes of other roads.[32]

Unrestrained by the traditional urban reliance on planters and cotton, Atlanta's businessmen were inclined to develop their interests along lines in keeping with the national, rather than the regional, economy. Led by the editors of two of the South's most prestigious and influential newspapers, the *Constitution* (1868) and the *Journal* (1883), they formed the most vocal and active leadership of the New South movement. Without close ties to the planter class, Atlanta's merchants and businessmen were less responsive to their influence and pressure.

Although it was Georgia's largest city, Atlanta's prominence did not go unchallenged. Savannah, Macon, Columbus, and Augusta— all important urban centers before the war—sought to regain their former positions and to short-circuit the growing influence of Atlanta. Only Macon, located in the geographic center of the state, offered any real competition. Macon's civic and political leaders, backed by the Macon *Telegraph,* worked constantly to undermine Atlanta's leadership. "There is no power on earth, nor under it, that can prevent Macon from becoming the industrial and commercial center of Georgia," wrote the *Telegraph's* editor in 1890. "The place is rightfully ours, belongs to us, and Macon proposes to claim her own."[33]

---

[30]Macon *Telegraph,* 20 August 1887; 18 January, 2 April 1890.

[31]Pressly and Scofield, *Farm Real Estate Values,* 47.

[32]The most important of these lines were the Western and Atlantic, the Georgia Railroad, and the Richmond Air Line.

[33]Macon *Telegraph,* 17 January 1890.

Like Atlanta, Macon was a center of railroad transportation, but unlike her rival, Macon's roads were mostly intrastate and connected the city with the older Black Belt. Despite its importance as a major collection and shipping center for cotton, Macon's railroads did not handle as high a volume of freight as Atlanta. The Macon Board of Trade, a quasi-governmental agency, worked to increase the number of roads serving the city by persuading the city council to offer free land, cash subsidies, and tax concessions to new roads willing to locate there.[34] The intense rivalry between Macon and Atlanta was reflected in the pages of the *Telegraph* as the editors kept up a running battle with the *Constitution* and *Journal* over the role each city played in the state's economy. Thoroughgoing believers in the New South, the *Telegraph's* editors were as impassioned on the subject as the editors of the Atlanta papers. Unlike the *Constitution* and the *Journal*, however, the *Telegraph* accepted the "Prussian Road" approach advocated by planters. All in all, what Macon and its supporters lacked in numbers they more than made up for in fervor. Thus, the *Telegraph* could confidently assure its readers that Macon would play a dominant role in a New South where the "wheels of our factories are turning, miners are delving in our hills, the smoke of our blast furnaces invades the heavens, and hope eternal beams upon the faces of our people."[35]

The antebellum ties between Macon's merchants and the old planter class survived the war intact, and the continued importance of cotton in the city's economy was a major factor in the willingness of her civic and political leaders to accept the "Prussian Road" concept of industrialization. In the hectic political struggles of the 1870s, 1880s, and 1890s, Macon was the center of opposition to politicians exclusively allied with the business interests of Atlanta. One indication of the strength of the city's ties with the planter class is the large vote Macon and Bibb County cast against the choice of Atlanta as the permanent capital of the state in 1877. Milledgeville, the antebellum capital and the alternative choice to Atlanta, was a small town located in the heart of the Black Belt, and it was dependent on Macon for supplies and railroad service. Rural in character and little more than a large village, Milledgeville offered Macon no economic or political competition.[36]

Railroad development was a critical part of the New South program. Under the Constitution of 1868, Georgia was committed to giving aid to railroads and other industries within the state, a resumption of the antebellum policy that had been discontinued in 1861. The postwar program

---

[34]Ibid., 20 August 1887; 24 November, 6 December 1888; 3 January 1889.

[35]Ibid., 30 July 1887.

[36]*Comptroller General's Report, 1877*, 82-86.

of aid exceeded that of the prewar period by several times.[37] The amount
to be granted by the state government after 1868 was calculated on a slid-
ing scale and ranged from $3000 to $15,000 per completed mile. By 1876,
Georgia was pledged to a possible expenditure of $30 million, although
the actual amount paid out was only $212,564,250.[38] During the period
of Republican control and until the ratification of a new constitution in
1877, aid was promised to all new railroads in the state, although only a
few actually collected it. On the average, the General Assembly chartered
forty new companies a year from 1868 until 1877.[39] Most of the proposed
routes were local ones connecting rural areas with major north-south, east-
west trunk lines, and most of the companies chartered by the legislature
never began construction. Although the amount of money that could have
been collected was rather large, the state actually paid out only slightly
more than one-third of the total amount it was committed to pay.

While railroad construction was a major objective of many New South
advocates, other projects also received their attention. One scheme widely
publicized in the 1870s was the construction of an intercoastal waterway
along the coastline of the Gulf of Mexico. A trans-Florida canal would
connect ports on the Gulf Coast with harbors on the Atlantic Coast. The
originator of this particular project, P. H. Raiford, wrote to Governor
Alfred H. Colquitt requesting a state appropriation of $7500 to study the
feasibility of his proposed "Landlocked Channel from the Mississippi River
via the Gulf Coast and Florida Peninsula to Harbors of the South Atlantic
Coast." In urging the governor to submit his request to the General Assembly, Raiford summed up the New South attitude toward the role of
government in fostering economic development. "I think, Governor," he
wrote, "you will agree with me in the opinion that to stimulate the indus-

TABLE 5.2

URBAN VOTE FOR LOCATION OF CAPITAL, 1877			
COUNTY	COUNTY SEAT	VOTE FOR MILLEDGEVILLE	VOTE FOR ATLANTA
Bibb	Macon	3071	358
Chatham	Savannah	1990	654
Fulton	Atlanta	52	5620
Muscogee	Columbus	845	1229
Richmond	Augusta	2675	1779

[37]Saye, *A Constitutional History*, 267-78.

[38]Thompson, *Reconstruction in Georgia*, 207-17.

[39]*Public Laws Passed by the General Assembly of the State of Georgia at the Session of
1870* (Atlanta: New Era Printing Establishment, 1870) 7.

tries and commerce of a country is the truest and best statesmanship, and to make available all the advantages which nature has given us, is the golden rule."[40] Raiford's canal, although never more than a pipe dream, was typical of the schemes seriously considered by the men of the New South.

Just as the expansion and modernization of railroads were considered essential to the development of the state's economy, so, too, were the expansion, diversification, and modernization of agriculture deemed necessary. The cry for crop diversification by proponents of the New South became a major irritant to planters, although they had once espoused the idea as an alternative to postwar wage-labor systems of cotton cultivation. As early as 1866, the State Agricultural Society, a planter-dominated group, urged them to give up their reliance on cotton and to concentrate their efforts on dairy farming, sheep raising, or the growing of cereal crops.[41] In 1867, the Conservative Convention, a political meeting of postwar planters, discussed crop diversification as a possible platform plank to be used against the Republicans. One speaker at the Convention, Dr. Ira E. Dupree, advised them to "abandon the cultivation of large, worn-out farms, cultivate little cotton, increase the production of cereals, improve our stock and make our means of support at home." Crop diversification, according to Dr. Dupree, was the panacea for the South's economic problems, and following such a course would allow planters to "restore our fallen country to its wonted political, financial, social, and religious condition."[42]

The introduction of sharecropping and the lack of available money to pay for necessary improvements, which would have to be made before diversification could be undertaken, halted most movement toward that end. Sharecropping encouraged the standardization of agriculture, and since cotton cultivation permitted this, planter interest in diversification lessened. Thus, after having been seriously considered and subsequently rejected by planters, diversification became a major tenet of the New South creed.[43]

The New South emphasis on this matter came in the form of verbal attacks on planters for refusing to grow alternative crops. Editors berated them for their continued dependence on cotton and placed the blame for the declining market squarely on their shoulders. "Cotton is just the thing of course," wrote the editor of the Greensboro *Herald,* "men, women and

---

[40]P. H. Raiford to Alfred H. Colquitt, 12 August 1878, Incoming Correspondence of Governor Alfred H. Colquitt, Georgia Department of Archives and History. Hereafter referred to as ICAHC.

[41]Range, *Georgia Agriculture,* 67, 119.

[42]Quoted in Conway, *Reconstruction of Georgia,* 123.

[43]Mandle, *Roots,* 52-70. Ransom and Sutch, *One Kind of Freedom,* 149-70.

children and horses can eat cotton and grow fat on it."[44] The editor of the *Meriwether Vindicator* rebuked planters for "their anxiety to plant all their land [in cotton] and plow all their mules" even though they had to "buy bacon and corn to feed laborers and stock at high rates of credit. They have done this every year in the hope of big crops and high prices."[45] Another editor went so far as to call planters who continued to raise cotton "dupes" and to urge them "to set the rest of the South a noble example by just doubling their grain crops for every rise that takes place in the cotton market from now until spring."[46] To planters, who were responsible for the major part of the state's economy, these criticisms amounted to stinging public reprimands from men who didn't know what they were talking about.

Despite their opposition to the New South rhetoric, planters were not opposed to industrial development and crop diversification. Indeed, they had often advocated many of the same kinds of programs as part of the state's prewar growth. The antebellum Whig party, which stressed internal developments and drew its leadership from the ranks of planters, had been very strong in Georgia.[47] Through the efforts of planters, Georgia entered the Civil War with the most extensive railroad network of any state in the Lower South. As early as 1840, state aid was given to an emerging textile industry, and by 1850 Augusta had over 16,000 spindles in operation. By 1860, 1,890 separate manufacturing concerns employing over 11,500 workers were annually producing goods valued at an estimated $17 million, although their initial capitalization was only $11 million. Antebellum industries engaged in a wide variety of activities, including the manufacture of paper; cloth; and iron, kaolin, and lumber products, as well as milling and iron mining. In addition to these operations, Georgia led the nation in the production of naval stores.[48]

Planters had invested considerable sums in prewar industries, and in some cases these investments provided the basis of the postwar recovery of their families.[49] Charles Colcock Jones, a wealthy coastal planter and minister, made substantial investments in railroads and iron foundries

---

[44]Greensboro *Herald,* 5 May 1881.

[45]Greenville *Meriwether Vindicator,* 14 January 1877.

[46]Lexington *Oglethorpe Echo,* 26 January 1877.

[47]Arthur C. Cole, *The Whig Party in the South* (Washington DC: American Historical Association, 1914) 104. Wiener, *Social Origins,* 137-61. Thomas Weiss, "The Participation of Planters in Manufacturing in the Antebellum South," *Agricultural History* 48 (1974): 277-97.

[48]Conway, *Reconstruction of Georgia,* 104-105. Ralph V. Anderson,"Slaves as Fixed Capital: Slave Labor and Southern Economic Development," *Journal of American History* 64 (1977): 24-46.

[49]Woodman, *King Cotton,* 204-41.

prior to the war that later were to provide his widow with a comfortable income. In 1866, the return from Jones's investment in Georgia Railroad stock, considered by his son to be the "very best security in Georgia," meant the difference between Mrs. Jones's living in poverty or living only slightly below her antebellum standards.[50] A family friend, Roswell King—developer of Georgia's outstanding mill village, Roswell—first acquired his fortune as a supervisor of a rice plantation in Liberty County before he turned to manufacturing.[51]

After the Whig party came to power in Georgia, generous provisions were made to subsidize industrial development in the state, a policy that was continued throughout the 1850s. Charters granted to new industries were liberal in the privileges they allowed, and the General Assembly also made substantial grants of land and money to railroads and factories.[52] By 1860, various legislatures had committed the state to nearly $8 million in aid to railroads alone.[53] While railroad construction accounted for most of the state aid granted, canals, banks, and riverboat companies also received large subsidies. All in all, the industrial progress made in prewar Georgia was significant, and most of it was due to the efforts of planters.[54]

Antebellum planters, unlike their postwar counterparts, practiced a diversified agriculture that stressed the cultivation of rice, corn, and cotton. In 1859, for example, the state's corn crop was almost 31 million bushels, while rice production amounted to 52.5 million pounds. Although cotton was the chief money-maker, grain crops accounted for a large share of the state's economy. In addition to cotton and grains, experiments in silk production and stock raising received a great deal of attention from planters.[55] Thus, when the apostles of the New South reproached them for their dependence on cotton, planters had good reason to regard such criticism as unwanted and unwarranted. Cotton production was an efficient way to maximize profits with a minimum investment.[56]

Not only did planters react strongly to the economic aspects of the New South program, they were also antagonistic to the New South rhetoric, which constituted a direct attack on their values. As James L. Roark has noted, it was easy for planters to become bitter when they saw themselves

---

[50]Charles C. Jones, Jr., to Mary Jones, 28 May 1866, in Myers, *Children*, 1338.

[51]Ibid., 23.

[52]Cole, *Whig Party*, 69-80.

[53]Coleman, *A History of Georgia*, 152-73.

[54]Donald Arthur DeBats, "Elites and Masses: Political Structure, Communication and Behavior in Antebellum Georgia " (Ph.D. diss., University of Wisconsin, 1973) 274-352.

[55]Thompson, *Reconstruction in Georgia*, 257-82. Woodman, *King Cotton*, 141-47.

[56]Higgs, *Competition and Coercion*, 49, 138-39.

depicted by editors as "soft, self-indulgent snobs who were doomed to extinction in a rawer, more competitive society."[57] William Browne, former Confederate Assistant Secretary of State and Professor of History at the University of Georgia after the war, spoke for many planters when he labeled the New South an "apostasy." To him, rejection of planter society made a mockery of four years of war and the deaths of thousands of Southerners.[58] The emphasis placed on the acquisition of outside capital and the concentration of industrial power in urban areas reversed the prewar pattern and largely excluded planters.[59]

The most significant disagreement planters had with New South exponents was over the question of who would control the industrial process. While great strides toward industrialization had taken place before the Civil War, they had been carefully regulated by planters, and industrialization always took a back seat to agriculture. Through their control of financial resources and labor, planters directed the location and rate of development of prewar factories. By dispersing factories throughout the Black Belt, they prevented the rise of a distinctive and independent business class and bound industrialists to them through an elaborate system of financial, social, and kinship ties.[60] By preventing the concentration of factories in urban areas and by co-opting the social allegiances of industrialists, planters managed to subordinate industry to agriculture and to protect their hegemony in the state.

The extent to which prewar planters were successful in controlling industrialization is best illustrated by the railroad networks of the period. Because planters were usually responsible for the construction and expansion of railroad and riverboat routes, either personally or through the allocation of state funds, these projects were limited in scope and served only the Black Belt.[61] In 1860, railroads in Georgia were confined to this region with the single exception of the state-owned Western and Atlantic Road. Similarly, most factories were located within the borders of the Black Belt where planters could directly supervise their activities.[62]

While planters were not opposed to industrialization per se, they were opposed to postwar patterns of industrial growth that removed control of

---

[57]Roark, *Masters,* 179-80. Woodman, *King Cotton,* 341-45.

[58]Hesseltine, *Confederate Leaders,* 40-41.

[59]Woodward, *Origins,* 20-21, 142-74. Wiener, *Social Origins,* 137-61. Roark, *Masters,* 179-81.

[60]Genovese, *In Red and Black,* 331-49. DeBats, "Elites and Masses," 448-74.

[61]Wiener, *Social Origins,* 141-44. Cole, *Whig Party,* 94-103.

[62]Woodward, *Origins,* 200. Woodman, *King Cotton,* 88. See also Robert W. Fogel, *Railroads and American Economic Growth: Essays in Econometric History* (Baltimore: Johns Hopkins Press, 1964).

the process from their hands. Unlike antebellum industrialists, advocates of the New South were not tied to the planting class and tended to ignore their interests. Instead of dispersing factories throughout the countryside, postwar developers adopted the New England pattern of mill villages near urban centers. Prewar planters had supported the expansion of railroads at state expense because it strengthened their economic power, but they opposed state aid in the postwar years because it had the opposite effect. Throughout the late 1860s and early 1870s, successive General Assemblies authorized subsidies to feeder lines, which weakened the power of the Black Belt by opening new areas of the state to cotton cultivation. Corporations, often controlled or owned by men outside the state, received favorable treatment from legislators.[63] Furthermore, control of many factories and railroads changed hands when planters found it necessary to sell their stocks in order to finance their planting operations.[64]

As Jonathan Wiener has pointed out, planters were willing advocates of industrialization as long as it did not interfere with or supplant agriculture as the dominant force in the Southern economy. Whether or not planters approved of it wholeheartedly was unimportant; they had to accept the inevitability of industrialization. Abolition, together with the Civil War, created new forces within the South—forces that could not be halted by the mightiest exertions of planters. Thus they found themselves confronted by a perplexing dilemma: to remain steadfast in their opposition to industrialization would result in the isolation and eventual destruction of the planter class, while conditional acceptance might allow them to ultimately gain control of the process and shape it according to their own wishes.[65]

Planter control of industrialization depended on their ability to control the state government. The Constitution of 1868, although written by Republicans, did not drastically alter the structure of state government, but the granting of suffrage to freedmen resulted in a temporary loss of power by planters. The gradual movement of the rural population to cities and the opening of marginal lands to cotton farming heightened the illusion that their political influence was waning. In reality, by resorting to physical violence and economic coercion. planters had regained much of their lost power by 1871.[66] Immediately after Rufus B. Bullock fled the state and Republican control ended, planters began to call for a convention to write a new constitution. From 1871 until 1876, their efforts were unsuc-

[63]*Journal of the House of Representatives, 1870*, 1344-47.

[64]Roark, *Masters*, 166-67, 198. Moore, *Dictatorship and Democracy*, 111-15.

[65]Genovese, *Roll, Jordan, Roll*, 661-65. Wiener, *Social Origins*, 141-61. Moore, *Dictatorship and Democracy*, 144-49.

[66]Trelease, *White Terror*, 226-45, 318-35.

cessful because of poor organization. The defection of such men as Benjamin H. Hill and John B. Gordon to the New South and the deaths of antebellum leaders like Howell Cobb and Linton Stephens had depleted their ranks.[67] Taking advantage of this situation, New South editors and leaders staunchly opposed the attempt to curtail business activities and privileges through the medium of a new constitution.[68]

To discredit the New South position, planters sought to equate opposition to a constitutional convention with approval of and support for the Republican party and Negro rule. The Columbus *Enquirer* was typical of planter oriented papers leading the call for a new convention when it described the Constitution of 1868 as a "foreign document." "The present constitution of Georgia was adopted by people inimical to the people of Georgia," blustered the *Enquirer's* editor, "[and] by those who represent the passions and hate of the enemies of Georgia and her true interests. It was effected under the shadow of Federal bayonets. The Constitution so framed cannot be regarded as the will of the people of the Empire State of the South."[69] Robert Toombs, the most vocal planter spokesman, proclaimed the document as "the handiwork of negroes, thieves, and Yankees."[70] By placing the issue of a new constitution in the context of Reconstruction, Republicanism, and Negro rule, planters made it increasingly difficult for white Georgians, regardless of economic persuasion, to offer opposition.

When the convention question was finally placed before the people in 1877, it was approved by a narrow margin of 9000 votes out of a total of 87,000 votes cast.[71] A year earlier, 144,000 Georgians had participated in the gubernatorial election won by Alfred H. Colquitt, a prewar Whig. The small number of voters casting ballots in the 1877 referendum was indicative of the attitude many Georgians had toward the 1868 Constitution. Businessmen and industrialists found the provisions of the constitution advantageous and had no desire to change it, but few were willing to take a public stand in favor of it.[72] Poor farmers, tenants, and sharecroppers—groups who had been responsible for the passage of the document—failed to vote, since to do so would be to invite economic reprisals.[73] The lack of

---

[67]Nathans, *Losing the Peace,* 61-62. Parks, *Brown,* 398-405.

[68]Atlanta *Constitution,* 15, 21, 28 January 1874; 26 January, 11 February 1875.

[69]Columbus *Enquirer,* reprinted in the Greenville *Meriwether Vindicator,* 14 January 1876.

[70]Atlanta *Constitution,* 15 January 1874; 26 January 1876.

[71]*Comptroller General's Report, 1878,* 72-79.

[72]Ward, "Georgia under the Bourbon Democrats," 226-45.

[73]Robert Toombs to Alexander H. Stephens, 24 April 1877. Alexander H. Stephens Collection, Emory University.

widespread support for a new constitution worried some planters. W. L. Peek, a prominent planter and later the Populist candidate for governor in the 1892 election, sent Governor Colquitt an urgent letter emphasizing the danger of apathy among white Georgians. "It is well known that but a few country people are taking any interest in this matter," he wrote, "and it is thought that the Republicans will take advantage of the occasion and defeat the measure which can be easily done with a small effort with the Negro who embraces every opportunity to vote."[74]

One of the most successful tactics employed by planters in their efforts to win support for the convention was to exploit the rivalries between Atlanta and other urban centers in the state. Since the location of a permanent capital was a matter to be considered by the convention, citizens in all the urban areas were very interested in the referendum. Of the five urban counties, only Fulton County failed to approve the convention call. Voters in the other four counties, allied to the planting class and hoping to deny Atlanta the prestige of being the state's capital, cast their ballots in favor of the convention.[75]

With a handful of urban allies and the power of racist rhetoric, planters won the opportunity to devise a new constitution in 1877. With the threat of further interference from the Federal government gone, planters sought to reestablish their hegemony over the political, social, and economic institutions of the state. Recognizing the inexorable trend toward urbanization and industrialization, they sought to bring these forces under their control through the creation of legal devices safeguarded in the fabric of a constitution.

Despite their success in gaining approval for a convention, the referendum revealed a considerable opposition to old Black Belt planters from the newer planters and merchant-planters in the recently exploited southwestern Black Belt. Thus the convention not only had to deal with

TABLE 5.3

VOTE OF FIVE URBAN COUNTIES ON CONVENTION CALL			
COUNTY	VOTES FOR	VOTES AGAINST	% VOTES FOR
Bibb	896	62	93.5%
Chatham	1779	607	74.6%
Fulton	94	1176	8.0%
Muscogee	874	375	70.0%
Richmond	1184	870	57.6%

[74]W. L. Peek to Alfred H. Colquitt, 12 April 1877, ICAHC.

[75]*Comptroller General's Report, 1877,* 82-86.

the business opposition, but also had to devise methods for controlling dissident elements within the agricultural community.[76] Black Belt planters from the older regions of the state were keenly aware that the 1877 convention offered them a single chance to reassert their dominance. If they failed, it was highly unlikely that they would be able to get another chance.

---

[76]Wiener, *Social Origins*, 83-93. Ransom and Sutch, *One Kind of Freedom*, 146-48. Roark, *Masters*, 169-81.

CHAPTER 6

A PLANTER CONSTITUTION

The Constitutional Convention of 1877 represented a critical juncture in the political fortunes of Georgia planters. Stripped of their political control of the state in 1868, they had seen their interests ignored in the post-Republican years of the early 1870s. For them, the convention was the last chance they would have to regain their power and to combat the growing influence of merchants and industrialists. When the delegates assembled in Atlanta on 11 July 1877, planters claimed a majority of those present. The leading member of the convention was Robert Toombs, the outspoken champion of the interests of planters from the old Black Belt. He was joined by other prominent men who had been members of or closely allied with the antebellum planter class. Some, like Alexander R. Lawton, Lucius J. Gartrell, and Ambrose R. Wright, were Confederate veterans and had served with distinction in the Civil War. Others, such as R. B. Nisbet, Thomas J. Simmons, and William T. Thompson, were younger planters connected with the antebellum elites by birth or by business and social ties. Still others were men who sympathized with the planters on issues concerning state aid to railroads, or who were concerned about the status of Negroes in postwar Georgia.[1]

Opposition to the planter delegates was led by prewar Unionists and postwar Republicans, such as Charles J. Jenkins and Joshua Hill. Jenkins, a widely respected politician, was an antebellum judge and had served as governor from 1865 to 1868. Hill, a staunch Unionist in 1860, was a Republican who had served as United States Senator from 1871 until 1873. Although both men had connections with the antebellum planter class, they had developed stronger ties to the postwar business class and were stout supporters of the New South movement. Jenkins, Hill, and the men they led were, nevertheless, a swing faction because of their natural con-

---

[1]Ward, "Georgia under the Bourbon Democrats," 230-32. Samuel W. Small, ed., *A Stenographic Report of the Proceedings of the Constitutional Convention Held in Atlanta, Georgia, 1877* (Atlanta: The Constitution Publishing Company, 1877). See also Kenneth Coleman, "The Constitutional Convention of 1877 " (Master's thesis, University of Georgia, 1940).

servatism and willingness to compromise on some issues. Despite his support of the New South, Jenkins was widely respected by all factions; and, because of his reputation for personal honesty, he was elected the permanent president of the convention.[2]

A third group was led by James R. Brown, a delegate from Cherokee County and a brother of Joseph E. Brown. Adamant supporters of continued state aid to railroads and industry, these men consistently refused to accept reductions or restrictions on such aid and represented the hard-core resistance to the planter majority. Although a minority in the convention, the staunch opposition they offered to planters tended to make the compromises of the Jenkins-Hill faction more palatable to the majority.[3]

Because of the large number of delegates in attendance, the members decided to use a committee system to write the new constitution. Thirteen standing committees, composed of one delegate from each congressional district, were appointed to write specific sections of the new document. A fourteenth, the Committee on Revision, was given responsibility for incorporating the recommendations of the others into the final version. Members of these committees were predominantly men sympathetic to planter interests, and the Committee on Revision was chaired by Robert Toombs, who also chaired the Committee on the General Assembly. As chairman of the two most important committees, Toombs dominated the convention, and the final draft of the new constitution bore the imprint of his thinking. As the Atlanta *Constitution* noted, he was "by all odds the most conspicuous figure in the Convention," a man who "has ideas on every subject, and no contingency finds him unprepared or unwilling to express them."[4]

Much of the convention's time was given over to discussions on measures that would limit the activities of industries in the state. Because railroads were the most visible and the wealthiest of Georgia's corporations, they received most of the attention. A variety of proposals was made to control both the growth of railroads and their operation. Toombs led the floor fight against the roads, and his major thrust was against the *carte blanche* charters granted to them by previous legislatures. Insisting that many of the roads were monopolies because of charters giving them "irrevocable privileges and immunities," he argued that the right to grant charters should be taken from the General Assembly and placed in the hands of some responsible state officer. Unless this was done, he continued, more monopolies would result and "Monopoly is extortion; it is spo-

---

[2]Small, *Stenographic Report*, 2-5. Saye, *Constitutional History*, 280-82.

[3]Ward, "Georgia under the Bourbon Democrats," 233. Atlanta *Constitution*, 1-12 July 1877. The *Constitution* provided short sketches of all the delegates to the convention.

[4]Atlanta *Constitution*, 24 July 1877. Saye, *Constitutional History*, 280-81.

liation." Warning delegates that corporations required strong regulations "or they will override the law," Toombs asserted, "Already, sir, they have defied the law a hundred times in the state of Georgia. They are too strong for the law, and even claim to have grown out of the power of the state." Urging the delegates to approve a provision to restrict the charter granting authority of the Assembly, Toombs neatly summed up the planters' attitude by basing his argument on "the solitary principle of whether the people of Georgia shall govern the [artificial] persons that they have thus created."[5]

Toombs's attack on railroads and corporations brought a strong response from Charles J. Jenkins, who left the president's chair to answer him on the floor. Arguing that corporations made possible achievements individuals could not accomplish by themselves, Jenkins attacked the removal of authority from the legislature in strong language. "I tell you this is a deadly blow aimed at the prosperity of the state," he informed the delegates. "It is calculated, and will have the effect, to some extent, to put a quietus on and an end to all industrial enterprises proposed in the state of Georgia." Pleading with the delegates to reject Toombs's argument, Jenkins warned them that "no prudent man will invest in any chartered enterprise when he knows that in one or two years it may be abrogated."[6]

Jenkins's arguments were seconded by other probusiness delegates. Nat J. Hammond, a delegate from Fulton County, rose from his seat to support Jenkins. The General Assembly needed the right to grant "irrevocable privileges," he argued, or much needed capital would be scared away from the state. "We want mining, banking and railroad companies," another supporter told his fellow delegates. "The state of Georgia owes as much of her prosperity and wealth to corporations in her midst as to any other collection of citizens in the state. What we need now is to have our vast and valuable means developed by such enterprises as these."[7] For men who agreed with the concepts of the New South, corporate rights to immunities and privileges were essential.

Despite the objections of Jenkins, Hammond, and others, a provision prohibiting the General Assembly from granting special privileges to corporations was included in the constitution.[8] In addition, the right to grant charters was given to the Secretary of State, whose actions would be regulated by a series of general incorporation laws enacted by the General

---

[5]Small, *Stenographic Report*, 404-10.

[6]Ibid., 106.

[7]Ibid.

[8]Constitution of 1877, Article 1, Section 3, in Lawton B. Evans, *A History of Georgia* (New York: American Book Company, 1911) 15. Hereafter referred to as C77.

Assembly.[9] To prevent corporations from attempting to influence the legislature in their favor, another provision prohibited lobbying. The General Assembly was instructed to enact "suitable penalties" for violations of the anti-lobbying law at its first session following the ratification of the constitution.[10]

The decision to take the right to grant corporate charters out of the legislature's hands was an essential first step in establishing planter control over the state's industrialization. Standardization of incorporation laws allowed for easier regulation, prevented the General Assembly from favoring one corporation over another, and made it much easier for corporations to be formed.[11] Planters favored the proliferation of corporations because it would reduce the possibility of a few wealthy and extremely powerful concerns emerging as the only outlet for investment. As long as it was easy for individuals to start small corporations, fewer concentrations of industrial wealth would exist, and industrial development would probably follow the antebellum pattern of small factories in small towns or rural areas.[12] With industries isolated in agricultural communities, planters could influence their growth and production in many ways. Local industries drew from the same labor pool as planters, a practice necessitating cooperation between them and their businessmen rivals. Furthermore, planters could, and did, invest surplus profits in these industries, thereby gaining a direct say in their management. Finally, isolated factory managers and owners turned to local planters for social contacts, and through these might absorb some of their attitudes. Planters did not oppose industrialization per se; they simply wanted it to be subordinate to agriculture. The greater the number of small industries, the better their chances of achieving their aims.[13]

---

[9]Ibid., Article 3, Section 7, 21.

[10]Ibid., Article 1, Section 2, 14.

[11]Wiener, *Social Origins,* 150. Wiener argues that standardization of incorporation laws was generally a probusiness measure and cites Alabama as proof. Republicans, he insists, favored business and enacted laws to standardize incorporation procedures to stimulate it. In Georgia, Republicans left the power to grant corporate charters in the General Assembly, but planters took it from that body in 1877 in order to prevent the accumulation of capital by only a few large corporations.

[12]Woodward, *Origins,* 131-35. Woodward describes the success planters had in this effort and notes that cotton mills were located "more typically in isolated Piedmont towns. Old market villages of a few hundred citizens that had drowsed from one Saturday to the next since the eighteenth century, were suddenly aflame with mill fever."

[13]Wiener, *Social Origins,* 141-44. Robert S. Starobin, *Industrial Slavery in the Old South* (London: Oxford University Press, 1970) 183-91.

Railroads were also the subject of regulatory legislation enacted into the constitution. Delegates used the opportunity of the convention to air their complaints against railroad practices, particularly the lack of standardization in rates and schedules. One delegate from Sumter County protested the use of the "long-and-short haul device" that allowed railroads to "extort" money from cotton growers on local freight runs. "In regard to the tariff on cotton from Americus to Macon, it was last season sixty cents on the hundred pounds, and to Savannah it was seventy-five cents," he charged. "I know that we in Americus were charged ten cents more on the bale than Albany, yet Albany is thirty miles farther from Savannah than we are."[14] Other delegates from rural areas agreed, and they rose to cite other instances of discrimination and unfair practices.

Railroads, however, had their advocates among the delegates, and charge was met with countercharge. The principal argument of the pro-railroad faction was that the roads were guilty of no wrongdoing because their charters entitled them to set rates for passengers and freight. To impose regulations on these rights, they countered, would be a violation of the contract between the state government and the railroad companies.[15] Once again, Charles J. Jenkins, the president of the convention and a railroad lawyer, provided the strongest defense against regulation.[16]

In the end, arguments against the railroads prevailed, and the convention incorporated a provision into the new constitution requiring the General Assembly, at its next session, to pass appropriate legislation to regulate railroad fares and practices. In addition to establishing rate schedules for the roads, the General Assembly was authorized to create penalties for corporations that created monopolies, entered into combinations, or created holding companies for the express purpose of restricting competition or fixing rates. Railroads were also prohibited from giving rebates or engaging in deceptive rate schemes. The Georgia system of regulation was among the most comprehensive in the nation, and despite many court challenges in the next several decades, it survived until the middle of the twentieth century. The Railroad Commission, the regulatory agency created in the General Assembly, continued to function until 1945 when it was replaced by the Public Service Commission, a general purpose regulatory agency.[17]

Further restrictions were placed on businesses by the convention. To prevent corporations from using their wealth as a lever to gain favors from various governments, the state, county, and municipal governments were

---

[14]Small, *Stenographic Report*, 390.

[15]Ibid., 389-410.

[16]Ward, "Georgia under the Bourbon Democrats," 234.

[17]C77, Article 4, Section 2.

prohibited from levying taxes for the purpose of subsidizing industries, from exempting businesses from taxation, and from becoming stockholders in any corporation. Railroads were denied state aid, and companies holding state bonds in 1877 were forced to accept either a reduction of their face value or complete repudiation.[18] Future state aid to any business or railroad was explicitly forbidden by the constitution. All in all, there were at least thirteen clauses in the new document restricting the activities of corporations and prohibiting state aid to them.[19] Planters used their control of the convention to ensure the total separation of government and industry. Cut off from government funds, industrialists had to turn to planters or to sources outside the South for necessary financing, and neither of these sources was particularly interested in creating large industrial organizations.[20]

Planter delegates in the convention also sought to restrict government spending in general. Because their wealth was based on extensive land holdings, and because property owners bore the brunt of taxation in the nineteenth century, planters imposed constitutional ceilings on the expenditures of the state government. The salary of the governor, for example, was limited to $5000 a year, and he was allowed to have only two secretaries. He would receive an additional $6000 a year for clerical personnel, which was regarded as a reform measure since previous governors had frequently rewarded political supporters by appointing them to staff positions. The Secretary of State, the Treasurer, and the Comptroller General, as well as Superior Court judges and the Attorney General, received only $2000 a year. Judges on the Georgia Supreme Court were paid an annual salary of $3000.[21] Some delegates were so determined to limit state spending that Robert Toombs attacked them as being ridiculous. "The whole finances of the state are not involved when we are talking of the governor's salary," he reminded them, "and you spend more [money] talking about it than your children will have to pay in forty years."[22] Ultimately, however, Toombs congratulated the delegates for their efforts to limit government spending. "You have put restraints upon and thrown instructions around the public treasury," he told them. "You have locked it, and you have put the key in the pockets of the people, and I thank God for it."[23]

---

[18]Ibid.

[19]Ibid.

[20]Woodward, *Origins*, 134. *One-Gallused Rebellion*, 89-97. Wiener, *Social Origins*, 164-69.

[21]C77, Article 5, Sections 1 and 2; Article 6, Section 13.

[22]Small, *Stenographic Report*, 115.

[23]Ibid., 407.

Although the delegates spent a lot of time discussing fiscal matters, their most important work in terms of the retention of power by planters in the future came when they undertook the task of revamping the system of representation in the General Assembly. Under the provisions of the Constitutions of 1861, 1865, and even 1868, senators—who exercised much of the power of state government—were elected for four-year terms. Generally regarded as the representatives of the "propertied" classes in the state, senators were traditionally empowered to elect all state officers, with the exception of the governor. The proposed Constitution of 1877, however, reduced the term of office for a state senator to two years and made state offices elective.[24]

The key to understanding why this apparently democratic revision emerged from a convention dominated by elites can be readily found in the adoption of the county unit system as the basis for statewide elections and the reapportionment of the House of Representatives. Previous constitutions had given the House little power, and it was dominated by planters, who were allowed by the Constitutions of 1861 and 1865 to count each slave or freedman as three-fifths of a person. Although counted in the general population, freedmen were not allowed to vote until the Constitution of 1868 was adopted. The Republicans, confident of freedmen support, changed the method of apportioning representation in the House from the system adopted in earlier constitutions—from a 2-1 system, in which the thirty-seven largest counties would be entitled to two representatives and the remaining counties one each, to a 3-2-1 system. Under the 1868 system, Negro participation would have been maximized since the six largest counties in population, white and black, had three representatives each; the next thirty-one largest, two each; and the remaining ninety-five counties, one each.[25] Because the most heavily populated counties were located in the Black Belt or urban areas, where support for their party was strong, Republicans viewed this system as being the most effective method of retaining political dominance of the state. By 1870, however, economic coercion by planters and the physical intimidation of blacks by the Klan had allowed planters to reestablish their command over Negro voters. Instead of preserving Republican control, the 3-2-1 system became the bulwark of revived planter power.[26]

By 1877, planters in the older section of the Black Belt were aware of the population shift from their counties to southwest Georgia. As commercial fertilizer allowed cotton growers to utilize marginal lands successfully, the population in these newer regions grew accordingly. In order

---

[24]C77, Article 3.

[25]Nathans, *Losing the Peace*, 56-69. DeBats, "Elites and Masses," 513-47.

[26]Nathans, *Losing the Peace*, 202-206.

to compensate for future population losses, planter delegates from the older Black Belt demanded and got a revision of the apportionment scheme. On the surface, the new system of allocating representatives appeared to be a copy of the 1868 scheme; there were, however, some important changes. Although the number of representatives remained the same (175), subtle differences in how they were apportioned ensured a planter majority in the lower legislative body. The six largest counties in population continued to have three representatives each, but only the next twenty-six largest would be allocated two representatives apiece, and the remaining 105 counties would be allowed one representative each. Although not a radical change from the 1868 system, the new system worked to the advantage of planters in the older Black Belt. Of the six counties allotted three representatives, three were located in the old Black Belt, as were eighteen of the twenty-six counties entitled to two representatives. Forty-one counties with one representative also fell within this region. Thus, out of 175 representatives, planters could count on eighty-six "sure" votes, which left them only two shy of an absolute majority. It was an easy matter to secure the additional votes when needed. To ensure their continued dominance of the House, delegates to the 1877 convention included a constitutional prohibition against the creation of any new counties in the state.[27]

The last structural change made in the organization of the state government concerned the office of governor. The Constitutions of 1861 and 1865 provided for two-year terms of office for the state's chief executive, but the Constitution of 1868 extended the term to four years. Delegates to the 1877 convention revised the constitution to limit the term to one of two years and to place a limitation of four years on continuous service. The incumbent governor, Alfred H. Colquitt, was exempted from this limitation.[28]

Although much of the rhetoric used by its proponents had stressed the specter of Negro domination in Georgia, the convention actually did little to restrict the suffrage rights of blacks. The right to vote was curtailed only by the normal requirements of age and residency, as well as the payment of an annual $1 poll tax. The Constitution of 1868 had also included a poll tax, but the new constitution made it cumulative, and citizens were required to pay all back taxes before they were eligible to vote. This restriction applied to whites as well as blacks, and it is doubtful that the cumulative poll tax provision prevented many Negroes from voting. Candidates simply paid any outstanding poll tax liabilities owed by their supporters.[29] For planters, control of land and economic resources gave them command of

---

[27]Rigdon, *County Unit System*, 16-22.

[28]C77, Article 5, Section 1.

[29]Shadgett, *Republican Party in Georgia*, 44-45.

the political machinery, and the threat of reprisals was usually sufficient to control black voters.[30]

Convention delegates, eager to secure ratification of the new constitution, failed to include two controversial issues in it. Pre-convention campaigning had focused a great deal of attention on the question of selecting a permanent capital for the state. The possibility of the capital's being moved from Atlanta, where it had been temporarily located since 1868, had lured many urban voters to the polls to cast ballots in favor of a convention. After listening to several proposals from other cities, delegates narrowed the choice to Milledgeville and Atlanta, but they decided to leave the final choice to the voters.[31] By divorcing the question of the capital from the ratification of the constitution, planters adroitly managed to direct criticism away from the new document and to force the probusiness Atlantans to concentrate their attention on defending their city as the best permanent state capital. The Atlanta *Constitution,* the recognized voice of the proAtlanta forces, offered only slight opposition to the constitution, describing it as being "more worthy of commendation than condemnation," and spent its energies on convincing Georgians that Atlanta was the ideal location for state government.[32]

A second potentially troublesome issue that faced the convention members was the question of a revised homestead exemption for debtors. The Constitution of 1868 allowed debtors to exempt $2000 in real estate and $1000 in personal property from attachment and forced sale.[33] The 1877 convention proposed a reduction in the combined exemption to $1600, which could be further reduced to $300 by waiver.[34] Although planters and farmers had approved of the exemption in 1868, it was now considered to be an obstacle to obtaining needed credit for sharecroppers and tenants. Planters, who had taken over the function of furnishing merchants in the old Black Belt, favored the reduction because it would tighten their control over their tenants.[35] However, most felt that to include the

---

[30]For a complete discussion of disfranchisement laws in Southern states, see J. Morgan Kousser, *The Shaping of Southern Politics: Suffrage Restrictions and the Establishment of the One-Party South, 1880-1910* (New Haven: Yale University Press, 1974), and Roger L. Hart, *Redeemers, Bourbons and Populists: Tennessee, 1870-1896* (Baton Rouge: Louisiana State University Press, 1975).

[31]The suggested cities were Savannah, Columbus, Macon, Milledgeville, Atlanta, and Augusta.

[32]Atlanta *Constitution,* August-November 1877.

[33]Nathans, *Losing the Peace,* 116-18.

[34]C77, Article 9.

[35]The 1877 version of the homestead exemption was overwhelmingly approved by a margin of 50,963 to 8,241.

reduced exemption in the new constitution would be to invite defeat, and the delegates separated this question from the issue of ratification. Once again, the citizenry would make the decision on this possibly explosive question.

When the convention adjourned on 25 August, it had produced a document that included some significant changes in the political and economic alignments in Georgia. The provisions of the document reestablished the planting class as the most potent political force in the state, and the restrictions placed on business subordinated that segment of the economy to planter control. The regulatory measures enacted by the convention were not anti-industry as such, but they did ensure that the progress of industrialization in Georgia would be along the lines of the "Prussian Road." By encouraging the development of many small industries in the small towns, planters assured themselves of a major voice in the direction of industrialization in the state. In the long run, this strategy produced a much greater and more complete victory than open conflict could have achieved.

Although some historians have attempted to place the Constitution of 1877 in the context of the New South, they are frustrated because of what seems to be a complete turnaround in political and economic directions. As much as anything else, the Constitution of 1877 marked the reemergence of the antebellum planting class as the dominant force in Georgia. Although none of the leading politicians of the 1870s were delegates, there was no absence of men familiar with the exercise of power. For some, like Toombs, the constitution marked their last hurrah. It became the most effective and lasting triumph of the old slaveholding order. Certainly Henry Woodfin Grady's description of the convention recognized the determination and skill of these "non-politicians, elder statesmen, or discredited politicians"[36] to reassert themselves as the true leaders of the state. The convention was, in his words, "probably the most self-reliant body of men ever assembled. The day they met they declared themselves independent of the Governor . . . [and the] third day they declared themselves independent of God Almighty by refusing to appoint a chaplain."[37] Unhindered by the presence of industrialists, planter leaders were determined to create a document to preserve and maintain their class.

The date set for ratification of the new constitution was 5 December 1877. During the time between the adjournment of the convention and the referendum in December, very little public opposition to the document materialized, and newspapers concerned themselves with debates over the homestead exemption and the merits of Milledgeville and At-

---

[36]Ward, "Georgia under the Bourbon Democrats," 243.

[37]Raymond B. Nixon, *Henry W. Grady, Spokesman of the New South* (New York: Russell and Russell, 1969) 144.

lanta. Robert Toombs attributed the lack of open opposition by New South papers, particularly the *Constitution*, to fear that it would cause a backlash against Atlanta and cost her the capital. "Both the *Chronicle* of Augusta and the *Constitution* of Atlanta are really opposed to ratification," he informed Alexander H. Stephens, "but they are afraid to move against it for fear of the people." He predicted that "if the fidelity of Atlanta to ratification becomes even suspected, the Capitol will be moved back to Milledgeville."[38] Earlier Toombs had written to Stephens that "the opposition is mostly secret and is composed of those who wish no additional safeguards against legislative burglary in the state."[39]

The campaign for ratification of the new constitution faced little open resistance, and the December referendum overwhelmingly favored the document. The majority of the opposition (74.6%) came from Black Belt counties, but it was not enough to defeat the measure. The strongest opposition came from counties that had previously returned Republican majorities. In the seaboard counties of Camden and McIntosh, for example, Negroes had controlled the local political machinery since 1868. On the northern edge of the Black Belt, Greene, Morgan, and Burke counties—which had been Republican strongholds in the late 1860s—also voted against ratification.[40]

Five counties in the southwestern Black Belt, located along the Alabama border, also rejected the constitution. This area, sparsely settled before the Civil War, was experiencing a period of rapid population growth in the 1870s. Commercial fertilizers and railroad development produced a minor economic boom in the region, which had proven very lucrative for furnishing merchants forced out of the older Black Belt counties. As they became a major influence in the area's economy, these men also began to play a central role in its politics. Of the eleven counties that rejected the constitution in December, ten were located in the peripheral areas of the Black Belt. Of the counties outside the Black Belt, only Fulton County failed to approve the new document. The patterns of opposition to the constitution were generally duplicated in all political contests for the next decade.

With the adoption of the Constitution of 1877, planters were firmly in command of Georgia's government. As the realization of that fact set in among the New South advocates, they began to make tentative contacts with planters concerning what role industrialists were to play in the state. Completely overwhelmed by the planting class politically, these men were quick to understand that if they wanted to have a voice in governing the

---

[38]Robert Toombs to Alexander H. Stephens, 27 November 1877, SC.

[39]Ibid.

[40]Nathans, *Losing the Peace*, 90-101, 112-13, 175-77.

state, it would have to be through some alliance with the Black Belt planters. More than likely, they also realized, their position would be that of a junior partner or a minority stockholder. Relatively few in numbers, especially when compared to the large agricultural population under the control of planters, industrialists were in no position to confront them in a face-to-face struggle for power. The absence of a permanent factory laboring class denied industrialists a base of support to be manipulated politically, and the proliferation of small corporations in rural towns and villages prevented the development of a single central manufacturing metropolis. Even Atlanta was dependent on the countryside for workers for its industries.[41]

Having established their dominance over state politics, planters were eager to placate their opponents. Continued opposition from monied sources within the New South could only create confusion and chaos that might allow Republicans to reorganize and recover their political power. Or, even worse, confrontation might encourage some dissidents to create a new political coalition to challenge both planters and industrialists. So, after a decade of conflict, the two factions merged into a coalition of elites to rule the state. Planters, operating from a position of strength, controlled the coalition; and industrialists, seeking to protect themselves against unknown enemies, accepted the secondary position allotted them. Thus was born the *entente cordiale* that ruled Georgia for the next one hundred years.

The most obvious indication that an agreement had been reached between planters and industrialists was the sudden cessation of attacks on planters and the Old South in New South newspapers.[42] Indeed, within a short time, New South orators adopted the myth of the Lost Cause and used it to justify their own efforts to industrialize. During the early years of the movement, industrialists had attacked planters as being the cause of the economic backwardness of the South. Benjamin H. Hill, one of the earliest advocates of the New South, had set the tone for these attacks in his address to the University of Georgia Alumni Association in 1871. "I only propose to show that slavery affected and most deleteriously affected the South States and people in general scientific, physical and educational progress, and especially in *material* and commercial development," he told the alumni, "and as a consequence delayed their growth in population, wealth, and physical power."[43] After 1877, the New South message

[41]Woodward, *Origins*, 205-55. Cash, *Mind*, 202-20.

[42]Gaston, *New South Creed*, 154-71. Cash, *Mind*, 142-71. See also Clement Eaton, *The Waning of the Old South Civilization* (Athens: University of Georgia Press, 1968) and Rollin G. Osterweis, *The Myth of the Lost Cause, 1865-1900* (Hamden CT: Archon Books, 1973).

[43]Pearce, *Hill*, 239-44. Coulter, "The New South," 179-99.

changed. Instead of vilifying planters, it glorified their virtues and idolized Confederate leaders and soldiers.[44]

The capitulation of the New South to the Old South came, as Jonathan Wiener points out, as "a sign, not of their strength, but of their weakness; it was not so much a successful use of the past to build a New South program, but rather a strategic attempt at accommodation with an opponent they were unable to beat—an opponent who was not simply 'mythic,' but one with extensive economic and political power."[45] The coalition of planters and industrialists that followed the ratification of the Constitution of 1877 formed the strongest political arrangement that could be made in postwar Georgia. Yet, despite the ascendancy of planters to the top of the political heap and the acceptance of a secondary role by industrialists, the coalition did not go unchallenged.

---

[44]Lexington *Oglethorpe Echo*, 6 November 1874. Cash, *Mind*, 124-47. Wiener, *Social Origins*, 215-21.

[45]Wiener, *Social Origins*, 219.

CHAPTER 7

THE NOT-SO-LOYAL OPPOSITION

The birth of the planter-industrialist coalition in Georgia politics was not an easy one. The alliance, representing planter elites from the older Black Belt and New South businessmen from Atlanta, Macon, and Savannah, excluded several large and important groups in the state. Immediately after the ratification of the Constitution of 1877—the event that brought the coalition into existence—these "out" groups began to fuse into a rival alliance seeking to challenge the coalition for political supremacy in the state.

The principal opposition to the planter-industrialist coalition came from southwest Georgia, a rapidly growing area of the "new" Black Belt that was enjoying a period of unprecedented prosperity as the use of commercial fertilizers expanded the cotton frontier. Merchants in this area, many forced out of the older regions of the Black Belt, quickly became the dominant voice in sectional politics. Products of the postwar mercantile class, such men had few ties to the antebellum planter class; and many were upset at what they viewed as abandonment by their former allies, the industrialists. During the political upheavals of the late 1860s and early 1870s, merchants from this area of the Black Belt had played important roles in state government; but the coalition of 1877, with its center in the old Black Belt, threatened to end their influence. The merchants were supported in their opposition by many planters in the region, particularly men who were new to the planter ranks and who were the products of the postwar systems of sharecropping and tenantry instead of slavery.[1]

Merchants and planters of southwest Georgia were apprehensive about possible attempts by the new coalition to limit the continued progress of that region. Their primary concern was over the creation and development of a transportation system to serve the area, which had largely been ignored in the prewar years. The Constitution of 1877 prohibited state aid to railroads, and this policy, unless modified, would restrict the rate of agricultural and commercial growth in the southwest counties. To planters

---

[1]Wiener, *Social Origins*, 83-93. Ransom and Sutch, *One Kind of Freedom*, 146-48. Roark, *Masters*, 169-81. Woodman, *King Cotton*, 309-14.

and merchants in the region, the intent of this prohibition appeared to be the continued dominance of other Black Belt areas and the permanent subordination of the southwest counties to the older, more developed counties. Subordination would mean a continuing inferior economic position. Unless new railroads were built, freight charges on goods and supplies coming into the region would make prices exceedingly high, thus consuming more of the annual income of area planters; while the same freight rates would reduce the amount of profit to be made on agricultural products shipped out of the region. Continued prosperity depended on the destruction of the coalition.[2]

Opposition to the coalition also came from the mountain and wiregrass sections of the state. Areas of small farms and anti-planter sentiment before the war, these sections had also provided strong Republican support in the late 1860s. Following the collapse of the Republican party in 1871, a powerful Independent movement opposed to the continued domination of the planting class developed in these areas.[3] Many former Whigs, opposed to the Democratic party and unable to stomach the Republican party emotionally, also became Independents.[4] In the mid-1870s, two Independent leaders, William H. Felton and Emory D. Speer, won seats in Congress.[5] Confronted with the coalition of planters and New South men and hampered by charges that Independentism encouraged Negroes to vote, the movement was less and less able to maintain its separate identity and organization after 1878. Despite their inability to combat the "Organized Democracy" under the control of planters, Independents remained a significant and potentially powerful force in state politics.

A third source of opposition to the planter-New South coalition came from the remnants of the Republican party. The resignation of Rufus B. Bullock in 1871 had been a deadly blow to them, and although the party structure remained intact, Republicans demonstrated little ability in regaining the momentum that had accounted for their gubernatorial and legislative victories in 1868. In 1876, Jonathan Norcross, a former Confederate blockade runner, attempted to build an all-white party, but his efforts were unsuccessful.[6] By 1880, the party was little more than a loose

---

[2]Small, *Stenographic Report,* 389-410.

[3]Nathans, *Losing the Peace,* 213-27. Woodward, *Origins,* 75-82. Gaston, *New South Creed,* 119-50.

[4]George L. Jones, "William H. Felton and the Independent Democratic Movement in Georgia, 1870-1890" (Ph.D. diss., University of Georgia, 1971) 1-10.

[5]Lexington *Oglethorpe Echo,* 8 November 1878.

[6]Unknown to J. M. Avendano, 18 November 1863, William McNaught Papers, Atlanta Historical Society.

conglomeration of federal officeholders or candidates for patronage jobs.[7] Nevertheless, some of its members, aided by others in the national party, hoped to bring about a revival of Republican fortunes in Georgia. To this end, they joined forces with discontented Democrats and Independents to oppose the coalition of 1877.[8]

The first challenge to the planter-New South alliance came in 1880. On 20 May, the people of Georgia were shocked to learn that General John B. Gordon had resigned from the United States Senate and that Governor Alfred H. Colquitt had appointed Joseph E. Brown to take his place. Although the Atlanta *Constitution* described the resignation as a "bolt out of the blue," the change had been in the works for several months.[9] A month before the actual deal was consummated, Henry W. Grady, the messenger for the principals, intimated to friends that Gordon would resign and that Brown would be appointed. In mid-May, Grady's prediction came true.[10]

Immediately after Brown's appointment, cries of "bargain and corruption" were raised throughout the state, particularly in newspapers outside the Black Belt. Even papers within the fold of the coalition found it hard to understand how Joseph E. Brown, renegade Democrat and former Republican, could be appointed to the Senate. The Savannah *Record* attacked the new senator as a "stench in the nostrils not only of the Democratic party, but of everything in the nature of a Southern element."[11] The Columbus *Daily News* declared, "Brown with his money, Gordon with his buttons, and Colquitt with his religion will make a combination that cannot be beaten."[12] Another observer wrote to the *Constitution* to express his dismay at Brown's appointment and to speculate that Colquitt's reward was to be Brown's support in the upcoming gubernatorial election.[13] Rebecca L. Felton, a constant critic of Brown and Gordon, suggested to the readers of the Athens *Southern Watchman* that Gordon had simply followed the dictates of his god, Mammon.[14]

---

[7]Ruth Currie McDaniel, "Black Power in Georgia: William A. Pledger and the Takeover of the Republican Party," *Georgia Historical Quarterly* 62 (1978): 225-39. Nathans, *Losing the Peace*, 222-27.

[8]Jones, "William H. Felton," 1-32.

[9]Atlanta *Constitution*, 20 May 1880.

[10]Telegrams, 15-19 May 1880, HT. Parks, *Brown*, 508-20.

[11]Savannah *Record*, 30 May 1880.

[12]Quoted in Jones, "William H. Felton," 155.

[13]Atlanta *Constitution*, 23 June 1880.

[14]Athens *Southern Watchman*, reprinted in the Cartersville *Free Press*, 17 June 1880.

Whatever the reasons for them, Gordon's resignation and the appointment of Brown in his place cemented the alliance of Black Belt planters and New South businessmen. The matter also provided the first test of their political strength when Colquitt sought reelection to the governor's chair. As early as April 1880, a month before the Brown-Gordon affair became public knowledge, Robert Toombs noted the mounting opposition in the state to Colquitt. To Alexander H. Stephens he wrote, "It seems that there are many aspirants for Gov[ernor] and that Colquitt will have strong opposition. I saw him in Savannah, he seemed very ernest [sic] and anxious on the subject, perhaps [he] has reason to be so."[15] Following Colquitt's appointment of Brown, Toombs again remarked on the governor's chances for reelection, commenting that he could probably be beaten by a "Black Negro."[16]

The months between Brown's appointment and the Democratic Convention in August were filled with considerable activity as would-be candidate after would-be candidate tested the political waters. When the convention met in Atlanta on 4 August, several men were on hand to try to secure the party's nomination. The adoption of the two-thirds rule, a requirement that any candidate nominated receive at least two-thirds of the delegates' votes, made it difficult for any of the contenders to win the nomination.[17] For six days, the delegates failed to select a candidate, although Colquitt received a majority of votes in all the ballots. On the seventh day, the convention "recommended" Colquitt to the voters of the state, but did not make him the official nominee of the party. In the first gubernatorial election with no Republican opposition since 1868, Georgia Democrats failed to make a nomination.[18]

Although Colquitt could not win the nomination outright, his supporters argued that recommendation was tantamount to nomination, and they proceeded to campaign on that assertion. His opponents, however, refused to accept his recommendation by the convention, and they called a second convention to select a candidate to run against him. Thomas M. Norwood, a former United States Senator from Savannah, received the nomination of the rump convention after both Alexander H. Stephens and William H. Felton refused it. Norwood, it was rumored by Colquitt supporters, wanted the senatorial seat held by Brown, and he felt his best

---

[15]Robert Toombs to Alexander H. Stephens, 25 April 1880, SC.

[16]Quoted in John E. Talmadge, *Rebecca Latimer Felton: Nine Stormy Decades* (Athens: University of Georgia Press, 1960) 61.

[17]Atlanta *Constitution*, 25 July 1880.

[18]Kenneth Coleman, "The Georgia Gubernatorial Election of 1880," *Georgia Historical Quarterly* 25 (1941): 89-119.

chance of gaining that prize was to defeat Colquitt.[19] As a candidate, Norwood intended to make the Colquitt-Brown-Gordon senatorial affair the primary issue of his campaign. Prior to the first convention, Norwood had noted the impact of the issue on Georgia voters when he wrote to his advisor, Leander Newton Trammell, about the reaction of delegates in the Chatham County Democratic Convention. "I noticed a general hiss followed a vote for Jo[seph E.] Brown in the convention," he wrote. "This is significant. My observation is that C[olquitt] and G[ordon] make no headway by their speeches. The *main question* has not been answered, and it won't be without *ruin* to the actors—*two* at least."[20]

After his nomination by the rump convention, Norwood made a *pro forma* offer to Colquitt that both men retire from the race in favor of some third candidate, but he did not seriously expect Colquitt to agree and immediately set about campaigning. In addition to the Brown appointment, Norwood questioned the entire record of the Colquitt administration, including the governor's refusal to pay the expenses of the constitutional convention of 1877.[21] Furthermore, his approval of the payment of Northeastern Railroad bonds,[22] his payment of $30,000 to two lobbyists, and the leasing of state convicts to Joseph E. Brown and John B. Gordon became campaign fodder for Norwood.[23]

The charge that Colquitt paid two lobbyists, Robert Alston and A. C. Garlington, $30,000 to influence Congress to appropriate $200,000 for claims made by the state against the federal government for damages to the Western and Atlantic Railroad during the Civil War was particularly damaging to his candidacy. Alston, a confidant of Gordon's, was a rather shady character whose involvement with the Gordon convict lease re-

---

[19]Ibid., See also Alexander H. Stephens to John A. Stephens, 30 May 1880, SC.

[20]Thomas M. Norwood to Leander Trammell, 12 June 1880, Leander Newton Trammell Collection, Emory University. Hereafter referred to as TC. Trammell was a unique figure in Georgia politics in the postwar period. He was Norwood's advisor, but he was also personal friends with Brown, Colquitt, Gordon, and Stephens. Trammell served throughout the 1880s as a member of the Georgia Railroad Commission.

[21]While the 1877 Convention was meeting, Colquitt refused to pay the delegates' expenses because he said he had not been authorized to do so by the General Assembly. Saye, *Constitutional History*, 282.

[22]While the 1877 Convention was still in session, bonds of the Northeastern Railroad came due; and Colquitt, as required by law, signed them and committed the state to pay them, although the Convention ultimately included a provision in the new constitution prohibiting state aid to railroads. Henry D. McDaniel to Alfred H. Colquitt, 17 January 1878, ICAHC.

[23]Columbus *Daily Times*, 21 May 1880. Greenville *Meriwether Vindicator*, 3 September; 15, 22 October 1880.

sulted in his assassination in the state Capitol in 1880. Alston was suspected of paying a considerable portion of his lobbyist fees to Gordon, a suspicion Norwood took great delight in emphasizing on the stump.[24] Because of his close association with Gordon and his appointment of Brown, Colquitt was labeled a "silent partner" in the convict leases granted the two men and was accused of profiting from them.[25]

Colquitt quickly responded to Norwood's charges. In all instances his defense was that he had simply carried out the functions of the governor's office. As far as the convict lease was concerned, he denied any connection with the lessees and argued that he was only continuing a practice dating from 1865. In granting the leases to Gordon and Brown, he insisted, he had carefully followed the letter of the law. In the matter of the payments to Alston and Garlington, Colquitt explained that he was merely fulfilling the provisions of a legal contract, standard in claims cases, that called for a percentage of the money collected to be paid to the lobbyists who presented and pursued the claims.[26]

Colquitt's appointment of Brown to the Senate was not so easily explained away. Although he insisted that Brown was the best man for the job and a true Democrat, this judgement was not readily shared by all Georgians.[27] To counter the hostile reaction in some quarters, both Gordon and Brown took to the stump in favor of Colquitt. Gordon applauded the appointment of Brown as his successor, although he admitted that "as a matter of sentiment, some of us would have preferred some other Georgian."[28] With Gordon's assurances that the resignation-appointment was all above board, the impact of the incident was lessened.

The campaign was not strictly a defensive one for Colquitt. Norwood, according to one historian, "had little personal support" in the state, but he benefited from the opposition that had developed to the planter-New South coalition, as well as the hostility many Georgians had for Brown.[29] On specific issues, Norwood was vulnerable on two points. While a member of the Senate, he had voted to increase the salaries of members of Congress, and Colquitt used this fact against him. In a letter to Leander N. Trammell, Norwood recognized the possible negative impact his vote on the so-called "Salary Grab" might have; but it was, he felt, "the only

---

[24]John B. Gordon to Leander Newton Trammell, 14 April 1887, TC. Talmadge, *Felton,* 59-61.

[25]Felton, *Memoirs,* 259.

[26]Ibid., 259-64.

[27]Savannah *Recorder,* 30 May 1880. Quitman *Reporter,* 27 May 1880. Albany *News,* 27 May 1880. Monroe *Advertiser,* 25 May 1880. Thomasville *Times,* 29 May 1880.

[28]Atlanta *Constitution,* 8 June 1880.

[29]Parks, *Brown,* 524. Coleman, "Election of 1880," 109-19.

charge against me, and if necessary, I can 'plead guilty and throw myself on the mercy of the court.' "[30]

Colquitt's supporters quickly leveled another and more serious charge against Norwood. During his early political career as a member of the "Know-Nothing" party in the 1850s, Norwood had at one time advocated the exclusion of Catholics from public office. While a Senator during the 1870s, he delivered an address to the student body of Emory College in Oxford, Georgia, in which he viciously attacked Negroes:

> Annoyed by their sloth, disappointed in our remuneration, mortified by our retardation in material prosperity, wearied to impatience by the incapacity of the few who are honest, and goaded to desperation by the crime of the vicious and idle, we will joyfully echo back from city, garden, and farm, "Cut him down. Why cumbereth he the ground?"[31]

Colquitt supporters used the refrain, "Cut him down. Why cumbereth he the ground?" as a telling argument against Norwood among black voters. In contrast to Norwood's bombastic statement, Colquitt's activities as a Sunday school teacher in black churches were highly publicized.[32] The success of the Colquitt camp in attracting Negro voters is evident in the inability of Republicans to agree on a resolution supporting Norwood at their 1880 convention.

Although most white Republican delegates were in favor of Norwood's candidacy, most black delegates opposed him. Jackson McHenry, a Negro Republican from Fulton County, expressed the feelings of many blacks as to which candidate was more deserving of their support. "Governor Colquitt," he was quoted as saying, "has done some little good for us; but my God, don't talk to me of Norwood. It scares me to hear of him. Norwood says he's opposed to Colquitt for preaching to niggers. I'm opposed to him because he don't."[33] William A. Pledger, Negro editor of the Athens *Blade,* also supported Colquitt. As early as 1877, Pledger assured Colquitt that Georgia Negroes would support him if he desired a second term. "I predict," wrote Pledger, "that your opponents at another election . . . will not be a united colored people and your supporters a united white people, but with unanimity—all *honest* and *true* men of *whatever race will be* invincible in the clamor for your re-election."[34] In 1880, Pledger was the

---

[30]Thomas M. Norwood to Leander Newton Trammell, 18 December 1876, TC.

[31]Greenville *Meriwether Vindicator,* 3 September 1880.

[32]Coleman, "Election of 1880," 109-19.

[33]Macon *Telegraph,* 9 September 1880.

[34]William A. Pledger to Alfred H. Colquitt, 22 April 1877, ICAHC.

chairman of the Republican Executive Committee in the state, and in that capacity he pledged the support of black Republicans to Colquitt.[35]

The contest between Norwood and Colquitt was a bitter one and revealed the depth of the opposition among some factions to the planter-New South coalition. As later incidents would confirm, the gubernatorial campaign of 1880 was merely the prelude to other bitter conflicts within the state during the next two decades. For some older politicians, like Lucius J. Gartrell and Rufus E. Lester, the Norwood candidacy provided an opportunity to emerge from the postwar obscurity to which they had been consigned and once again occupy the limelight of state politics. For some younger politicians, like Thomas E. Watson, the Norwood campaign offered the first opportunity to gain statewide recognition.[36] Many of the personality conflicts that came to light in the 1880 campaign persisted for the next twenty years.

The importance of the 1880 election extended far beyond the governor's office; at stake was the future control of the state's economy, political system, and philosophical commitment. If Colquitt won reelection, the planter-New South coalition would remain in control of the Democratic party; and from their positions as party leaders, they could direct the state down the Prussian Road at a well regulated pace. A Norwood victory, on the other hand, would be tantamount to a rejection of the planter-New South coalition, a loss of power for Atlanta businessmen, and a repeal of the state aid and regulatory provisions of the Constitution of 1877.

With such high stakes, it was not surprising that both Norwood and Colquitt supporters worked hard to get every eligible voter to the polls. When the balloting ended on October 6, over 182,000 Georgians had voted. Of the 137 counties in the state, 122 recorded Colquitt majorities. In the popular vote tallies, he received a total of 118,349 to only 64,004 for Norwood.[37] An analysis of Colquitt's votes reveals that the coalition worked to perfection. The majority of the ballots cast for him came from the heavily populated counties of the old Black Belt and the urban counties of Bibb, Richmond, and Fulton. Colquitt won sixty-three of the sixty-eight counties with Negro majorities. The Atlanta *Constitution* estimated that of the 30,000 Negro ballots cast, he received 20,000.[38] The heavy Negro vote for Colquitt demonstrated both the tremendous appeal he had for blacks and the ability of planters to control the votes of their tenants and sharecroppers.

---

[35]McDaniel, "Black Power," 225-35. Atlanta *Constitution*, 24 August 1880. Coleman, "Election of 1880," 103-104.

[36]Nixon, *Grady*, 174-77.

[37]*Georgia House Journal, 1880* (Atlanta: Constitution Printing Office, 1880) 37.

[38]Atlanta *Constitution*, 9, 10 October 1880.

For Norwood, the election results spelled complete disaster. Of the fifteen counties he won, Chatham and Muscogee were the only urban counties to give him a majority. Since Chatham was his home county, Norwood's victory there was to be expected. Muscogee County, the scene of the Ashburn murder in 1868, voted against Colquitt. Citizens of that county still considered Joseph E. Brown, the federal prosecutor in the Ashburn case, an anathema. Three Black Belt counties gave Norwood a majority, but they had voted against the Democrats in all contests since 1868.[39]

Although some historians have suggested that the bulk of Norwood's votes came from "towns," this assertion is questionable at best. The major sources of his strength were those areas that had opposed the ratification of the Constitution of 1877 and had been allied with the Republicans in the 1860s and 1870s. The newer Black Belt counties of southwest Georgia, in particular, accounted for the largest portion (50.8%) of the Norwood votes.[40] Excluding Chatham and Muscogee Counties and the Black Belt counties mentioned above, his remaining votes were distributed among counties in the wiregrass and mountain sections of the state. For all intents and purposes, the gubernatorial campaign of 1880 was a replay of the ratification election of 1877.[41]

The importance attached to the gubernatorial race is evident in the increased number of voters participating in the election. Approximately 31,000 (17%) more voters cast ballots in 1880 than in 1877. In several counties, the turnout exceeded the number of eligible voters as certified by the Comptroller General.[42] With the sole exception of Muscogee County, which had a voter turnout of 125.5 percent, counties where ballots outnumbered eligible voters were strong Colquitt supporters. Voter turnout throughout the state ranged from sixty percent in some counties to ninety percent in others, an unusually high percentage for a gubernatorial election. In Black Belt counties, it jumped nineteen percent over that in the 1877 ratification election. Colquitt benefited the most from this increase because Norwood received only about 2,000 of the additional ballots. Within the older Black Belt, enough votes went to Colquitt to elect him without any support from other sections of the state. The election of

---

[39]Parks, *Brown*, 412-17. Joseph E. Brown to Leander Newton Trammell, 4 September 1879, TC.

[40]*Comptroller General's Report, 1880*, 87-89.

[41]Coleman, "Election of 1880," 117.

[42]*Comptroller General's Report, 1880*, 87-89.

1880 was the first test of the alliance of planters and New South men, a test they passed with flying colors.[43]

Colquitt's election did not end the opposition to the alliance, and when the General Assembly convened in early November, it had to deal with a second challenge to the coalition. At stake was the office of United States Senator, since Brown's appointment to fill Gordon's empty seat was temporary. Brown was a candidate for reappointment, as was General Alexander R. Lawton, a Norwood supporter from Savannah. Lawton's hope was to defeat the coalition by defeating Brown, but the Colquitt majority in the gubernatorial campaign had also translated into a pro-Brown majority in both houses of the Assembly. Alexander H. Stephens, a friend of Lawton's, wrote to the General's wife urging her to get him to withdraw. "Brown in my opinion," he wrote, "is a great deal stronger in Georgia than Colquitt. But for Brown, Colquitt would have been defeated by Gen[eral] Lawton or any other good man. . . . Now I may be greatly mistaken; but my opinion is that Brown will have over $2/3$ in his favor for election to the Senate."[44] Stephens's estimate of Brown's strength was accurate, but it did not take a political genius to predict the outcome of the election.

On 13 October 1880, the Atlanta *Constitution* published its estimate of how the members of the General Assembly would vote, and it reported "a trifle over two-thirds are open and confirmed in their support of Brown, one-sixth are anti-Brown and one-sixth are doubtful."[45] When the final results were in, Brown received more than the necessary two-thirds majority. Just as Colquitt had done to Norwood, Brown defeated Lawton by a two-to-one margin.[46] Although Grady described Brown's victory as the "first substantial victory achieved by the New South over the Old South," Brown owed his election to those very forces of the Old South that Grady was attacking.[47]

Despite the overwhelming victories of the planter-New South coalition, significant opposition remained throughout the state. In 1881, Thomas M. Norwood wrote to Leander N. Trammell about a chance meeting he had with Gordon and Colquitt in Atlanta. It was a friendly encounter, and all three men "shook hands as if nothing had occurred in 20 years." Although Gordon and Colquitt were apparently willing to forget the past,

---

[43]The actual figures for voter turnout in the Black Belt were 88,406 in the 1877 ratification election and 105,189 in the 1880 gubernatorial contest. The Black Belt vote against the constitution was 30,541. Norwood polled 32,493 Black Belt ballots.

[44]Alexander H. Stephens to Sarah A. Lawton, 13 October 1880, SC.

[45]Atlanta *Constitution*, 13 October 1880.

[46]Ibid., 17 November 1880.

[47]Nixon, *Grady*, 177.

Norwood was reluctant to do so. "I find a very strong 'Norwood' feeling yet," he wrote, "[and] the feeling of the last October contest survivors in much force. Perhaps," he mused, it was time for "another fight."[48]

While Norwood was thinking about another fight, other men in the state were arriving at the same conclusion. "It appears to me," wrote Jonathan Norcross to William H. Felton, "the time has come in our state when something can be done and should be done to produce a reform in our state affairs." Norcross reminded Felton that "there is before the country no great questions to be decided or upon which the two great parties now stand divided, consequently it appears [to] me a reform party or a coalition for the purpose of reform in our state affairs, (which God knows are about as bad as they can be), could or should be easily and readily brought about."[49] Norcross, the unsuccessful Republican gubernatorial candidate in 1876 and the last Republican candidate of the nineteenth century, read the results of the Norwood-Colquitt contest as an indication that a strong opposition party could be created in Georgia. Instead of a death sentence, he saw the election of 1880 as a birth certificate of a new two-party system in the state.

By seeking the support of Dr. Felton, Norcross hoped to effect a combination of the two strongest groups opposed to the Democratic party, which was now firmly in the hands of planters and their allies. The first element—the Republicans—offered a regular party structure, some patronage positions at the federal level, and the possibility of financial aid from the national organization. Seeking to overcome their Reconstruction label as a party of corruption and pro-Negro feeling, Republicans hoped to use the dissatisfaction generated by the planter-New South coalition as a means of refurbishing their image and regaining their political importance.

There were deep divisions within Republican ranks over the issue of Negro participation in the party hierarchy and over the distribution of federal patronage jobs in the state.[50] In 1876, a revolt by black Republicans led by William A. Pledger had resulted in a split of the party into the "Lily Whites," who wanted it to cater to whites only, and the "Black and Tans," who wanted to continue the party's policy of including blacks in leadership roles.[51] As the leader of the "Lily Whites," Norcross had the

---

[48]Thomas M. Norwood to Leander Newton Trammell, 20 July 1881, TC.

[49]Jonathan M. Norcross to William H. Felton, 19 May 1881, William H. and Rebecca L. Felton Collection, University of Georgia. Hereafter referred to as WRFC.

[50]Brewton Cameron to Benjamin H. Brewster, 25 June 1882; E. A. Angier to Benjamin H. Brewster, 4 June 1882; Henry P. Farrow to President Chester A. Arthur, 10 June 1882, Henry McCay Papers, Atlanta Historical Society.

[51]McDaniel, "Black Power," 225-39.

support of a newcomer to Republican politics in Georgia, General James Longstreet. Like John B. Gordon, Longstreet was one of "Lee's Lieutenants" and a Confederate hero with impeccable military credentials. Unlike Gordon, however, Longstreet joined the Republican party immediately after the war and served in a variety of minor governmental positions in Louisiana. In 1881, he was appointed United States marshal for north Georgia and moved to Gainesville. Hoping to play a dominant leadership role in the state party, Longstreet added his voice to that of Norcross; and in December 1881, he urged Felton to join in a "combination . . . by which ideas may be so modified as to be acceptable to all."[52]

Longstreet's support of the combination of Independents and Republicans was the force that pushed the idea to fruition. The General had considerable influence with the Arthur administration, and he persuaded the President that he could achieve in Georgia what General William Mahone had accomplished in Virginia.[53] The prospect of establishing a successful Republican-Independent party in Georgia was enough to win Arthur's approval, and the President gave his blessings to the effort. In January 1882, Arthur informed Pledger that "party leaders who cannot win are useless. They ought to and they must give way long enough for others to try the experiment [of fusion with Independents]. I am determined to work only for those who can show me some results."[54]

The object of the Republican fusion efforts was to bring the strong Independent movement into their fold. The acknowledged leader of Georgia's Independents was Dr. William H. Felton—a physician, farmer, and Methodist preacher from Bartow County. Felton had won election to Congress in 1874, 1876, and 1878. Although defeated in his 1880 bid for reelection, he was still considered the most powerful Independent leader in the state. It was hoped that Felton's participation in a Republican-Independent alliance would attract the support of thousands of white voters who were unhappy with the planters' return to dominance. Felton's fellow Independent, Emory Speer, was invited to join the fusion effort, but he refused.[55]

In theory, the fusion of Independents and Republicans gave the Coalition, as it described itself, an excellent chance of winning state elections. Henry P. Farrow, a former chairman of the state Republican Party and an

---

[52]James Longstreet to William H. Felton, 3 December 1881, WRFC.

[53]Vincent P. DeSantis, "Negro Dissatisfaction with Republican Policy in the South, 1882-1884," *Journal of Negro History* 36 (1953):148-59. Vincent P. DeSantis, "President Arthur and the Independent Movements in the South in 1882," *Journal of Southern History* 19 (1953): 346-63.

[54]Atlanta *Constitution*, 26 January 1882.

[55]W. H. Hiddell to Rebecca L. Felton, 4 December 1883, WRFC. Jones, "William H. Felton," 183-89.

ardent supporter of the fusion movement, gave his assessment of that chance to General Longstreet in 1882. According to Farrow, the Coalition could count on the votes of 80,000 black and white Republicans across the state, to which another 15,000 Independent votes would be added. In addition to these, 10,000 more votes would come from urban areas within the state. With 105,000 votes, Farrow predicted, the Coalition would sweep the upcoming October elections.[56] Farrow's optimism was shared by other Republicans in Georgia. "There is no doubt but that a very large class of our people are anxious for an opportunity to break the shackles that bind them to Bourbonism and [to] assist . . . Independentism," wrote W. H. McWhorter of Green County. "They have been gulled by ringsters . . . long enough and are ready for revolt."[57] A. H. Cox, a LaGrange Republican, echoed McWhorter and predicted a great victory for the people, who would "no longer submit to methods subversive of all power of the people over their own affairs."[58] Certainly the prospects for success appeared bright when the leaders of both Republicans and Independents met to plan their strategy at Atlanta's Markham House on 29 December 1881.

The Markham House Conference was attended by four Republicans and three Independents. Longstreet, Farrow, Alexander N. Wilson, and Judge John S. Bigby represented the Republicans; Independents were represented by Felton, Judge James S. Hooks of Augusta, and Dr. H. V. M. Miller—a former United States Senator. The meeting produced an eleven-point platform designed to appeal to as many voters as possible without alienating any. The major features were planks calling for the abolition of the convict lease system, the creation of a system of free public schools, state funding of internal improvements, the payment of the national debt, and "free ballots and fair counts" in all elections. All in all, the Markham House platform was a mild document, designed to harness virtually every reform cause in the state and to offend no one.[59]

Having settled on a suitable platform, the delegates then discussed the possibility of finding a candidate for the gubernatorial campaign in 1882. Three names presented themselves immediately. The logical choice was Felton, but the old Independent warhorse refused to become a contender because he wanted to regain his former congressional seat. The second possibility was General Lucius J. Gartrell, a participant in the bitter Democratic convention fight in 1880 and an active candidate for the nomination

---

[56]Henry P. Farrow to James Longstreet, 20 April 1882, FC.

[57]W. H. McWhorter to William H. Felton, 27 January 1882, WRFC.

[58]A. H. Cox to William H. Felton, 28 January 1882, WRFC.

[59]Jones, "William H. Felton," 185. Warren Lee Jones, "Alexander H. Stephens, Governor of Georgia, 1882-1883" (Master's thesis, University of Georgia, 1942) 22.

in 1882. In the opinion of the Markham House conferees, Gartrell's candidacy had no popular base and no chance for success. The third possibility, and the one favored by the planners, was to nominate a man whose personal following, when combined with the Coalition's support, would be sufficient to defeat any Democratic candidate. Of all the prominent men in Georgia who were available, only Alexander H. Stephens was acceptable to all elements of the Coalition. From January until May, the fusion movement courted Stephens, trying to persuade him to become its candidate.[60]

The fusion movement touched off a bitter controversy within the Republican party in Georgia. Despite the assurances given to the Independents by Longstreet and Farrow that the Republicans would support the Coalition, the Republican Executive Committee refused to endorse the movement as a separate political party. Meeting on 2 January, just hours after the Markham House Conference ended, the Executive Committee would only approve a resolution that supported the fusion attempt as long as it took place within the organizational framework of the Republican party. This lack of an enthusiastic, and official, endorsement of the Coalition by the party hierarchy hampered the effectiveness of the movement.[61]

The refusal of the Executive Committee to give its unqualified approval to the Coalition was the result of internal party struggles over the distribution of federal patronage. Longstreet, as the leader of the pro-fusion Republicans, wanted a clean sweep of federal officeholders in the state and their replacement by men pledged to work for the Coalition. Only through a massive redistribution of patronage jobs could the old, ineffective leaders of the party be ousted from control.[62] The Atlanta *Constitution*, a critical observer of the fusion movement, accused the Coalition of trying to build a second party in the state at the expense of the American taxpayer.[63]

The struggle over patronage erupted into an open fight within the Republican party when Longstreet persuaded President Arthur to remove Andrew Clark and E. C. Wade, opponents of the fusion movement, from their jobs in the Internal Revenue Service in Georgia. Clark was removed with a minimum of fuss, but Wade's dismissal touched off a major flap. Republicans in the national organization, in addition to other members of the state party, protested Wade's firing. Sherman H. Merrill, a clergyman from Washington, D.C., wrote Felton a letter denouncing the attempt to purge nonfusionist Republicans from federal jobs. As far as Longstreet,

---

[60]Alexander H. Stephens to Rebecca L. Felton, 10 January; 7, 18 May 1882, WRFC. Jones, "William H. Felton," 198.

[61]Zachary B. Hargrove to William H. Felton, 20 January 1882, WRFC.

[62]James Longstreet to William H. Felton, 23 January 1882, WRFC.

[63]Atlanta *Constitution*, 3 August 1882.

Farrow, and other Republican fusionists were concerned, Merrill warned, "There are 20,000 Republican voters, white and colored . . . in Georgia and not one hundred of them would follow the lead of these men."[64] Jesse Wimberly, an employee of Wade's in the IRS, voiced similar sentiments. "I have travelled over forty of fifty counties in South G[eorgi]a within the last three months," he wrote, "and find that the people are ripe for revolt against 'bourbon' rule." But, he warned, "If Col. Wade is removed . . . the appointment of any of the men who are seeking Col. W [ade] removed will result in forcing the independents back into the ranks of the bourbons."[65]

The internecine warfare between Republicans over patronage prevented the Coalition from achieving its full potential, a situation that was aggravated by a controversy over the role Negroes would play in the new alliance. Many of the Republican fusionists wanted to prohibit blacks from joining the Coalition as a means of preventing the loss of some white voters. Zachary Hargrove, a leading Republican from Rome, had previously been a strong advocate of Negro participation in party affairs, but he changed his mind and joined the "Lily Whites" of the Coalition. "In the new movement in G[eorgi]a," he wrote to Felton, "the Negroes will divide *and* it may be best if they should."[66] W. J. White, Negro editor of the *Georgia Baptist,* expressed his opinion of the Coalition in a letter to Henry P. Farrow. "My views are that since colored men find themselves denied recognition because they are colored then it devolves upon them to look out for themselves," he commented. "[White Republicans and Independents] do not accord colored men as a class that recognition to which I believe they are entitled."[67]

While Republicans were arguing over race and patronage, Independents were also experiencing problems. The Independent movement in Georgia drew its strength from the personalities of its various leaders and possessed no statewide organizational structure. Generally concerned with local issues and local elections, Independents were frequently regular Democrats who temporarily deserted the party when they disagreed with its position on a specific issue, when individuals failed to receive rewards of nominations they thought were due them, or when local party leaders had lost the confidence of the party membership.[68] In most instances, men who ran as Independents in one election were active in the Democratic party in the next contest.

---

[64]Sherman Merrill to William H. Felton, 11 February 1882, WRFC.

[65]Jesse Wimberly to William H. Felton, 11 February 1882, WRFC.

[66]J. R. Gibbons to William H. Felton, 3 November 1880; Zachary B. Hargrove to William H. Felton, 20 January 1882, WRFC.

[67]W. J. White to Henry P. Farrow, 17 June 1882, FC. McDaniel, "Black Power," 225-39.

[68]Jones, "William H. Felton," 94-98.

Even the candidacy of Norwood in 1880 was considered by party leaders to be an insurgency rather than a permanent split in party ranks. In 1882, Independents within the Coalition were discovering that allegiances to specific men or strong feelings about certain issues did not provide the structure upon which a new party could be constructed.

The most damaging charge leveled against Independents was that they were in league with Republicans. This charge, made in the past against insurgents, took on a new importance in 1882, and it became the greatest obstacle to the success of the Coalition. Republicanism in Georgia was equated with Negro rule, and the Democratic press used this theme repeatedly in its campaign against the Coalition. The *Meriwether Vindicator* warned its readers that Independents were "more dangerous to the success of the Democratic party than the veriest Radical could possibly be."[69] The Columbus *Enquirer* agreed, noting that "Independents and Radicals are regarded as the same," although "the Independent is the worst of the two."[70] The Albany *News* followed suit and denounced Independents for making Negro rule a possibility in the state. "It's a hard matter," wrote that paper's editor, "for one to decide who or what our independent candidate is. Is he a white-washed Democrat, black-washed Republican, or a mixture of both? Mongrel—that's the word. Who is there to join the mongrel party?"[71]

The Coalition, weakened by internal struggles in the Republican party and by a lack of organization among Independents, was also hampered by the charges of race mixing that appeared in the Democratic newspapers. The only real hope it had for attracting enough white votes to win the October gubernatorial election was to nominate a candidate whose reputation was such that the Democratic charges would have no impact. Among Georgians, only Alexander H. Stephens had enough personal prestige to overcome the racist tactics of the Democrats. Stephens, who had maintained his distance from state politics since his unsuccessful bid for the United States Senate in 1868, was reluctant to join the Coalition. In January 1882, he informed Rebecca L. Felton that he was through with politics and that he did not expect to ever be a candidate for public office again. When his term in Congress ended, he intended to retire to his home in Crawfordville.[72] Yet despite his protestations about leaving public service, Stephens refused to firmly and finally reject the overtures of the Coalition.[73]

---

[69]Greenville *Meriwether Vindicator*, 29 September 1876.

[70]Columbus *Enquirer*, quoted in Greenville *Meriwether Vindicator*, 13 October 1876.

[71]Albany *News*, quoted in Greenville *Meriwether Vindicator*, 20 September 1878.

[72]Alexander H. Stephens to Rebecca L. Felton, 10 January 1882, WRFC.

[73]Ibid., 7, 18 May 1882.

In the absence of a firm commitment from Stephens, General Lucius J. Gartrell attempted to pressure the Coalition into backing his candidacy. Despite pleas from Felton and others to wait, in early February Gartrell announced his decision to run as an Independent candidate for governor. "He is a very suspicious man," wrote a mutual friend to Felton, "and is afraid that everybody is like himself—wants to be governor—hence his hot haste [to announce his candidacy.]"[74] The inability of Coalition leaders to persuade Gartrell to stay out of the race demonstrated a critical weakness of that organization. Without a formal party structure, a party purse, or party patronage, the Coalition had no leverage to use to control dissidents within the movement. Gartrell's candidacy not only complicated the Coalition's efforts to get Stephens to accept its nomination, but his early announcement gave the Democrats a target for, and time to mount, an extensive anti-Coalition propaganda campaign.[75]

The prospect of a Stephens candidacy in behalf of the Coalition was frightening to the Democrats who did not have an abundance of attractive candidates to choose from, and none who could match the popular appeal of the "Old Commoner." Alfred H. Colquitt, the incumbent, was prevented by the Constitution of 1877 from succeeding himself. Joseph E. Brown, a possible candidate, was occupying one of the state's Senate seats while Benjamin H. Hill, a remote possibility, held the other seat. Hill was suffering from cancer of the tongue and mouth, and was not expected to live out the year. John B. Gordon, another possible candidate, was engaged in constructing the Georgia-Pacific Railroad (one of the few successful ventures of his business career) and was not interested. A fourth possibility—and a man who very much wanted the job—was Augustus O. Bacon of Macon. Bacon, a veteran politician and Speaker of the Georgia House, was in disfavor with Colquitt and Brown because he had backed Norwood in 1880.[76]

Faced with a lack of acceptable, available, and popular candidates, Democratic leaders decided to defuse the Coalition threat by stealing their candidate. In early March, the *Constitution* published an open letter from Henry P. Farrow accusing the Democrats of making Stephens an offer of their party's nomination.[77] Governor Colquitt, acting as the party's spokesman, made the offer during a trip to Washington. According to some observers, he was eager for Stephens to accept because he wanted

---

[74]W. A. Wright to William H. Felton, 22 February 1882, WRFC.

[75]Atlanta *Constitution*, 7, 26 January; 2 February; 9 March 1882.

[76]Augustus O. Bacon to Joseph E. Brown, 22 May 1882; Joseph E. Brown to Augustus O. Bacon, 25 May 1882, Elijah E. Brown Collection, Atlanta Historical Society. Hereafter referred to as EEBC.

[77]Atlanta *Constitution*, 2 March 1882.

to eliminate the Congressman as a possible rival for Hill's soon-to-be-vacated Senate seat.[78]

The publication of Farrow's angry letter brought a swift response from Stephens. On 8 March, he wrote to Farrow and admitted that Colquitt had indeed made him an offer of the Democratic nomination, but he insisted that he had refused it and planned to retire from politics altogether.[79] Despite his avowed intention of abandoning politics, Stephens was still courted by both the Democrats and the Coalition. For both sides, success hinged on the final decision of a frail, egocentric seventy-year-old man described by his best friend as being "in his dotage."[80]

While the Coalition and the Democrats pursued Stephens, Lucius Gartrell conducted a vigorous campaign throughout the state. Members of the Coalition were put in an awkward situation, since they could neither deny nor support his candidacy until they secured a firm acceptance or rejection from Stephens. Gartrell insisted that he was in the contest to the finish and that he would continue his independent campaign with or without the Coalition's approval. Only the people of Georgia, he vowed, could end his efforts by rejecting him at the ballot box.[81]

Despite the Democrats' overtures to Stephens, the members of the Coalition were confident that their offer would be the one he chose. A second conference was called for the Markham House in May to finalize plans for a nominating convention. On 30 April, a few days before the planning conference was to meet, Stephens was quoted in the Atlanta *Constitution* as having accepted the Democratic nomination.[82] When Mrs. Felton fired off a letter to him questioning that report, Stephens responded ambiguously. "I have simply given my assent to serve the people of Georgia as Governor," he wrote back, "if they shall by unmistakable demonstration show me that is their desire for me to do so." Only his "desire to produce harmony in the state" and his desire to spare it the "horrible effects of divisions and factions" forced him into giving his unqualified acceptance to the Democrats.[83]

Coalition leaders were dismayed by Stephens's action. For more than a year, they had counted on his ultimate acceptance of their nomination, and his apparent defection to the Democrats created additional confusion

---

[78]Anonymous to Henry P. Farrow, 12 April 1882, FC. Jones, "William H. Felton," 201.

[79]Alexander H. Stephens to Henry P. Farrow, 8 March 1882, FC.

[80]Rudolph von Abele, *Alexander H. Stephens: A Biography* (New York: Alfred A. Knopf, 1946) 304-13.

[81]Atlanta *Constitution*, 12 April 1882.

[82]Ibid., 30 April 1882.

[83]Rebecca L. Felton to Alexander H. Stephens, 9 May 1882, WRFC.

among Coalition members. William H. Felton assessed the impact of Stephens's cooperation with the Democrats in a letter to Henry P. Farrow. "If we fail to make him our candidate in some way," he prophesied, "the 'organized Bourbons' will shout with delight—and they will nominate him and leave us in the lurch." Felton proposed to force Stephens into becoming the Coalition candidate by formally nominating him before the Democratic convention met. "I am in favor," he continued, "of throwing upon him the responsibility of accepting our proffered support—in unmistakable words—he must in written language let all the world know that he is thankful and appreciates our help, for without us he cannot be Governor." If this ploy did not work, Felton had little hope for the Coalition's success, since "*we* cannot succeed *now* without Mr. Stephens."[84]

Although Stephens had accepted the Democratic nomination in advance of the party's convention, some members of the Coalition clung to the belief that he would prefer theirs instead. James Longstreet assured Felton that "Mr. Stephens wants to run for Governor as the Independent candidate." To make sure that the Coalition leaders would be united in their response to the Stephens announcement, Longstreet called for a meeting on 5 May. This, he explained to Felton, was necessary so that "a concert of action should be had among our friends as to the proper course to be pursued."[85] Henry P. Farrow added his sentiments to those of Longstreet, and he urged the Coalition not to reject Stephens until Stephens had rejected the Coalition.[86]

The 5 May meeting produced an agreement among Coalition leaders that the scheduled planning session of 15 May would be used as an early nominating convention. Still hoping that Stephens could be persuaded to accept their bid, they concurred with Felton's suggestion to nominate him before the Democrats could. In Washington, Emory Speer, Georgia's lone Independent in Congress, acted as the liaison between the Coalition and Stephens. On the eve of the 15 May meeting, Speer wired Felton that he had sent an important telegram to the Coalition. When the convention met the next morning, Felton disclosed the contents of that telegram. Apparently successful in his efforts to get Stephens to accept the Coalition's nomination, Speer informed the members of the meeting that the Congressman would "positively . . . not reject such recommendation, and that if elected he will be governor of all the people without regard to party."[87] Interpreting the telegram as the assurance they had been seeking, the Co-

[84]William H. Felton to Henry P. Farrow, 9 May 1882, FC.

[85]James Longstreet to William H. Felton, 5 May 1882, WRFC.

[86]Henry P. Farrow to William H. Felton, 8 May 1882, WRFC.

[87]Emory Speer to William H. Felton, Telegrams, 14, 15 May 1882, WRFC.

alition leaders nominated Stephens and cancelled their scheduled June meeting.[88]

Despite his approval of the Speer telegram, Stephens refused to publicly accept the nomination. On 18 May, he wrote to Mrs. Felton that the Coalition's action was "about the best thing that could have been done." However, he intimated that he would accept no nomination because of his health problems. "How it will all end, even in case my health should improve, I do not know," he lamented. "The times are uncertain and ominous."[89] The same day he wrote to Dr. Felton to congratulate him on how well he "had managed matters in Atlanta," and to assure him that the Coalition had looked after "the best interest of the state." But here again, Stephens failed to give an unqualified acceptance of the Coalition's nomination.[90]

Democratic reaction to the news was swift. Prominent Democratic leaders, aware that the Coalition now had a formidable—if reluctant—candidate, hurried to Washington to confer with Stephens. The outcome of these conferences was apparent when the *Constitution* printed a letter from Stephens to Charles E. Smith on 23 May. In his letter, Stephens publicly reacted to the Coalition's action for the first time and announced that he, regardless of who nominated him, would not run against the nominee of the Democratic party. The *Constitution* assured its readers that despite the feeble efforts of the "coalition colonels," Stephens would be "the candidate of the regular Democracy or not at all." Everything was settled; all that remained was to formally nominate him at the party convention on 19 July.[91]

The publication of Stephens's letter created a sensation among some Democrats. Within the party, a strong movement had developed around the possible candidacy of Augustus O. Bacon. The day before the letter appeared in the *Constitution*, Bacon wrote to Joseph E. Brown to get his reaction to a possible nomination. Brown's reply, written two days after the story broke in the press, stressed party unity as the primary consideration of all Democrats. Stephens's nomination was essential, he informed Bacon, because he could "do more to unite the Democracy and can probably carry a larger vote as the nominee of the party than any other candidate could carry." Brown reminded Bacon that "you are a young man in the vigor of manhood and the prime of your intellect, and if the Democracy on this occasion should call Mr. Stephens to the chair, I am well aware that it by no means disposes of your prospects to fill that high po-

---

[88]Atlanta *Constitution*, 16 May 1882.

[89]Alexander H. Stephens to Rebecca L. Felton, 18 May 1882, WRFC.

[90]Alexander H. Stephens to William H. Felton, Ibid.

[91]Atlanta *Constitution*, 23 May 1882. Jones, "William H. Felton," 211.

sition."[92] Brown's answer was an unspoken promise to Bacon that if he would forego his aspirations in 1882, he would be favorably considered by the party at some later date. In the interest of party harmony, Bacon gave up his ambitions temporarily, but they were to surface again in 1883, 1884, and 1886.

While disconcerting to some Democrats, Stephens's letter was even more traumatic for the Coalition. By refusing to run against the Democratic nominee, he had, at last, rejected them. Felton, a friend of Stephens, felt betrayed. Two days after the publication of the Stephens letter, he wrote to Henry Farrow that he would "announce myself as an independent candidate for Governor" if General Gartrell could be persuaded to withdraw from the contest.[93] Although Felton would have been a much better candidate, Gartrell refused to bow out of the race and continued to campaign.

Stephens's rejection of the Coalition halted their ambitious plans to create a new party in the state, and within three weeks the alliance dissolved. Without an acceptable candidate to unify its factions, the Coalition had no reason for existing, and problems that would have been overlooked in the frenzy of a statewide campaign took on exaggerated importance. The event that triggered the breakup was the appointment of Judge W. H. Underwood, an avowed enemy of Felton in the Seventh District, to a federal office. The Atlanta *Post-Appeal* (a paper formerly owned by Stephens) gleefully announced this news, taunting the Coalition with the fact that Longstreet—who thought himself the new boss of federal patronage in Georgia—could not prevent it. Calling Underwood's appointment "one of the worse stabs the Independents could have had," the *Post-Appeal* continued, "Judge Underwood has bitterly fought Dr. Felton in the Seventh District every time, and is now the representative of the anti-Felton party in that district."[94]

Although the failure to secure Stephens's acceptance of its nomination had sealed the fate of the Coalition, the Underwood appointment provided an excuse for Independents and Republicans to point accusing fingers at each other. In a bitter letter to Henry P. Farrow, Felton blamed the failure of fusion on Republicans who were caught up in "this war for federal patronage." He concluded, "The cause of Independentism has been irreparably damaged by the unseemly fight in Washington among Georgia Republicans over the federal offices in the gift of the President." The continued squabbles among party members had measurably affected the appeal of the Coalition, he railed, "[and] the great mass of the people . . . are disgusted and indifferent as to who may be appointed." The tragedy

---

[92]Augustus O. Bacon to Joseph E. Brown, 22 May 1882; Joseph E. Brown to Augustus O. Bacon, 25 May 1882, EEBC.

[93]William H. Felton to Henry P. Farrow, 25 May 1882, FC.

[94]Clippings from Atlanta *Post-Appeal*, 14, 17 June 1882, FC.

of such intraparty struggles was that the Coalition was the chief casualty, "a good cause ruined by the personal factions among Republicans."[95] Mrs. Felton voiced similar sentiments when she served notice on Farrow that "if Judge Underwood's appointment is not revoked, you may all understand that Dr. Felton is done with all efforts to resist the tyranny of the Bourbons."[96]

Despite the collapse of the Coalition, Stephens's election to the governor's chair was not automatic. In the Democratic convention, which met on 20 July in Atlanta, a few delegates opposed Stephens and pushed for the nomination of Augustus O. Bacon. After delaying action for one day, the Bacon delegates—aware that their candidate could not possibly win—gave up their opposition, and Stephens was nominated by acclamation. When the Republican convention met, it formally endorsed Gartrell's candidacy, a not totally unexpected decision.[97]

The campaigns of the two candidates were as different as the personalities of the men themselves. Gartrell, a Civil War veteran, carried on an aggressive campaign throughout the state. Hampered by ill health, Stephens "made a leisurely jaunt through the state, speaking in Atlanta, Macon, Columbus, and last of all in Augusta."[98] William E. Simmons, a Lawrenceville Democrat, became alarmed at the relaxed pace of the Stephens effort, and he wrote to him to warn that twenty-five percent of the "true democracy, enough to secure your defeat, was indifferent to the election."[99] Stephens himself was aware that Gartrell was a tough opponent, and he urged Leander Newton Trammell, "you who got me in the present position," to see that everything went smoothly.[100] In August, Stephens again wrote to Trammell about Gartrell. "My opinion is that Gen[eral] Gartrell will get a much larger white vote than is generally credited to him," he warned, "and I am satisfied that he will get an almost solid colored vote unless means are taken to prevent it."[101]

Stephens's fears were unfounded. The Democratic party, under the control of the planter-New South alliance, functioned perfectly. When the final tallies were made, Stephens amassed a total of 107,253 votes to Gartrell's 44,896. Of Georgia's 137 counties, only eleven returned Gartrell

---

[95]William H. Felton to Henry P. Farrow, 16, 17 June 1882, FC.

[96]Rebecca L. Felton to Henry P. Farrow, 14 June 1882, FC.

[97]von Abele, *Stephens*, 310.

[98]Ibid., 311.

[99]William E. Simmons to Alexander H. Stephens, 19 August 1882, SC.

[100]Alexander H. Stephens to Leander Newton Trammell, 1 June 1882, TC.

[101]Ibid., 19 August 1882.

majorities.[102] Of these, six were located in the mountain section, and the remainder were in the Black Belt. Three of the latter—Burke, McIntosh, and Liberty—were consistent Republican counties. Official election returns for each county were never published by the Comptroller General, and a detailed analysis of the votes is not possible. One unusual aspect of the 1882 election is the low voter turnout when compared to that of 1880. Thirty thousand fewer (16.6%) voters cast their ballots in the Stephens-Gartrell contest than had voted in the Colquitt-Norwood election.

The Coalition was a last-ditch effort to revive the old alliance the Republicans had momentarily created in 1868. Against the combination of Black Belt planters and New South businessmen, it had little chance of success. The Norwood candidacy of 1880 had made a better showing than the Coalition because the movement of 1882 was tainted by direct Republican participation. General William T. Wofford, a political ally and business partner of Felton, explained why Georgians failed to rally to the Coalition. In a letter to William King, a Felton supporter, Wofford argued that the Coalition did not represent a factional split within the Democratic party, but was considered to be a frontal assault on it. Once Stephens received the Democratic nomination, he argued, Felton and other Independents sacrificed their status as renegade Democrats and became Republicans.[103] In Georgia, Independentism was acceptable only so long as it was kept within the framework of the Democratic party.

The election of 1882 revealed the failure of white Republicans to control the Negro vote. Despite the optimistic appraisals of those in the Coalition that 80,000 Republicans would vote for its candidate, this figure was based on the belief that all Negroes would vote for the nominee approved by the white party hierarchy. This view failed to take into consideration the growing schism between white and black Republicans in the state and the factional divisions over patronage. Although white Republicans wanted (and counted on) the Negro vote, they pursued a policy of segregation and exclusion. Such a policy alienated many black politicians, and it was responsible for the creation of two Republican party organizations in Georgia.[104] The Coalition's dependency on Negro votes also failed to take into account the tremendous power white planters had over the voting habits of their black sharecroppers and tenants.[105] A black

---

[102]*Georgia House Journal, 1882* (Atlanta: Constitution Printing Office, 1882) 38-39. Atlanta *Constitution,* 10 October 1882. Augusta *Chronicle and Constitutionalist,* 10, 11, October 1882.

[103]William T. Wofford to William King, 3 November 1882, WRFC.

[104]W. J. White to Henry P. Farrow, 17 June 1882, WRFC.

[105]Peter Kolchin, *First Freedom: The Responses of Alabama's Blacks to Emancipation and Reconstruction* (Westport CT: Greenwood Press, 1972) 174.

sharecropper or tenant was far more likely to vote the Democratic ticket under the watchful eye of his landlord than he was the Independent or Republican ticket. Voting for a non-Democratic candidate could result in economic or physical reprisals.

Just as the election of 1882 demonstrated the weaknesses of Independents and Republicans, it also revealed the power of planters. The Black Belt, with its large population, responded to the wishes of planters who controlled the region's economy; and where planters led, the rest of the state had no choice but to follow. The election of Alexander H. Stephens ended the last serious challenge to planter hegemony until the Populist uprising in 1892. Independentism and Republicanism were dead, and the Augusta *Chronicle and Constitutionalist* pronounced their last rites. The election of Stephens was "the death blow . . . and there is no hope for them to gain possession of the State of Georgia. The die has been cast."[106]

---

[106]Augusta *Chronicle and Constitutionalist*, 11 October 1882.

CHAPTER 8

THE BOURBON TRIUMVIRATE

The coalition of Black Belt planters and New South men was anchored by an ad hoc committee known as the "Bourbon Triumvirate." Although usually portrayed as a cohesive unit that functioned to implement the goals of the New South, the real purpose of the Triumvirate was to serve as a visible expression of the tenuous balance of power between planters and industrialists.[1] With Alfred H. Colquitt and Joseph E. Brown as permanent members and a third member who changed with each new occupant of the governor's chair, the Triumvirate served as an effective buffer against opposing political movements in the state. Dissident politicians, men who might successfully lead such a movement or who might splinter the surface unity of the Democratic party, were occasionally offered the governorship as a bribe for continued party loyalty.[2] In the absence of a significant opposition threat, rival groups within the party fought for control of the governor's chair. With planters firmly in command of both houses of the General Assembly and the governor's powers reduced considerably by the Constitution of 1877, the office was more important in determining the influence of rival cliques within the Democratic ranks than it was in effecting the balance of power in the state.

General Alfred H. Colquitt—Confederate hero, prewar planter, and former slave owner—represented planter interests in the Triumvirate. A member of a distinguished and politically active Georgia family, Colquitt was a Princeton graduate who had been prominent in antebellum politics. In 1852, he was elected to Congress, and in 1857 he lost the Democratic gubernatorial nomination to Joseph E. Brown.[3] A member of the 1861

---

[1]Woodward, *Origins*, 14-17. Wiener, *Social Origins*, 210-12. Parks, *Brown*, 517-19. Although the traditional portrayal of the Triumvirate is that of a cohesive unit, the Triumvirate was more a part of political folklore than a reality. It existed more as a symbol of cooperation between the Old South and the New South than as a collective repository of political power. Each of the members operated independently in the political arena.

[2]See the discussion of the elections of 1882 and 1884 in the previous chapter.

[3]Parks, *Brown*, 25. Richard H. Clark to Joseph E. Brown, 21 April 1877, HT.

secession convention, Colquitt entered the Confederate Army as a captain and rose to the rank of major general.[4] While on active duty in 1864, he distinguished himself at the Battle of Olustee, an important engagement that checked the advance of federal troops into central Florida.

After the war, Colquitt resumed his agricultural activities and became one of the most successful planters in the state. He was active in the Georgia Agricultural Society, an organization made up of planters, and served one term as its president. When the Grange was organized in Georgia in the 1870s, Colquitt was elected vice-president. A devout Christian and a Methodist lay preacher, he was widely respected for his missionary work among Negroes. Throughout his lifetime, Colquitt spent most Sundays teaching in Negro Sunday schools. An active prohibitionist, he also often spoke at temperance meetings. Colquitt's private life was exemplary, and even his most virulent political enemies acknowledged his personal honesty.

In addition to his planting activities, Colquitt also had extensive business interests. A partner of John B. Gordon, he was involved in "two Southern railroads, a New England textile mill, a Tennessee fertilizer factory, and in coal mining," businesses that, according to C. Vann Woodward, netted $1 million in "less than a year."[5] Colquitt's contemporaries were less complimentary about his financial abilities, and they accused him of squandering his family's fortune and those of his two wives.[6] His involvement in many enterprises started by Gordon did little to add to his reputation in business. He was vice-president of the Southern Life Insurance Company—which failed in 1876, a partner in a land development scheme that failed, and one of the incorporators of a company proposing to drain the Everglades.[7] All of these ventures were started by Gordon, and it is doubtful whether any of them ever made a profit. In 1887, the Macon *Telegraph* described Colquitt's business career as one of continual failures. "The presumption is a reasonable one," wrote the paper's editor, "[that] Colquitt is deficient in business knowledge, because he has failed where other men have succeeded. . . . He has failed as a planter, cotton factor, and farmer's exporter."[8]

Although a questionable business success, Colquitt was an unqualified political one. First elected governor in 1876, he was exempted from the provisions of the Constitution of 1877 limiting a governor to four consecutive years in office. Identified by the state press as part of the "bargain

---

[4]Woodward, *Origins*, 17.

[5]Ibid.

[6]Undated and unidentified newspaper clipping in Alfred H. Colquitt Scrapbooks, University of Georgia.

[7]W. M. McIntosh to Alfred H. Colquitt, 18 October 1882, ICAHC.

[8]Macon *Telegraph*, 22 August 1887.

and corruption" scandal that saw Gordon resign from the United States Senate and Joe Brown appointed in his place, Colquitt was still the planters' choice to serve an additional two years. His election in 1880 was the first real test of the planter-New South coalition, and his victory clearly demonstrated the strength of the new alliance.[9] The death of Benjamin H. Hill in 1882 created a vacancy in the U. S. Senate, which Colquitt was elected to fill. His connections with both the planter class and the New South businessmen made him an ideal representative on the Triumvirate, particularly for planters. Familiar with the "ins" (and unfortunately the "outs") of high finance, he was nevertheless firmly linked to the planter class. In many ways, the career of Alfred H. Colquitt epitomized the careers of many postwar planters.

Although suspected of being little more than a pawn of Brown and Gordon in the resignation controversy of 1880, Colquitt quickly proved himself free of Brown's influence when he entered the Senate in 1882. As the representative of Georgia's business community, Brown supported high tariffs, hard money, and favorable legislation for industry. In 1888, the Americus *Recorder,* commenting on Brown's tariff stand, accused him of being an "assistant republican."[10] Colquitt, on the other hand, faithfully represented the interests of planters and consistently opposed Brown on economic questions.

The diversity of opinion between the two men made Colquitt's appointment of Brown to the Senate unusual. Indeed, had not a compromise been worked out between planters and industrialists, Brown would probably have never received it. Herbert Fielder, a second-rate politician and Brown's paid biographer, remarked on the "startling alliance" the appointment created. It "brought men together who had stood at a cold and selfish distance—men who up to that time sought honors by different and opposing popular currents."[11] What made Colquitt's decision to name Brown even more remarkable, wrote Fielder, "was the poor opinion you had of Colquitt expressed to me only a few weeks prior to his making you Senator."[12]

The "poor opinion" Brown had of Colquitt was returned in kind. Colquitt was a source of frustration for Brown, effectively blocking many of his political schemes. In 1886, Julius L. Brown, the Senator's eldest son and his business associate, noted Colquitt's opposition to the younger Brown's possible appointment to the federal judiciary. "Colquitt will *not be* for me," wrote Julius to his father. "He will not forget Prohibition, and

---

[9]See previous chapter.

[10]Americus *Recorder,* 22 March 1888. Parks, *Brown,* 554-57.

[11]Herbert Fielder to Joseph E. Brown, 30 October 1882, HT.

[12]Ibid.

he would fear my rulings on that subject."[13] Two years later, the differences between the two former governors became a public sensation when the Georgia Democratic convention chose delegates to the national convention who were in favor of lower tariffs. Despite Brown's attempts to get them to ignore the tariff and to select men who were moderates on that question, Colquitt was able to persuade the convention to elect a full slate of strong anti-tariff delegates. Brown suffered an even greater humiliation when the convention refused to give Patrick Walsh, the pro-Brown editor of the Augusta *Chronicle,* a place on the delegation.[14]

Evan P. Howell, co-editor of the Atlanta *Constitution* and another Brown supporter, wrote to him about Colquitt's activities, assuring the Senator that "in all this we will get even with Colquitt." Howell's plan for revenge was to defeat Colquitt's bid for reelection to the Senate by getting the General Assembly to elect Henry W. Grady in his place. To this end, Howell urged Brown to "write me a strong letter in favor of Grady . . . and say all the good things you can. The wider I can make the breach between Grady and Colquitt *the better it will be for both of us."* The essential thing, he informed Brown, "above everything else is to beat Colquitt."[15]

Grady and Howell discovered that planters were not willing to abandon the popular Colquitt for the editor of a New South newspaper, and Grady's candidacy died a quiet death.[16] The tariff question, however, disrupted the coalition of planters and industrialists. In 1888, Roger Q. Mills of Texas introduced a bill into Congress calling for significant tariff reductions. Planters, faced with increasing costs for manufactured goods and decreasing market prices for cotton, supported the Mills proposal. As their spokesman, Colquitt's support was critical, and he vigorously worked for the bill's passage. Brown was strongly opposed to the Mills Bill and made several Senate speeches against it.[17] The disagreement over the tariff was symptomatic of a growing rift in the planter-industrialist alliance, and tariff reform provided an issue for a final battle between the two camps.

The year 1888 was a decisive one for Georgia politics. A slump in the price of cotton and the formation of the Farmers' Alliance produced a new class consciousness among planters, a feeling that manifested itself in the

---

[13]Julius L. Brown to Joseph E. Brown, 1 August 1886, HT.

[14]Joseph E. Brown to General Phillip Cook, 12 May 1888, HT.

[15]Evan P. Howell to Joseph E. Brown, 10 May 1888, HT.

[16]Americus *Recorder,* 2 February; 5 April; l6, 23 November 1888. Parks, *Brown,* 571-73. Nixon, *Grady,* 280.

[17]Ward, "Georgia under the Bourbon Democrats," 184. Parks, *Brown,* 554-57.

rapid growth of the Alliance[18] In Georgia, the tariff controversy served to unite planters even more by providing an issue that polarized attitudes on economic questions. Planters and the Alliance were opposed to protective tariffs and demanded their repeal, while industrialists still argued that protection was necessary for America's developing industries. Brown and Colquitt became the symbols of opposing tariff views in the state.

Brown, as the spokesman for the protariff New South, received support from most of the large, urban daily newspapers, such as the Augusta *Chronicle*, the Macon *Telegraph*, and the Atlanta *Constitution*. Colquitt, as the leader of the antitariff planters, was widely supported by county newspapers, which published less frequently. Indeed, many rural editors welcomed this opportunity to take potshots at their rival, the *Constitution*. "Georgia is not ready to be handed over by Joe Brown and the Atlanta *Constitution* to the Republican doctrine of protecting monopolies," wrote the Albany *News*.[19] The Americus *Recorder* concurred in its opinion. "Senator Brown and his tariff policy are not meeting with an expression of approval from the Democratic conventions of the State," editorialized the *Recorder*. "The fact is the Democrats of Georgia are not pleased with Senator Brown's course on the tariff."[20]

While Brown and the *Constitution* were criticized in the rural press, Colquitt was highly praised. As far as his bid for reelection was concerned, the *Recorder* assured him that "the Legislature to be elected, and which will elect Mr. Colquitt's successor will not denounce Mr. Colquitt." Instead, the General Assembly would "elect as Georgia's next Senator a man who holds the same views on certain questions as does Senator Colquitt," and, the *Recorder* promised, "only your Uncle Joseph E. will get left."[21] Brown's response to the furor over the tariff was to denounce Colquitt privately as being one of the "class of public men [who are] pandering all the time to the lowest public prejudices and taste, and who are doing a great deal of harm."[22]

Joseph Emerson Brown—Civil War governor, Chief Justice of the state's Supreme Court, prewar slave owner, United States Senator, Republican, Democrat, lawyer, and industrialist—was accustomed to being the center of political storms. From 1857 until 1888, Brown was perhaps the single most powerful man in Georgia. A master politician, he rose from the ob-

---

[18]Lewis N. Wynne, "The Farmers' Alliance: Georgia's Experiment in Agrarian Politics," *Atlanta Historical Bulletin* 17 (1972) 21-30. Lewis N. Wynne, "The Alliance Legislature of 1890" (Master's thesis, University of Georgia, 1970).

[19]Albany *News*, reprinted in the Macon *Telegraph*, 7 October 1887.

[20]Americus *Recorder*, 26 April 1888.

[21]Ibid., 5 April 1888.

[22]Joseph E. Brown to Leander Newton Trammell, 23 May 1888, TC.

scurity of the Georgia hill country in 1857 to serve an unprecedented eight years as governor of the state. Immediately after the Civil War, Brown surfaced as the guiding force in the Republican party and was appointed Chief Justice of the Georgia Supreme Court by Rufus B. Bullock, the state's only Republican governor. His ability to change positions and parties rapidly and with little apparent loss of influence made him, according to one historian, "first in secession, first in reconstruction, and very nearly first in the restoration of home rule."[23] Suspected by the masses of Georgia as being untrustworthy, Brown was a political power broker whose occupancy of public office depended on behind-the-scenes deals instead of popular elections.[24]

A shrewd businessman, Brown managed to come through the chaos of Confederate defeat and Reconstruction as one of the state's first millionaires. During Bullock's administration, he put together a corporation that, through some rather suspicious dealings, managed to lease the state-owned Western and Atlantic Railroad.[25] A few years later, during a Democratic administration and under equally suspicious circumstances, Brown secured the right to lease most of the state's convicts.[26] Control of the convict lease was the basis of Brown's successful operation of a variety of corporations in North Georgia. Convicts provided the necessary labor for the Dade Coal Company, the Rising Fawn Iron Company, the Walker Iron Company, and the Chattahoochee Brick Company.[27]

Brown's business activities were not limited to these companies, however, and he was one of the state's largest dealers in real estate. In addition to his many holdings in Georgia, he owned 28,000 acres of prime Texas land.[28] His control of the Western and Atlantic Railroad also gave him

---

[23]Thompson, *Reconstruction in Georgia*, 207-34.

[24]Parks, *Brown*, 576-78.

[25]Thompson, *Reconstruction in Georgia*, 223-34. Nathans, *Losing the Peace*, 206-18. Parks, *Brown*, 450-68. Wiener, *Social Origins*, 211.

[26]Rebecca L. Felton to Henry P. Farrow, undated letter, WRFC. Mrs. Felton provided Farrow with information to use against former Governor James M. Smith in the event Smith decided to run for public office in 1882. According to her, Smith "refused a bid for all able-bodied long term men at 52 dollars per capita—and he let Brown have 300 of that class at $11 per capita, losing to the State in the 20 years [of the lease] a vast amount—

$$20 \times \$11 \times 300 = \$ \ 66,000$$
$$20 \times \ 52 \times 300 = \ \underline{612,000}$$

$556,000 loss to the State on 300 slaves."

[27]Derrell C. Roberts, "Joseph E. Brown and the Convict Lease System," *Georgia Historical Quarterly* 44 (1960): 399-410. Idem, "Joseph E. Brown and His Georgia Mines," *Georgia Historical Quarterly* 52 (1968): 285-92.

[28]Parks, *Brown*, 560-78.

considerable influence in the Southern Railroad and Steamship Association, a group of transportation companies that attempted to reduce competition by agreeing on rates to be charged for passengers and freight.[29] Possessed of extraordinary business judgement, Brown's ability to make money was legendary, and ownership of stock in a Brown enterprise was a gilt-edged guarantee of profit.[30] His success in business was the key to his political success in the postwar era, and Brown rewarded political supporters with jobs in his various enterprises.

Brown's prewar political strength was based on the support of yeoman farmers from "Cherokee" Georgia, and he carefully cultivated his image as a simple man of the people. Largely fiction, the image served him well. A graduate of Yale Law School, he had married into a prominent South Carolina family, and his wife had brought with her a considerable dowry.[31] He was a successful lawyer who invested his considerable earnings in slaves, land, and mineral leases. These leases provided him with a solid foundation for many of his postwar businesses.

Brown's wealth and his ready acceptance of Reconstruction made him an anathema to white Georgians in the immediate postwar period. In 1869, while Chief Justice of the Georgia Supreme Court, Brown wrote the decision recognizing the right of Negroes to hold public office in the state.[32] A year earlier, he had alienated many whites when he made a speech at the Republican national convention and condemned Southern resistance to Reconstruction. For this speech, the Atlanta *Constitution* labeled him a "traitor" to the South.[33] By 1876, Brown had managed to rejoin the Democratic party in a leadership capacity, and for his efforts on their behalf in the disputed presidential election, the *Constitution* now considered him to be a "very smart man."[34]

---

[29]Small, *Stenographic Report*, 407. In his major speech on the subject, Toombs referred to the Southern Railroad and Steamship Association when he argued for regulation because "I think I can make rates for these railroads as well as those fellows who meet here in the Kimball House and New York to decide upon how much of the people's substance they will take to themselves. Their proceedings are secret, and nobody knows what they are doing until it comes out."

[30]Parks, *Brown*, 563-64. So widely recognized was Brown's ability to make money that even his political enemies sometimes consulted him on business matters. Joseph E. Brown to Rebecca L. Felton, 23 July 1883, WRFC.

[31]Paul D. Escott, *After Secession: Jefferson Davis and the Failure of Confederate Nationalism* (Baton Rouge: Louisiana State University Press, 1978) 159-67. Parks, *Brown*, 1-8.

[32]Nathans, *Losing the Peace*, 152-59.

[33]Atlanta *Constitution*, 10, 24, 25, 26 July; 16,18, 22 November 1876.

[34]Atlanta *Constitution*, 17 June; 10, 24 July 1868; 16, 18, 22 November 1876.

Not all Georgians readily forgave Brown for his political apostacy during Reconstruction. One of his most persistent and vocal critics was Robert Toombs, who never relented in his efforts to ruin Brown politically. Although Toombs and Brown had been political allies in the 1850s and although both had opposed the policies of Jefferson Davis during the war, each had gone in different political directions afterward.[35] Toombs, the unreconstructed rebel who was barred from holding public office because of his refusal to swear allegiance to the United States, emerged as one of the most active planter spokesmen in the postwar years. As a staunch advocate of planter supremacy, he conducted running battles with Republicans, railroads, the New South, and its leading proponent—Joseph E. Brown. So strong was the animosity between Toombs and Brown that the two men almost fought a duel in 1872.[36]

Following Ben Hill's defection to the New South in 1870, Toombs became the best known leader of Georgia planters. Although his constant ascerbic comments on the New South and Joseph E. Brown provided newspapers with good copy, his most important leadership contribution came in the Constitutional Convention of 1877. The provisions in the new constitution that dealt with the legislative power, corporate restrictions, and the Railroad Commission were the handiwork of Toombs. In fact, much of their actual wording derived from court decisions involving Toombs and various railroads in the state.[37] Throughout his postwar career, he worked diligently to disrupt the activities of the New South. Toombs, unlike Hill, never succumbed to the blandishments of the state's industrialists.[38]

His constant bickering with Toombs did not affect Brown's ability to reconcile himself with other planter spokesmen. In particular, he successfully maintained cordial relations with Alexander H. Stephens. Like Toombs, Stephens was an antebellum political power, and his opposition to secession in 1860-61 was in direct contrast to Brown's fervent support. By 1863, however, both men were united in their opposition to the policies of Jefferson Davis, and they cooperated closely in various efforts to weaken his authority.[39] The two men maintained a friendly correspon-

---

[35]Escott, *After Secession*, 121, 159-67. Joseph E. Brown to Robert Toombs, 5 January 1878, HT.

[36]Parks, *Brown*, 467-74.

[37]Thompson, "Robert Toombs and the Georgia Railroads," 56-64.

[38]Pleasant A. Stovall, *Robert Toombs, Statesman, Speaker, Soldier, Sage* (New York: Cassell Publishing Company, 1892).

[39]Escott, *After Secession*, 159-67.

dence throughout the Reconstruction period, and Brown allowed Stephens to purchase a half-share in the Western and Atlantic lease in 1870.[40]

Although Stephens and Brown remained on close personal terms, politically they maintained their distance during Reconstruction. Stephens even returned his half-share of the railroad lease when Toombs and others protested that by owning it, he appeared to be a party to Brown's underhanded dealings.[41] Rebecca L. Felton, fiery wife of Dr. William H. Felton and bitter enemy of Brown, observed that a general truce existed between the two men. "Mr. Stephens was never at 'outs' with Governor Brown after the Confederacy collapsed," she wrote in 1911. "He might have been fractious if Governor Brown had ever put his finger in his congressional campaigns—but they agreed to stand apart and each 'tote his own skillet.' "[42] The only postwar campaign in which Brown and Stephens cooperated was in 1882 when Stephens ran for governor. Brown, to the chagrin of his brother James and Augustus O. Bacon, backed Stephens and discouraged possible rivals.[43]

Regardless of what political group he associated himself with, Brown quickly occupied a position of leadership. As a Republican during the Bullock administration, he became the final arbiter of federal patronage in the state. Robert Toombs acknowledged this fact when he described Brown as the covert "Gov[erno]r of Georgia [for] nearly two years, administering the patronage of the military, and had the whole patronage of Bullock at his feet."[44] Brown's influence with various national Republican administrations continued even after he rejoined the Democratic party in 1872. As late as 1882, Georgia Republicans, trying to revive their party, had to contend with him. James Atkins, Republican politician and federal office seeker, recognized the extent of Brown's power when he advised his fellow Republican, Henry P. Farrow, "You have got to belong to the carpet-baggers; and is it not better to belong to [Colonel Alfred E.] Buck and Joe Brown than to [John E.] Bryant and Joe Brown?"[45]

The issue of patronage and the interference of Brown in the internal affairs of the state Republican party were instrumental in breaking up the Coalition in 1882. In a complicated piece of political maneuvering, Democrat Brown was able to persuade Republican Chester A. Arthur to appoint Democrat John W. H. Underwood, the archenemy of Independent

---

[40]Thompson, *Reconstruction in Georgia*, 229-31.

[41]Ibid.

[42]Felton, *Memoirs*, 69.

[43]Joseph E. Brown to Augustus O. Bacon, 25 May 1884, EEBC.

[44]Robert Toombs to Alexander H. Stephens, 9 August 1868, quoted in Thompson, *Reconstruction in Georgia*, 193.

[45]James Atkins to Henry P. Farrow, 11 August 1882, FC.

William H. Felton, to a federal judgeship in Felton's district.[46] Mrs. Felton, disgusted at the inability of state Republicans to control patronage matters, railed out against leaders who could not prevent the appointment of Underwood, who "has bitterly fought Dr. Felton in the Seventh District every time and is now representative of the anti-Felton party in that district."[47] "The republicans," she wrote to Farrow, "are as much the slaves of Brown as the Democrats are, and the only regret I have is that Dr. Felton went to the front to bear the burden of abuse and to expose the villainy of Brown and Co[mpany]."[48]

One of the keys to Brown's political success was his willingness to reward supporters with jobs, either in corporations he owned or in government. A conservative in financial matters, he nevertheless realized that money was a critical ingredient in successful campaigns.[49] Unlike Colquitt and Gordon, who were not wealthy, Brown frequently purchased the support of minor politicians in the state. A shrewd businessman, he made sure that every dollar spent in politics paid some kind of return.[50]

Brown's political and business activities were bolstered by his close connections with Evan P. Howell and Henry W. Grady, editors of the Atlanta *Constitution*. While it is impossible to prove, Brown probably controlled the *Constitution* financially. Individuals who were stockholders in various Brown companies also held stock in the *Constitution*, and Brown may have had something to do with arranging the financing for Grady's share of the paper.[51] After editing papers critical of Brown in Rome and Atlanta, Grady became an intimate of his in 1876, and the relationship grew even closer after Brown's appointment to the Senate in 1880. Certainly no other newspaper in the state was as consistent in its support of Brown as was the *Constitution*. As late as 1889, the paper argued for Brown's views on the tariff despite their unpopularity with most Georgians. "The Atlanta *Constitution*," wrote the editor of the Americus *Recorder*, "does not support the Mills Bill. It repudiates it—calls it a Republican measure, and wants the country, congress, president and the foreign nations to vote for one that

---

[46]See previous chapter.

[47]Atlanta *Post Appeal*, 17 June 1882.

[48]Rebecca L. Felton to Henry P. Farrow, 14 June 1882, FC.

[49]Parks, *Brown*, 467-74, 494.

[50]Julius L. Brown to Joseph E. Brown, 23 September 1883, HT. Ibid., 6 March 1884. See William Anderson, "The Resignation of John B. Gordon from the United States Senate in 1880," *Georgia Historical Quarterly* 52 (1968): 438-42.

[51]Nixon, *Grady*, 167-69. Cyrus W. Field to Henry W. Grady, 8 May 1880. Henry W. Grady Collection, Emory University. Hereafter referred to as HWGC. See various telegrams between Brown and Grady, 15-19 May 1880, HT.

its Josef B. will prepare—the man of pikes, fame, and convicts."[52] The *Constitution's* importance to Brown's political fortunes was noted by the Albany *News* in 1887. "Gordon and Colquitt with their war records, Joe Brown with his money judgement, and the *Constitution* with its soft soap and monumental cheek," complained the *News*, "has [*sic*] constituted a combination that has been invincible, and it will be a fine day for Georgia when it is broken."[53]

Because of his wealth, political experience, and conservative views, Brown was the logical representative of industrialists in the Triumvirate. His public acceptance of the Constitution of 1877 and the Railroad Commission, despite his private opposition, greatly facilitated their acceptance by other industrialists in the state.[54] Furthermore, despite his heresy during Reconstruction, Brown was a known political quantity to planters, many of whom had followed him in the 1850s and had admired his actions as Georgia's wartime governor. Although he had authored the court decision giving Negroes the right to hold office, Democratic control of the political system had rendered that decision practically worthless, and Brown's general social and political views were conservative enough for most planters.[55]

Businessmen also benefited from Brown's presence on the Triumvirate. His political acumen and his ability to compromise on critical issues ensured moderation in state government. His knowledge of Georgia politicians and his willingness to aid supporters with money and patronage gave him a formidable power that translated into political influence for the business community far beyond what simple numbers would ordinarily dictate. Brown's domination of the editorial policy of the Atlanta *Constitution* was important, since it was the most important newspaper in Georgia and the entire South. Henry W. Grady, the eloquent editor of the *Constitution*, used its pages to expound the glories of the New South and the blessings of industrialization, and businessmen reaped the benefits of his rhetoric.

Colquitt and Brown provided the balance that made the coalition of planters and industrialists work. The third position in the Triumvirate was that of governor. Initially considered unimportant, the governor's office was used as a "safety valve" to release the frustrations of ambitious younger

---

[52]Americus *Recorder*, 5 April 1888.

[53]Albany *News*, reprinted in the Macon *Telegraph*, 7 October 1887.

[54]Ward, "Georgia under the Bourbon Democrats," 243-45. Atlanta *Constitution*, 5 June 1877. Joseph E. Brown to Julius L. Brown, 6, 9 June 1877, HT.

[55]Parks, *Brown*, 481-85. Although Brown authored the decision recognizing the right of Negroes to hold public office, Parks insists that the ruling was based on "the pressure of necessity" and that he "steadfastly opposed social equality."

politicians within the Democratic party—men who might upset the alliance of planters and businessmen. In particular, the governor's office became the bone of contention between politicians in Macon and Atlanta as well as between the *Constitution* and its chief rival, the Macon *Telegraph.* [56] The election of John B. Gordon as governor in 1886 gave the office real importance, and ultimately it became the most important position in the Triumvirate.

If any politician ever deserved the name "opportunist," it was John B. Gordon. A bona fide Confederate hero, he had risen from the rank of captain to that of Lieutenant General. On Lee's staff, Gordon was present at the surrender of the Army of Northern Virginia at Appomattox. He was every inch the personification of the dashing Confederate officer, complete with a prominent scar on his cheek from a Union minie ball, and his political stock-in-trade was to capitalize on his fame as a general. "Bob Toombs once said," wrote the editor of the Marietta *Journal* in 1886, "that if Gordon's scar was somewhere else than on his face he would be a failure as a politician."[57]

Gordon's political career began in 1868. That was the year the Ku Klux Klan began operations in Georgia, and he was reputed to be the state's Grand Dragon.[58] He was unsuccessful as a Democratic candidate for governor in 1868, but his loss did nothing to lessen his popularity with white Georgians.[59] Gordon's reward for opposing Bullock and the Republicans was his election to the United States Senate when the Democrats regained control of state government. In the Senate, he was regarded as a servant of the railroad interests and as a man whose vote could be readily purchased.[60] Reelected to the Senate in 1878, Gordon served until 1880 when he resigned to go into business. From 1880 until 1886, he was involved in a number of railroad building projects, most of which were unsuccessful.

Gordon's financial ability, like Colquitt's, was suspect. A born promoter, he regularly involved himself in one grandiose scheme after another in futile attempts to make a fortune. His popularity as a war hero and his ability to gain public office enabled him to attract investors for numerous railroad, land development, industrial, insurance, and farming ventures. Throughout his career, Gordon used his public offices to promote his private business projects. In 1887, for example, while governor, he became a partner in the Tallapoosa Land Company and used the pres-

---

[56]Nixon, *Grady*, 207-11.

[57]Marietta *Journal*, 13 June 1886. See also Allen P. Tankersly, *John B. Gordon: A Study in Gallantry* (Atlanta: Whitehall Press, 1955).

[58]Trelease, *White Terror*, 20, 74-79.

[59]Nathans, *Losing the Peace*, 84-93. Conway, *Reconstruction of Georgia*, 156-61.

[60]Felton, *Memoirs*, 484-85. Woodward, *Origins*, 37-46.

tige of his office to entice investors into the company.[61] In 1888, still governor, he used the official stationary of the Executive Department to urge a group of Georgia citizens to invest in a company to develop the town of Rockmart. A natural promoter, Gordon described the town's prospects in glowing terms. Like all Gordon-backed enterprises, this one was portrayed as a guaranteed money-maker. "Over $200,000 has been taken in in the last few days," he wrote to Dr. George L. Smith of Toombsboro, "and I am anxious that just as many of our own folks shall be interested as possible." The money invested in Rockmart, Gordon continued, was "not really an investment but a temporary loan on the amplest security, and will be promptly returned with interest, leaving your entire stock in the enterprise clear profit."[62]

In addition to using his office to attract investors in his own projects, Gordon also authorized the use of his name and position to aid his son, Hugh H. Gordon—a lobbyist, in soliciting customers. In 1887, Hugh Gordon contacted various Southern railroad companies and asked them to hire him to lobby Congress for damages incurred during the Civil War. He listed as his major qualification the fact that his father was "General Gordon, who is well known both officially and personally in Washington, [and who] has promised to aid me in every way in his power . . . and with my Father's influence and cooperation, we can certainly succeed if success is possible."[63] While he was busy soliciting business from the railroads, Hugh Gordon was also peddling his services and his father's influence to persons and corporations who wanted favors from the Georgia General Assembly. Virtually nothing was impossible, he assured one potential customer, because "the leaders of the House—the ablest and most influential members—are my personal friends."[64]

Gordon's willingness to sell the influence of the governor's office was not the first instance of his using a public trust to make money. His guiding principle was summed up in a letter he wrote to an employee of the International Railroad, a Gordon corporation in Florida. "Discretion, caution, secresy [sic] and the blinding of the public to our real designs," he wrote, "is absolutely necessary to the accomplishment of my purposes."[65] Although writing about a business project, Gordon had followed

---

[61]Macon *Telegraph*, 21 August 1887.

[62]John B. Gordon to Dr. George L. Smith et al., 24 October 1888, John B. Gordon Letterbooks, 1886-1890, Georgia Department of Archives and History. Hereafter referred to as GL.

[63]Hugh H. Gordon to W. C. Wickham et al., 29 December 1887, Hugh H. Gordon Letterbooks, Georgia Department of Archives and History. Hereafter referred to as HGL.

[64]Hugh H. Gordon to Messers. Miller, 5 October 1887, HGL.

[65]John B. Gordon to Captain Charles F. Smith, 17 May 1883, GL.

this philosophy while a U. S. Senator in the 1870s. In 1876, he was named in a scandal that erupted in the Senate over an attempt to get congressional approval for $223 million to finance the construction of Thomas A. Scott's Texas-Pacific Railroad.[66] Gordon's involvement with Scott was so intimate that he was referred to as one of "Tom Scott's Democrats" in the Washington press.[67]

In 1880, Gordon was accused of selling his Senate seat to Joseph E. Brown. Despite denials by both men, recent evidence has been made public proving beyond any shadow of doubt that collusion was present and that money changed hands. The price Gordon received for his resignation from the Senate was a job as a lawyer with the Louisville and Nashville Railroad at a salary of $14,000 a year.[68] Although it was a major political scandal, Gordon managed to survive the resignation controversy with little damage to his popularity with Georgia voters.

Like his friend Colquitt, Gordon was a business failure, but failure did not prevent him from trying new ventures. In 1876, the Southern Life Insurance Company, a Gordon enterprise, was forced into bankruptcy despite having assets of over $1.5 million. On the very day the bankruptcy petition was filed in federal court in Atlanta, Gordon was busy soliciting policies from unwary customers.[69] Individuals who had purchased stock and policies from the company, largely on the strength of Gordon's reputation as a war hero, eventually received only $11 per thousand invested in the bankruptcy settlement.[70] Following his resignation from the Senate, Gordon became an attorney for the L & N but left this position to become president of the Georgia-Pacific Railroad in 1883. By 1885, he was involved in building the International Railroad in Florida, a project that died when the state's legislature failed to grant him a subsidy. The failure of this project exhausted Gordon's finances, and he had great difficulty in meeting even his household expenses.

Even after his election as governor in 1886, Gordon's creditors continued to hound him for payment.[71] "There is no truth whatsoever," he wrote to one creditor, "in the statement that I have made a million or any other

---

[66]Felton, *Memoirs*, 79-143. Woodward, *Origins*, 31-44.

[67]Washington (DC) *Union*, 20 February 1877, quoted in Woodward, *Origins*, 44.

[68]Telegrams between Henry W. Grady and Joseph E. Brown, 15-19 May 1880, HT. Anderson, "Resignation," 438-42.

[69]Felton, *Memoirs*, 632-40.

[70]W. M. McIntosh to Alfred H. Colquitt, 18 October 1882, ICAHC.

[71]John B. Gordon to Jno. R. Dos Passos, 2 December 1886, GL. Gordon asked Dos Passos not to file a suit to recover money Gordon owed him since it would be embarrassing and would not result in payment. Gordon insisted he had no money with which to pay his creditors.

sum—I wish it were true. My whole railroad enterprise is at a stand[still] and has been for a long time. I am greatly embarrassed to meet the most pressing obligations."[72] To another creditor he wrote, "The money I owe you shall be paid to the last farthing. It is due, however, to myself, to tell you frankly that I cannot pay it at present and that you must bear with me."[73] After a string of unsuccessful business ventures, Gordon was broke. The only commodity he had left in 1886 to sell was his popularity as a Confederate hero, and that, like everything Gordon had ever had, was up for sale to the highest bidder.

The gubernatorial election of 1880 was the last campaign in which Gordon had actively worked. Despite his six-year absence from the state—or perhaps because of it—he possessed considerable appeal for Georgia voters.[74] When the Atlanta-based clique of politicians led by Henry W. Grady faced losing their control of the governor's office to Augustus O. Bacon and Macon politicians, Gordon was brought out of political retirement to meet the threat. For Grady, seeking a candidate with enough personal appeal to overcome the machine Bacon had been building for over ten years, Gordon appeared to be the logical choice to guarantee success.[75]

There were those who saw Gordon's candidacy in another light. One political observer wrote to Dr. Felton, an avowed Gordon hater, that the General's comeback was being orchestrated by Joseph E. Brown, who wanted "to secure a man as Governor friendly to him in the convict lease business—his present lease expiring in a year, and he wishes for this privilege of special slavery to him continued and hence he will be for Gordon—*though he despises him.* "[76] Gordon's reputation as a political prostitute was enough to convince his enemies that he was entering the gubernatorial race in order to sell that office to special interests in the state. Because Brown's convict lease and his lease on the Western and Atlantic Railroad were due to expire soon, he was suspected of being the mastermind behind Gordon's sudden candidacy.[77]

Regardless of the reasons behind his decision to return to politics, Gordon's entry into the gubernatorial race of 1886 and his subsequent victory marked a turning point in his life.[78] While he exploited the power and in-

---

[72]Ibid.

[73]John B. Gordon to Morton Rose and Company, 2 December 1886, GL.

[74]James Gaston Towery, "The Georgia Gubernatorial Campaign of 1886" (Master's thesis, Emory University, 1945) 15.

[75]Tankersly, *Gordon*, 329-33.

[76]W. H. Hiddell to William H. Felton, 2 May 1886, WRFC. Italics mine.

[77]Ward, "Georgia under the Bourbon Democrats," 176-89. Parks, *Brown*, 560-64. Macon *Telegraph*, 6 December 1888. Americus *Recorder*, 1 March 1888.

[78]To be discussed more fully in the next chapter.

fluence of the governor's office to rebuild his finances, he also gave the state four years of efficient, scandal-free government. In many ways, he fulfilled the earlier expectations Georgians had for him. When he returned to the U. S. Senate in 1891, Gordon left behind him a record of reform unequalled by any previous postwar governor.[79]

Gordon's election also marked a turning point in the planter-industrialist coalition that had governed the state since 1877. On the surface, Gordon appeared to be an ideal candidate to perpetuate the alliance, since he symbolized the dynamic fusion of the Old and New Souths. When he was elected in 1886, few. people expected much from him in the way of innovation, and fewer still expected him to escape from office unscathed by scandal.

---

[79]Gordon made some small efforts in upgrading the care and conditions of convicts by fining lessees for inflicting excessive punishment and for failing to provide adequate care. Although his efforts were only nominal, the fines imposed represented the first real attempt by the State to reassert its authority over and responsibility to convicts.

CHAPTER 9

THE GORDON YEARS

The election of Alexander H. Stephens as governor in 1882 ushered in a new era of postwar politics in Georgia. The rout of the Coalition in October and the subsequent defeat of William H. Felton in his November bid to reclaim his old congressional seat marked the end of an active two-party system in the state for at least a decade.[1] The planter-New South alliance had proven its ability to defeat any possible political opposition, and the debacle of 1882 left Independents and Republicans suspicious and resentful of each other and quite unwilling to attempt fusion again. For the first time since 1868, the Democratic party faced no opposition in Georgia.[2]

The absence of opposition guaranteed Democratic control of all state offices and most local ones as well. Consequently, the need for party unity was less acute, and feuds and rivalries buried during the 1870s blossomed into vicious interparty fights during the 1880s. The most important of these was the rivalry between Macon businessmen, led by Augustus O. Bacon, and Atlanta industrialists, led by Henry W. Grady, over who would dominate the New South movement in the state. The prize both groups sought was control of the governor's office and the prestige that came with it. Planters, secure in their command of the General Assembly and the Democratic party, encouraged the businessmen to fight among themselves. As long as the men of the New South were so engaged, they could not effectively challenge the hegemony of planters whose power was strengthened by each division in the business community.

The unexpected death of Stephens in early 1883, after only three months as governor, created a vacuum in state politics. Because it was so soon after the rancorous fight with the Coalition, the Democrats had no candidate groomed to take Stephens's place. Under the provisions of the Constitution of 1877, James S. Boynton, the president of the Georgia Senate, became the acting governor until a new governor could be chosen in a special election. Acting quickly, the General Assembly scheduled the

[1]Jones, "William H. Felton," 235-55.

[2]Shadgett, *Republican Party in Georgia,* 76-89.

election for the first week in May, less than two months after the death of Stephens.

The short time between March and May made it necessary for the Democratic party to nominate a candidate quickly. The Democratic Executive Committee, responding to the urgency of the situation, called for a party convention to be held on 10 April in Atlanta. Four men announced their intentions to seek the nomination. Henry D. McDaniel, Philip Cook, and James S. Boynton, all relatively unknown in state politics, were considered to be weak candidates, while the fourth hopeful, Augustus O. Bacon, had served ten years as the Speaker of the Georgia House and was given the best chance of winning the nomination. Bacon, the leader of Macon's Democratic organization, had the backing of the Macon *Telegraph*, the state's second most influential newspaper, and he was popular with most members of the General Assembly.

In Atlanta, the prospect of a Bacon victory caused a great deal of consternation. Henry W. Grady, the ramrod of the Atlanta *Constitution*, regarded a Bacon triumph as a personal defeat at the hands of his archrival, the *Telegraph*. Despite his lackluster political past and his lack of experience, Boynton received the backing of Grady and the *Constitution*. Charging Bacon with destroying the party "harmony" achieved with Stephens's election, Grady urged him to forsake his ambitions.[3]

Grady's admonition to Bacon was only the first sally in a bitter squabble between the *Telegraph* and the *Constitution*, between Macon and Atlanta, and between Bacon and Boynton that dominated the pre-convention activity. Bacon and the *Telegraph* responded by attacking the *Constitution* and the "Atlanta Ring" as being dictators within the party and by advising Democrats to abandon their allegiance to old political leaders. Due bills, they argued, had been issued in the past in return for party unity, and one of these bills—the promise of the gubernatorial nomination for Bacon—was to be collected in 1883. When asked to withdraw his candidacy in 1880 and 1882 in the interest of party harmony, Bacon had complied, and in exchange Democratic officials had given their tacit approval for a campaign at some later date. Since the Democrats faced no opposition in 1883, Bacon supporters called upon the party to honor the commitments made in previous years.[4]

When the convention assembled on 10 April, no one could predict the outcome of the balloting. On the first vote, the Bacon and Boynton forces appeared to be fairly evenly matched. Boynton received 139 votes, Bacon gathered 136, Henry D. McDaniel pulled 36, and Philip Cook won only 20. The balloting continued the second day, and although Bacon man-

---

[3]Nixon, *Grady*, 208-09. Ward, "Georgia under the Bourbon Democrats," 162.

[4]Augustus O. Bacon to Joseph E. Brown, 22 May 1882; Joseph E. Brown to Augustus O. Bacon, 25 May 1882, EEBC.

aged to gain a slight edge over Boynton, he could not get enough votes to secure the majority necessary for nomination. As the second day ended, Cook withdrew his name from consideration, and shortly thereafter McDaniel announced that he would drop out of the race the next morning. With McDaniel and Cook apparently out of contention, it appeared that Bacon would be nominated on the first ballot the following day. Most of the delegates pledged to McDaniel—enough to give Bacon a clear majority—were expected to switch to him. The Macon/Bacon group seemed to be on the verge of defeating the Atlanta/Grady/Boynton forces.[5]

Although Bacon's victory seemed assured, Henry W. Grady worked through the night to prevent it. Hurrying from delegation to delegation, he abandoned Boynton and adopted McDaniel as a compromise candidate. From Judge Rufus T. Dorsey, the leader of the Boynton forces, he secured a promise to commit Boynton delegates to McDaniel if it appeared that Bacon would be able to gain a majority. The next day, he managed to keep Cook and McDaniel from withdrawing and thus prevented Bacon from getting the necessary votes. Finally the convention decided to refer the nomination to a special committee as a means of breaking the deadlock. Each candidate was allowed to select members of the eighteen-man committee according to the number of votes he had received in the balloting. Boynton and Bacon, as the top contenders, were allowed to pick six members each; while McDaniel, as the candidate with the third highest vote total, was given the right to name four members. Cook, despite his earlier announcement of withdrawal, could name two members.

When the committee met, McDaniel asked that his name be withdrawn from consideration. With three candidates still in the running, Bacon received a plurality on the first ballot. Before a second ballot could be taken, Judge Dorsey announced that the Boynton delegates were switching their support to McDaniel. With his original four votes and the six additional Boynton votes, McDaniel received a majority. Despite the protests of Bacon and his supporters, the committee recommended McDaniel to the convention, which promptly ratified the committee's decision.[6]

The nomination of Henry D. McDaniel was an important, and almost singlehanded, victory for Henry W. Grady who regarded Bacon's defeat as a personal triumph of the greatest magnitude. In a letter to Estelle Cuyler Smith, a house guest he had missed seeing because of his lobbying efforts, Grady explained his reasons for opposing Bacon. "To have had Bacon elected by the [Macon] *Tel[egraph]* and *Mess[enger]* would have disgraced and hurt me," he wrote. "Almost everyone gave it up but me. But I was determined to die with it if necessary. There I was at the hotel with the very ground slipping from under my very feet—fighting against odds

---

[5]Ward, "Georgia under the Bourbon Democrats," 162-64. Nixon, *Grady*, 208-11.

[6]Atlanta *Constitution*, 10-13 April 1883. Macon *Telegraph*, 10-13 April 1883.

and a hopeless fight. But I tell you now that if I had come home that night Bacon would have been Governor."[7]

The Democratic nomination assured McDaniel of election because the Republicans and Independents did not name a candidate. Although the Macon/Bacon group had been defeated in the convention, the conflict over the leadership of the New South movement had not been resolved. From his position as Speaker of the House, Bacon began a careful campaign to win the gubernatorial nomination in 1886. Although a Democratic convention would meet again in 1884 to select a nominee for that year's election, Bacon was willing to concede the nomination to McDaniel. The next open convention would be in 1886, and Bacon intended to control it from start to finish.

McDaniel was renominated in 1884, and he was elected with no Republican or Independent opposition once again. Although he was legally eligible to serve another term, he decided not to stand for reelection in 1886. A governor, he announced, "should not ask for reelection unless there were pending some great political question which divided the people, and in which he was the *natural representative* of his party, or unless there had been such an arraignment of his administration that an appeal to the people was necessary." Since the McDaniel administration had not aroused much opposition and because there were no divisive political questions to be answered, McDaniel refused to become a candidate again "merely for the purpose of holding office another term."[8]

McDaniel's decision not to run again strengthened Bacon's claim on the nomination. With no other candidate on the horizon, it appeared that the 1886 convention would be only a *pro forma* exercise of the obvious. In the years after his 1883 defeat, Bacon had built a statewide network of approximately 1500 former legislators and local politicians who were pledged to work for his nomination.[9] Because the method of selecting convention delegates was left to local party bosses, Bacon's extensive organizational efforts were expected to produce enough delegates to give him a first ballot victory.

When Henry McDaniel refused to seek another term of office, Grady, the *Constitution,* and the Atlanta industrialists were left with no candidate to represent them. Bacon's political machine precluded the kind of behind-the-scenes maneuvering that had been successful in 1883, so it was necessary for Grady and the *Constitution* to come up with a candidate who could short-circuit Bacon's plans. In February 1886, a second candidate from the Macon area, Judge Thomas J. Simmons, announced his desire

---

[7]Henry W. Grady to Estelle Cuyler Smith, 18 May 1883, HWGC.

[8]Atlanta *Constitution,* 14 March 1884.

[9]Nixon, *Grady,* 225-26.

to become the Democratic gubernatorial nominee. A popular judge, Simmons was regarded by some Georgians as a stalking horse for the yet unnamed candidate of the "Atlanta Ring." Bacon and the *Telegraph* reacted immediately to the judge's announcement. Simmons, they claimed, was guilty of a serious conflict of interest because he continued to hold his judicial office despite his announced candidacy. If he wanted to become a candidate, he should resign his judgeship.[10] The *Constitution* defended Simmons, and it argued that no conflict existed until Simmons actually received the nomination.[11]

A few days after he announced his intention to run, Simmons proposed a test of the viability of his candidacy. If he did not receive two-thirds of the delegates to the Democratic convention in primary elections in Bibb, Houston, Crawford, Monroe, Jones, and Twiggs Counties, he would withdraw from the race.[12] The Columbus *Sentinel*, a strong Bacon supporter, called the proposal "fair" and urged Bacon to accept Simmons's offer. It had "the true ring of magnanimity" and obviously came "from the heart of one who has the good of our state in view."[13] Bacon, confident of his organization, accepted the challenge, and both men began to campaign vigorously.

While Bacon and Simmons engaged in their pre-convention battle, the *Constitution* injected a new element into the contest by frequently mentioning John B. Gordon as a possible candidate.[14] Gordon had been inactive in state politics since the election of 1880. After resigning his seat in the U. S. Senate, he had been involved in a number of business ventures, most of which had not been successful. In 1886, he was living a precarious existence in New York while seeking financial backing for several projects in Florida. His attempts to secure either a cabinet position or a diplomatic appointment had failed, and the publication of the Collis P. Huntington letters, which revealed that he had sold his vote while in the Senate, made it unlikely that a government appointment would be forthcoming. Broke and apparently without prospects, Gordon was, as his biographer described him, "down at the elbows."[15] Despite his tarnished reputation as a financier and politician, nothing could detract from Gor-

---

[10]Macon *Telegraph*, 9 February 1886. Lala Carr Steelman, "The Public Career of Augustus Octavius Bacon" (Ph.D. diss., University of North Carolina, 1950) 73.

[11]Atlanta *Constitution*, 18 April 1886.

[12]Ibid., 28 February 1886.

[13]Columbus *Sentinel*, reprinted in the Atlanta *Constitution*, 7 March 1886.

[14]Atlanta *Constitution*, 28 March 1886. Macon *Telegraph*, 6, 18, 21 April 1886. Steelman, "Bacon," 73.

[15]Tankersly, *Gordon*, 328-29. Nixon, *Grady*, 225-27.

don's record as a Confederate hero; it was this record that Grady hoped
to sell to the people of Georgia.[16]

The rumors of Gordon's impending candidacy received mixed reac-
tions from the state's newspapers. The Hartwell *Sun,* a Bacon advocate,
labeled the rumored candidacy an "unwarrented [sic] intrusion upon the
wishes of the people of Georgia."[17] The Americus *Recorder,* a neutral paper, took a more evenhanded approach. "Gen[eral] Gordon has just as
good a right to run for Governor as any other man," it argued, "and the
people have just as good a right to sit down upon his aspirations as any
other man. They have paid him all they owe him, and honors are easy."[18]
Bacon viewed the possible entry of Gordon into the race with considerable apprehension. "Up to now I have regarded my nomination as certain," he wrote to the editors of the Acworth *News and Farmer,* "but now I
am not so sure."[19]

The opportunity for Gordon to make his official entry into the race for
the Democratic nomination soon appeared. Jefferson Davis, through
Grady's manipulations, had been invited to lay the cornerstone of a mon-
ument to the Confederate dead, an event scheduled for early May in
Montgomery. Gordon also accepted an invitation to attend the ceremony,
and the spectacle of two former Confederate leaders on the same platform provided Grady with the perfect occasion to create a "spontaneous"
Gordon for governor movement.[20] All eyes would be focused on Montgomery, on Jefferson Davis, and on Gordon; it was too good to pass up.

Davis's appearance in Montgomery touched off a wave of nostalgia for
all things Confederate. On a widely publicized trip from Montgomery to
Atlanta, Davis and Gordon were met by thousands of former Confederate
soldiers who lined the railroad tracks hoping to get a glimpse of their former commander-in-chief. When the Davis-Gordon entourage reached
Atlanta, an estimated 100,000 people were on hand to greet them. Their
joint appearance boosted Gordon's chances as a gubernatorial candidate,
although he was very careful to avoid any reference to the upcoming convention. For almost a week, Davis's visit occupied the front pages of
Southern and national newspapers, and John B. Gordon was promi-
nently mentioned in most of the stories.[21]

After several days in Atlanta, Davis and Gordon journeyed to Savannah
to participate in the centennial celebration of the Chatham Artillery. On 7

---

[16]Woodward, *Origins,* 15-17.

[17]Hartwell *Sun,* reprinted in the Atlanta *Constitution,* 10 May 1886.

[18]Americus *Recorder,* 7 May 1886.

[19]Acworth *News and Farmer,* reprinted in the Marietta *Journal,* 13 May 1886.

[20]Nixon, *Grady,* 225-31.

[21]Atlanta *Constitution,* 25 April-10 May, 1886.

May, while still in the city, Gordon released a letter to the public in which he proclaimed that he was bowing to the "absolutely spontaneous" demands of the people of Georgia and becoming a candidate for the Democratic gubernatorial nomination. His announcement took no one by surprise because it had been expected all week and because it merely stated formally what was already so painfully apparent to Bacon: years of hard work were in jeopardy—his nomination was no longer certain.[22] At Gordon's formal announcement, Judge Simmons immediately withdrew from the race. Although he cited ill health as his reason, Simmons had done his work well; with Gordon in the running, there was no need for him to continue.[23]

Gordon's entry into the race for convention delegates produced a rather unusual and shortlived coalition of political leaders. William H. Felton, long an opponent of the Macon *Telegraph* and A. O. Bacon, offered his support to Bacon since he found the alternative of "Gordon, Colquit [*sic*], Brown and Co[mpany]" even more unpalatable.[24] Dr. Felton offered to stump the state for Bacon, and Mrs. Felton volunteered to write letters to the press attacking Gordon.[25] Correspondence between the Feltons and Alexander H. Stephens, written during their happy association in the 1870s, was widely published in anti-Gordon newspapers. One letter by Stephens referred to Gordon as a man who was "hollow hearted, deceitful, unprincipled and dishonorable and unreliable in every way."[26] In addition to supplying copies of the Stephens correspondence to the press, Mrs. Felton wrote articles that revived the charges of corruption against the General.[27]

The willingness of the Feltons to forget old quarrels and to throw their support to Bacon was questioned by both pro-Bacon and pro-Gordon papers. Many editors, after years of fighting the Feltons, were suspicious of their motives. The Athens *Banner*, a strong Bacon paper, accused Felton of trying to create chaos so that he could "get in a position where gubernatorial lightning will probably strike him."[28] Similar statements were made by the editors of the *Constitution*, the Atlanta *Journal*, the Columbus *En-*

---

[22]Americus *Recorder*, 8 May 1886. J. F. Hanson to Rebecca L. Felton, 30 April 1886, WRFC.

[23]Macon *Telegraph*, 9 May 1886.

[24]J. F. Hanson to Rebecca L. Felton, 30 April 1886, WRFC.

[25]Thomas C. Crenshaw to William H. Felton, 15 May 1886; Augustus O. Bacon to William H. Felton, 15 May 1886, WRFC. Mrs. Felton's letters were printed under the nom de plume "Plaintalk."

[26]Alexander H. Stephens to Rebecca L. Felton, 14 September 1880, WRFC.

[27]Atlanta *Journal*, 1 June 1886.

[28]Athens *Banner*, 3 June 1886.

quirer-Sun, and various other newspapers in the state.[29] The coalition of the Feltons and Bacon was an uneasy one at best, and neither side completely trusted the other. Nevertheless, the participation of Dr. and Mrs. Felton in the campaign enlivened an already interesting contest.

One of the questions that intrigued Georgians in 1886 was just how much support Gordon would receive from Alfred H. Colquitt and Joseph E. Brown. Gordon played down the involvement of these two men, and he publicly stated that "Senator Brown did not desire him to stand for Governor." As far as his friend Colquitt was concerned, Gordon "thought Senator Colquitt was [also] opposed to his making the race."[30] Even the editor of the Macon *Telegraph* was undecided about the extent to which the two permanent members of the so-called "Triumvirate" welcomed Gordon's candidacy. "Reports are conflicting as to the attitude of Brown and Colquitt," he wrote to Rebecca L. Felton. "Some say they tried to keep him out of the race while others attribute such [a] position to Brown and claim that Colquitt, through Grady, has done the work of bringing him out. I don't know how this is."[31] This interpretation of events was probably correct because Joseph E. Brown had little respect for the man from whom he had purchased his Senate seat. Regardless of what the facts were, Gordon, Colquitt, and Brown were linked together in the public's mind.

The *South Georgia Clarion,* a Bacon paper, informed its readers that Gordon would "undoubtedly have the backing of Brown and Colquitt in what is called the Atlanta Ring, and who doubts their tremendous power?"[32] The Cuthbert *Liberal* was equally sure that the two Senators were manipulating Gordon for their own purposes. "Try to disguise the fact as much as we may, pooh-pooh at it if you will, but it is a fact," wrote the *Liberal's* editor, "that a knot of Atlanta politicians have for some time directed the affairs of the State."[33] The Athens *Banner* assured its readers that Gordon's entry into the race for the nomination was only one aspect of the struggle "between the people and the Atlanta ring."[34] William H. Hidell, the editor of the Rome *Courier* and a close friend of the Feltons, concurred. "It is the people of the whole State," he wrote to Dr. Felton, "[versus] the most corrupt ring *in Atlanta* that ever disgraced any state capital in the United States."[35] Through-

---

[29]Atlanta *Constitution,* 17 June 1886. Atlanta *Journal,* 1 June 1886. Columbus *Enquirer-Sun,* 21 May; 2 June 1886. Sparta *Ishmaelite,* reprinted in the Atlanta *Constitution,* 7 June 1886.

[30]Barnesville *Gazette,* reprinted in the Americus *Recorder,* 19 June 1886.

[31]J. F. Hanson to Rebecca L. Felton, reprinted in Felton, *Memoirs,* 631.

[32]*South Georgia Clarion,* reprinted in Americus *Recorder,* 19 May 1886.

[33]Cuthbert *Liberal,* ibid.

[34]Athens *Banner,* ibid., 22 May 1886.

[35]William H. Hiddell to William H. Felton, 2 May 1886, WRFC.

out the contest for convention delegates, Brown and Colquitt maintained complete silence on Gordon's candidacy.[36]

Once he had entered the race for the nomination, Gordon was forced to wage an aggressive campaign in order to offset the advantages Bacon's organization gave him. Gordon concentrated his attack on the issue of popular primaries versus county conventions as a means of selecting delegates to the state convention.[37] "Since the restoration of Georgia to the Union," he told an audience in Haralson County, "I have hoped and prayed that the primary system of selecting candidates would become established practice in Georgia."[38] In previous state contests, Gordon had made no such plea for primaries, but in 1886 they were the only possible way for him to defeat the "machine" Bacon had been building for years. In a popularity contest, the Gordon wit, reputation, and oratorical ability would certainly triumph over the less flamboyant Bacon.

Primaries were not the only issue used by Gordon. In a series of speeches in May and June, he developed a five-point program to solve some of the controversial questions in state politics. Gordon's platform enunciated some rather strong positions, and none attracted as much comment as his stand on the Railroad Commission. Created by the General Assembly in 1878 after the Constitution of 1877 had mandated it, the Railroad Commission was a bone of contention between planters in the older section of the Black Belt and merchants/planters in the more recently opened areas of southwest Georgia. Where antebellum railroads were still in operation, planters supported the Commission as an effective check on the power of industrialists and as a means of limiting competition from the newer cotton growing regions of the state.[39] In the newly developed southwest, planters and merchants blamed the Commission for preventing needed railroad construction.[40]

By advocating a strong Commission, Gordon did not alienate Atlanta industrialists because new railroads would only increase competition for existing roads and lessen their power. Furthermore, Gordon's stand on this issue appealed to the planters in the old Black Belt, and these were

---

[36]Brown's most recent biographer, Parks, *Brown,* fails to even mention the election of 1886 in his account of Brown's postwar political career.

[37]Towery, "Campaign of 1886," 25-41.

[38]Marietta *Journal,* 16 May 1886.

[39]Small, *Stenographic Report,* 105-106, 389-410.

[40]Americus *Recorder,* 1 February; 25, 27 June 1884. Columbus *Enquirer-Sun,* reprinted in the Americus *Recorder,* 21 February 1885. The Commission was attacked as being responsible for "impeding commerce and scaring away capitalists," for hindering "the flow of outside capital," and for standing "in the way of the building of some new railroads."

men he wanted to impress the most.[41] His support of the Commission also won Gordon the backing of many small farmers, sharecroppers and tenants, who would lose more of their limited income if freight rates were allowed to go unregulated. The selection of the Railroad Commission as an issue with which to attract the interest and support of the people was a stroke of genius for Gordon, and his strong stand in favor of the Commission won him many followers.

The second and third planks in his platform concerned the state-owned Western and Atlantic Railroad. This road, controlled by a syndicate headed by Joseph E. Brown, was scheduled to be returned to the state in 1890, and many people feared that Brown would be awarded a new lease. The original lease, signed during the controversial Bullock administration, had been granted under suspicious circumstances, and despite a legislative investigation that cleared Brown, many Georgians believed that he had bribed Bullock in order to get the lease.[42] Gordon suggested that the state resume operation of the Western and Atlantic instead of leasing it. His proposal drew immediate criticism from Bacon supporters, and they accused Gordon of wanting the lease himself or of wanting to run the road "in the interest of Atlanta, and not the State of Georgia."[43]

Quickly responding to his critics, Gordon refuted the charges that he wanted control of the W & A by reminding them that he had had an opportunity to become a partner with Brown in 1870. "I had a chance to own part of it once," he protested, "and my action in the matter you can find in the record in Atlanta. I could have made $5,000 in five minutes at a time when I was much in need of it." He had passed up the chance, he went on to say, because he considered the circumstances surrounding the awarding of the lease to be "dishonorable." "I tried to persuade myself that I could honorably do anything Hill, Stephens, and others could do," he continued, "but I could not do it."[44] Gordon might well have had such an opportunity, but nowhere does his name appear on the lists of stockholders for any of the companies that competed for the lease. Although his stand on the Western and Atlantic lease might have been construed as a direct attack on Brown, no response or protest was forthcoming. Brown's

---

[41]Parks, *Brown*, 501, 567-68. Brown, Georgia's leading railroad magnate, approved of regulation in limited form. In 1882, he was offered $50,000 to "change the State Constitution and alter the whole Commission business." If he was successful, he would receive an additional $50,000. There is no evidence in either the public records or his private correspondence to indicate he tried. Julius L. Brown to Joseph E. Brown, 23 September 1883, HT.

[42]Thompson, *Reconstruction in Georgia*, 231-34. Nathans, *Losing the Peace*, 206-20. Conway, *Reconstruction of Georgia*, 192-97.

[43]Albany *News*, reprinted in the Americus *Recorder*, 18 June 1886.

[44]Americus *Recorder*, 13 May 1886.

biographer maintains that he had decided as early as 1883 to divest himself of the road because it was no longer paying dividends.[45]

The last two planks in the Gordon platform called for the reformation of the convict lease system. Gordon had been a partner in one of the companies granted a convict lease, but in 1886 he called for the abolition of the system. Instead of leasing convicts, he proposed that the state devise some humane way of dealing with its prisoners.[46] Despite his earlier connection with the lease, Gordon claimed that he was no longer involved with any company using convict labor, and he argued that his former association with the lessees gave him a special insight into the problem. Interestingly, he managed to place responsibility for the horrors of the system on Bacon, who, as a member of the General Assembly, had approved the leases. With his call for reform of the convict leases, Gordon created strong ties with members of Georgia's emerging reform movement.[47]

Bacon was caught off guard by the Gordon platform, and he belatedly issued one of his own. Bacon's three-point platform reflected his training as a lawyer, and although he echoed Gordon's stand on the Commission, convict lease, and the Western and Atlantic lease, he softened his positions by offering an explanation of the legal problems involved in changing the status quo. While he agreed with Gordon that convict leases should be abolished, Bacon argued that the state could not tamper with the existing leases since they were valid contracts. As for his responsibility for approving the leases, he explained that he was only one of many legislators who had voted for the leases. Such leases were necessary, he continued, because of the state's inability to clothe and house prisoners in the immediate postwar period. Bacon's stands on the Railroad Commission and the lease of the Western and Atlantic were equally lackluster. Although he approved of the Commission in principle, he was willing to see its powers curtailed. As far as the lease of the state railroad was concerned, he advocated its continuation, but with the stipulation that all stockholders in the leasing company be residents of the state. In a campaign that he had expected to be routine, Bacon now found himself having to fight for every delegate, and his "me too" response to Gordon's platform failed to impress many voters.[48]

In an attempt to regain the initiative, Bacon launched a vicious attack on his rival's past record in public office. Through the pages of the Macon *Telegraph*, he zeroed in on Gordon's activities in the Senate and on his sud-

---

[45]Parks, *Brown*, 563-64. Atlanta *Constitution*, 5 December 1886.

[46]Tankersly, *Gordon*, 339. Americus *Recorder*, 13 May 1886. Macon *Telegraph*, 2, 10 September 1887.

[47]Towery, "Campaign of 1886," 8-9.

[48]Americus *Recorder*, 14 May 1886.

den resignation in 1880. The General, Bacon charged, had turned his back on the people of Georgia when "he quietly and secretly arranged to vacate his seat in the Senate and to exchange their service and love for the sordid cumulation of Mammon." Why did Gordon choose to run for governor in 1886? "Has his gold turned to dust, and has he, like the prodigal son, who would 'fain have filled his belly upon the husks on which the swine fed,' concluded to return to his first love . . . the affections of the people of Georgia?"[49] Other Bacon newspapers followed the *Telegraph's* lead, and they filled their columns with charges that Gordon was merely the tool of Collis P. Huntington in the Senate.[50]

For each of the charges Bacon leveled against him, Gordon had a ready and often amusing answer. To the charge that he had been guilty of misconduct by resigning from the Senate, Gordon argued that he had done nothing illegal, and he added sarcastically, "Generally a fellow's not cussed or fussed after for trying to get out of office; the row occurs over his trying to get into office."[51] As for the charge that he was the tool of large corporations and railroads, he responded by making the same charge against Bacon, a corporation lawyer for the East Tennessee, Virginia, and Georgia Railroad. "I know my competitor is the candidate of the corporations, and I know their power, and if they defeat me all right," he assured an audience on 12 May, "but they are not going to beat me."[52] Because Bacon had also attacked his record as a businessman and railroad entrepreneur, Gordon felt compelled to defend his association with the Georgia-Pacific Railroad. He reminded Georgians that "three months after it was built the price of coal all over Georgia was reduced [by] one-half." With tongue in cheek, Gordon admitted that his record might be lackluster compared to Bacon's, since "I suppose he has built five or six railroads at least."[53]

May, June, and early July were filled with activity for both candidates as they canvassed the state seeking delegates. Although Bacon assumed an early lead in the delegate count, Gordon managed to reverse the trend by mid-June. In early July, the Gordon lead became a rout, and even the staunchest Bacon newspapers were admitting that their candidate was in trouble.[54] When the convention met in Atlanta on 28 July, many Bacon delegates, convinced that all was lost, refused to attend. On the first ballot

---

[49]Macon *Telegraph*, 8, 9 May 1886.

[50]Rome *Courier*, quoted in Felton, *Memoirs*, 541-44. Macon *Telegraph*, 30 May 1886.

[51]Atlanta *Journal*, 13 May 1886.

[52]Marietta *Journal*, 13 June 1886. Americus *Recorder*, 13 May 1886.

[53]Towery, "Campaign of 1886," 69-72. Atlanta *Journal*, 13 May 1886.

[54]Macon *Telegraph*, 13 June 1886. Americus *Recorder*, 30 July 1886.

252 of the 332 delegates present cast their votes for Gordon. When a motion was made to have the General's nomination declared unanimous, ten Bacon delegates refused to agree.[55] For Augustus O. Bacon, Gordon's nomination was an even greater humiliation than McDaniel's had been in 1883.

The Bacon-Gordon contest for convention delegates revealed several interesting facts about Democratic politics in Georgia. First, it reflected the mounting dissatisfaction of businessmen outside Atlanta with the leadership of Grady and the Atlanta business community. Bibb and Richmond Counties, claimants to the title of New South leader, sent strong pro-Bacon delegations to the convention. Clarke County, another emerging urban center, also supported Bacon, despite being Grady's home county. Gordon, as the candidate of Atlanta, was opposed by merchants in other cities who wanted to curtail Atlanta's growing importance. In the southwestern section of the state, three counties in the new Black Belt also supported Bacon.

Second, the campaign demonstrated that opposition to the planter-New South coalition had not dwindled in areas outside the Black Belt. Counties in North Georgia and in the Wiregrass voted against Gordon, and the coastal counties—traditional Republican strongholds—joined them. Although no complete data is available on which counties held primaries and which held conventions, apparently the counties with primaries went into the Gordon column. In some cases, Gordon was able to overcome the traditional anti-planter bias. Last, it would appear that he was also able to overcome the antagonism that had separated planters in the new and old sections of the Black Belt in previous contests.[56]

The nomination of the Democratic party was tantamount to winning, and Gordon was formally elected in October. At his inauguration in November, the worst fears of Gordon's enemies seemed confirmed when he was escorted into the Georgia Senate chamber by Joseph E. Brown, Alfred H. Colquitt, and the man Gordon supposedly made president: Rutherford B. Hayes. To all but the most knowledgeable observer, it appeared that the "Bourbon Triumvirate" reigned supreme.[57]

Despite their public show of solidarity at the inauguration, the members of the Triumvirate had serious differences of opinion on a number of issues. To a great degree, the conflicts between Gordon, Colquitt, and Brown were caused by the growing dissatisfaction of planters and men of the New South with their alliance. Although the Triumvirate was regarded by many Georgians as the dominant force in state politics, the real

---

[55]Atlanta *Constitution*, 29 July 1886. Tankersly, *Gordon*, 337. Nixon, *Grady*, 234.

[56]Americus *Recorder*, 30 July 1886. Atlanta *Constitution*, 29 July 1886.

[57]Atlanta *Constitution*, 10 November 1886.

power rested in the hands of planters in the old Black Belt. Through their control of their sharecroppers and tenants, these men dominated the General Assembly.[58] In the years following the ratification of the Constitution of 1877, these planters had voluntarily shared their power with industrialists as a means of avoiding the formation of a separate probusiness party. The political skills of Joe Brown and the influence of the Atlanta *Constitution* gave the New South men a voice in state politics far out of proportion to their numbers. Gordon's victory demonstrated that planters were capable of electing any candidate they chose, and in the absence of an Independent or Republican threat, they did not have to rely on their New South allies. The changing economic situation, the development of a new class consciousness by all agriculturists, and the aging of Joseph E. Brown tended to weaken the importance of the New South men to the alliance.

Another factor in the slow disintegration of the Triumvirate was the personal popularity of John B. Gordon. As long as the governor's office was filled by men like Alexander H. Stephens and Henry D. McDaniel, an aged has-been and a political neophyte, Colquitt and Brown were able to maintain a balance between the interests of planters and businessmen. When Grady resurrected Gordon from political limbo in 1886, it is doubtful that he or Brown expected the General to be anything other than the Senator's sycophant.[59] The victory over Bacon revitalized Gordon, and his election to the office of governor restored his confidence in himself. It was not long before Gordon served notice that he did not intend to be the servant of either Brown or Grady, but that he did intend to be a vigorous reform governor.[60]

Gordon's declaration of independence came just three weeks after he took the oath of office. In an address to the General Assembly, he attacked the convict lease system as a detriment to the state and proposed a self-sustaining experimental farm as a replacement. Gordon detailed a long list of abuses committed within the convict system: the indiscriminate housing of women and children with hardened male criminals, the imposition of excessive physical and mental punishment, the lack of proper medical care, and the lack of proper food. In addition to these evils, Gor-

---

[58]Woodward, *Origins*, 14-17. Atlanta *Constitution*, 9-10 October 1880. Albany *News*, reprinted in Macon *Telegraph*, 7 October 1887.

[59]Nixon, *Grady*, 255-56. Nixon discusses a "coolness" that developed between Gordon and Grady after the 1886 election and blames it on the prevalent rumor that Grady had made Gordon governor and that Gordon was Grady's "man."

[60]E. Merton Coulter, *James Monroe Smith: Georgia Planter, before Death and After* (Athens: University of Georgia Press, 1961) 90-91.

don pointed out that convict labor was unfair competition for free labor, and he asked the General Assembly for immediate reform legislation.[61]

Gordon's assault on the convict leasing system was widely interpreted as an attack on Senator Brown, the largest employer of convict labor in Georgia. Brown was aware that such a move might be forthcoming, just as he was cognizant of the growing unpopularity of the system in the state. In August 1886, Julius L. Brown, the Senator's son and chief legal advisor, refused consideration as a nominee for a federal judgeship because of the possibility of action against the lease system by "the mob through the legislature." He further advised his father against considering a person he did not name because of the candidate's "Communist record and tendencies" that might "hurt us and our interests, *especially when to defend our convict lease we may have to go into that Court.*"[62]

Despite Gordon's request, the 1886 General Assembly refused to enact any sort of corrective legislation, but it did pass a law that allowed the governor to reduce a convict's sentence for good behavior.[63] Gordon was unwilling to let the matter drop, and using his power as governor, he began an extensive investigation of the system. George S. Hillyer and Hoke P. Smith, prominent Atlanta lawyers, were named to supervise the probe. The hearings began on 8 September 1887 and continued for two months.[64] When they ended, officials from the various companies that held leases were found guilty of violating the terms of their contracts with the state. Although Gordon could have revoked the charters of the companies, he chose to levy a fine of $2500 on each of them. The imposition of monetary penalties did not alter the day-to-day operations of the lease system, but it marked a "first" for Georgia. For the first time in the history of the convict lease system, the state government had taken action, however limited, to restrict the power of the lessees. It was a step that won widespread approval for Gordon.[65]

There were those, of course, who questioned Gordon's motives in investigating the convict lease system. Some suspected that the inquiry was the beginning of an attempt by the governor to take over the leases himself. The Augusta *Gazette* cautioned its readers to be wary of the "present forced, stuffed, and extraordinary outbreak of lamentation over the convicts as a simpering and suspicious piece of mimicry." After all, it warned, Gordon was a "year ago a convict lessee on the largest scale."[66] The Macon

---

[61]Tankersly, *Gordon*, 338-39.

[62]Julius L. Brown to Joseph E. Brown, 1 August 1886, HT. Italics mine.

[63]Parks, *Brown*, 506, 557, 575.

[64]Ibid.

[65]Roberts, "Convict Lease," 394-410.

[66]Augusta *Gazette*, reprinted in the Macon *Telegraph*, 1 September 1887.

Telegraph seconded the *Gazette* and expressed doubt as to Gordon's sincerity because the men accused of negligence were his former business partners.[67]

While the convict lease hearings were claiming headlines in the state, Georgians were exposed to another sensational story. On 10 July 1887, Joseph E. Brown released a public letter asking Governor Gordon to grant him a renewal of the lease on the Western and Atlantic Railroad.[68] If Gordon failed to approve a new lease, Brown threatened to return the road to the state in the same condition it had been in when he took control in 1870. What that meant was simply this: all rolling stock and improved track purchased or built between 1870 and 1890 would be sold to other railroads or used to start a competing railroad.[69]

Brown's letter touched off a storm of angry debate throughout Georgia. The Macon *Telegraph*, ever eager to attack Brown, denounced the letter as an attempt to blackmail the state into renewing the lease.[70] In the General Assembly, William H. Felton introduced a bill to make "disimproving" state property a criminal offense.[71] Throughout the remaining months of 1887 and most of 1888, the arguments over the Western and Atlantic filled Georgia newspapers. Even the repudiation of the lease by Brown in another letter to Gordon failed to quiet the public outcry; instead, it heightened the controversy by injecting the question of "betterments" into the debate. All in all, Brown wanted the state to pay his company $1.5 million for improvements made during the period the railroad had been under his management.[72]

The question of the lease became the most important issue in the state election of 1888, and candidates based their campaigns on either supporting Brown or on actively denouncing him. The Americus *Recorder* suggested that each candidate for the General Assembly be asked the question, "Is he in favor of voting a couple of millions of dollars to Joe Brown for betterments or in favor of standing by the betterments?" If a candidate replied that he favored payments to Brown, the *Recorder* suggested he "be left at home."[73] The debate became so bitter that Brown felt

---

[67]Macon *Telegraph*, 2 September 1887.

[68]Ibid., 10-15 July 1887. Augusta *Chronicle*, reprinted in the Americus *Recorder*, 21 June 1888. Atlanta *Constitution*, 10 July 1887.

[69]Parks, *Brown*, 563. Macon *Telegraph*, 10 July 1887. Americus *Recorder*, 11 July 1887.

[70]Macon *Telegraph*, 11-15 July 1887.

[71]Jones, "William H. Felton," 301-302. Atlanta *Constitution*, 10 July 1887.

[72]Macon *Telegraph*, 6 December 1888. Parks, *Brown*, 563-64. Brown eventually received $100,000 from the General Assembly.

[73]Americus *Recorder*, 1 March 1888.

it was necessary to publicly deny any attempt on his part "to control the election of members of the Legislature in a single county in the state."[74] Despite his strong stand on the Western and Atlantic lease during his campaign against Bacon, Gordon refused to be lured into the controversy; he simply repeated his proposal that the road be operated by the state.

The bitter feelings the betterments question aroused were symptomatic of a general change in the attitudes of the people of Georgia. If the opinions of newspaper editors can be taken as an indication of the popular feelings of their readers, many people thought that it was time for the era of the exploitation of public resources for personal profits to end. "What has Brown . . . ever done for the Democratic party that [he] should be allowed to lord it over [his] fellows?" asked the Brunswick *Herald*. The paper then answered its own question, "Nothing, except to put money in [his] pocket."[75] Brown was also aware of the growing restlessness of the population, and he wrote to Leander N. Trammell in 1888 to voice his concerns. "There is an agrarian tendency among our people. I do not know what it will finally result in, *but fear it does not promise well.*" Brown pointed an accusing finger at the "popular politicians," who were "pandering all the time to the lowest public prejudices and taste, who are doing a great deal of harm."[76]

The "agrarian tendency" Brown referred to was the Farmers' Alliance, an organization that had swept the state since its introduction in 1887. A product of the discontent of the agricultural community with the continuing agricultural depression of the 1880s, the Alliance managed to unite farmers of all kinds under its banner. Sharecroppers, tenant farmers, yeomen, and planters, faced with rising production costs and decreasing market prices, rallied to the Alliance in the hopes of being able to solve their economic difficulties. Alliance lecturers rode circuits in the rural areas of the state; and they carried with them tracts, pamphlets, and books—available to farmers at little or no cost—that blamed the problems of the agricultural community on tight money, high tariffs, trusts, and monopolies. In such a milieu, Brown's laissez-faire, high tariff views were no longer acceptable.[77]

The extent to which Brown had lost touch with the great mass of Georgians was vividly illustrated at the state Democratic convention, which met

---

[74]Augusta *Chronicle*, reprinted in the Americus *Recorder*, 21 June 1888.

[75]Brunswick *Herald*, reprinted in the Americus *Recorder*, 31 July 1886.

[76]Joseph E. Brown to Leander Newton Trammell, 23 May 1888, TC.

[77]Wynne, "Alliance Legislature," 27-43. Robert C. McMath, Jr., *Populist Vanguard: A History of the Southern Farmers' Alliance* (Chapel Hill: University of North Carolina Press, 1975). *Henry County Weekly*, 16 March 1888. *Middle Georgia Progress*, 13 May 1890.

on 9 May 1888 to select delegates to the party's national convention. Although Brown was still in Washington attending to his senatorial duties, he sent a lengthy letter to the convention recommending certain policy positions. In it, Brown took issue with the tariff reduction stand of President Grover Cleveland, and he lectured delegates on the need for high tariffs to protect the developing industries of the United States. Even cotton farmers in the South benefited from high tariffs, he argued, because they prevented the importation of cotton from Brazil, Egypt, and India. Brown's position was identical to those taken by the New South press and offered nothing new in the way of argument.[78] At the end of his discourse on the benefits of tariffs, he asked the convention to select a delegation to the national convention that would not be committed to the idea of tariff reduction.[79]

The convention, under the personal direction of Alfred H. Colquitt and in response to the influence of the increasingly powerful Alliance, rejected Brown's proposal and elected a delegation of strong anti-tariff men. The convention also gave a strong endorsement to the Mills Bill, the tariff reduction measure pending before Congress. When General Philip Cook, a Brown ally, attempted to address the delegates on the Senator's tariff philosophy, he was roundly booed.[80] "Senator Brown and his tariff policy are not meeting with any expressions of approval from the Democratic conventions of the State," one newspaper editor had written, and it was certainly true in the statewide convention of May.[81]

Brown's stand on the tariff, his running battle with the General Assembly over the Western and Atlantic lease, and the public controversy over the convict leases did not "endear him to the people of the state."[82] Noting that Brown would come before the General Assembly for reelection in 1890, the editor of the Americus Recorder warned him that the legislature would be made up of men "unalterably in favor of tariff reform," which meant the "protectionist Senator would not find that body so easy to control in such a case."[83]

Brown's failure to dominate the state convention and Colquitt's activities during the meeting left some Brown supporters bitter. Henry W.

---

[78]Macon Telegraph, 22 August 1887. Atlanta Constitution, 28 October 1888. The Telegraph, a strong advocate of protection before the organization of the Alliance, abruptly changed its policy in October 1887. The Constitution continued to back high tariffs until the Alliance took control of state government in 1890.

[79]Joseph E. Brown to B. H. Bigham, 10 March 1888, HT.

[80]Evan P. Howell to Joseph E. Brown, 10 May 1888, HT.

[81]Americus Recorder, 26 April; 18 May 1888.

[82]Joseph E. Brown to Philip Cook, 12 May 1888, HT. Parks, Brown, 573-74.

[83]Americus Recorder, 26 April; 18 May 1888.

Grady and Evan P. Howell, Brown's alter-egoes on the Atlanta *Constitution*, were determined to get revenge for what they saw as Colquitt's public humiliation of Brown. Their plan to "get even with Colquitt" was to have Grady defeat the Senator in his bid for reelection in 1888. With Brown's approval, they began to organize a "spontaneous" Grady candidacy.[84] Grady, occasionally mentioned as a possible running mate for Cleveland in 1888, was eager to move from his position as a behind-the-scenes manipulator in the Democratic party to that of an active politician.[85] His desire to move into the ranks of political officeholders is not hard to understand. Possessed of a tremendous ego, he had become convinced of his own popularity following his famous "New South" speech in 1887.[86] Joseph E. Brown encouraged Grady in challenging Colquitt; for Brown, suffering from a chronic illness and despondent over the convention's rejection of his leadership, the possibility of Colquitt's defeat must have offered some solace for a battered ego.[87]

The success or failure of Grady's bid for the Senate depended on the support of John B. Gordon. While his backing would not necessarily be a guarantee of success, the lack of it would certainly be a guarantee of failure. When Evan P. Howell first approached Brown with the idea of a Grady candidacy, he assured the Senator that "Gordon will be squarely for him if he does [run]." Howell's certainty of the governor's intentions was based on the fact, as he wrote Brown, that "he told me so."[88] Despite any private promises he might have given Howell, Gordon quickly reversed himself and actively worked against Grady.[89]

His refusal to throw his support for Grady was indicative of a growing rift between the two men that followed Gordon's election as governor. As early as 1887, rumors were rampant in the state that Gordon was "at odds" with Grady; they became so prevalent that Grady thought it necessary to publish a statement praising Gordon as an "excellent governor."[90] The denial of a split between Grady and Gordon did not convince many Georgians, and some editors continued to refer to their estrangement in print.[91] One of the reasons why the Grady-Gordon rift developed was the pur-

---

[84]Evan P. Howell to Joseph E. Brown, 10 May 1888, HT.

[85]Nixon, *Grady*, 291-93.

[86]Americus *Recorder*, 2 February 1888.

[87]Parks, *Brown*, 573-74. Tankersly, *Gordon*, 344. Nixon, *Grady*, 253-55.

[88]Evan P. Howell to Joseph E. Brown, 10 May 1888, HT.

[89]Atlanta *Constitution*, 16 November 1890.

[90]Atlanta *Journal*, 2 June 1887. Macon *Telegraph*, 3 June 1887. Atlanta *Constitution*, 16 August 1887.

[91]Nixon, *Grady*, 290-96. John B. Gordon to Henry W. Grady, 24 June 1889, GL.

chase of the Atlanta *Journal* by Hoke Smith, whose brother, Burton, was
Gordon's son-in-law. After years of little or no competition in Atlanta, the
Constitution faced a rival newspaper with important political connections.[92] It is also likely that Grady and Gordon parted company because
the governor considered Grady a possible candidate for the Senate in 1890
when Brown was certain to retire, and he did not want to help a potential
rival for that seat.

Without Gordon's support, Grady had no chance of unseating Alfred
H. Colquitt. Although he continued to campaign for votes in the General
Assembly, Grady never officially announced his candidacy. "It is said that
Henry Grady will contest the United States Senatorship with Gov[ernor]
Colquitt," the editor of the Americus *Recorder* informed his readers, "but
we have little faith in the rumor. Henry still remembers how badly he got
set down in a little contest he had with Gov[ernor] Colquitt a few months
ago, and we doubt if he cares to renew the experiment."[93] Whether or not
Grady wanted to renew the experiment was unimportant; 1888 was not a
year in which a confirmed and uncompromising man of the New South
could be elected to public office in Georgia. When the vote was taken in
the General Assembly, Grady received only two votes. It was as much a
rejection of Grady's vision of the New South as it was a rejection of Grady,
the man.[94]

The election of Alfred H. Colquitt to the Senate in 1888 marked the end
of a chaotic period that had seen significant social, political, and economic
developments take place in Georgia. The decade of the 1880s was itself
the culmination of a longer era of drastic change in the state's politics. In
a span of twenty-eight years, Georgia had gone from being a state within
the Union to being an independent republic, a state within the Confederacy, and, finally, a state within the Union again. Politically, it had gone
from being dominated by planters to being controlled by Republicans,
businessmen, and, finally, planters once more. Ironically, Colquitt's election also signaled the beginning of another equally chaotic period of political activity—a period marked by further challenge to the hegemony of
the planter class in Georgia.

---

[92]Nixon, *Grady*, 254-56.

[93]Americus *Recorder*, 16 November 1888.

[94]Nixon, *Grady*, 290-96, 337-39.

EPILOGUE

The last two years of Gordon's administration were turbulent years in Georgia politics. The alliance between planters and New South businessmen, created by the Constitution of 1877 and administered by the so-called Triumvirate, dissolved under pressure caused by Grady's death in 1889 and by the rise of the Farmers' Alliance. Rapidly gaining strength following its introduction into the state in 1887, the Alliance had an estimated 85,000 white and 20,000 black members by 1889.[1] Three years of continued depression, low prices for cotton, and the failure of Congress to lower tariffs provided the favorable conditions for this organization to develop. Stressing self-help, self-sufficiency, and self-consciousness, the Alliance swept over Georgia in a matter of months. Its system of paid and non-paid lecturers, pioneered by the Grange in the early 1870s, provided a means of communication between farmers who had previously been isolated from each other.[2]

Although the Alliance theoretically represented the interests of all classes of farmers and although the message of agricultural unity was the favorite topic of Alliance lecturers, the leadership positions in the organization were quickly assumed by planters from the older sections of the Black Belt. As early as 1888, the original organizers of the Alliance—particularly the small farmers like R. H. Jackson, its first president—were forced out of the important offices. In their place, planters like Leonidas F. Livingston and William J. Northen, former officers in the Grange and in the planter dominated Georgia Agricultural Society, took command. While the rhetoric of the Alliance remained "radical" in its demands for an expanded national currency, the regulation of industry, and the creation of "sub-treasuries," the most important change brought about by the planter takeover was the organization's entry into state politics. Despite a specific disavowal of political action contained in the Alliance creed, planters were not willing to allow the potentially powerful organization to remain outside the political arena.[3]

The Alliance, once it moved into the mainstream of state politics, made use of the Democratic party structure. Alliancemen controlled county conventions, and they mobilized all classes of farmers to vote for candi-

---

[1]*Middle Georgia Progress*, 13 May 1890. Statesboro *Eagle*, 22 August 1889.

[2]Wynne, "Alliance Legislature," 27-43.

[3]Ibid., 84-112.

dates who were members of the Alliance or sworn to uphold its principles. Out of a possible 219 seats in the General Assembly in 1890, the Alliance captured 192. In addition, the Alliance elected William J. Northen to the governor's chair, replaced six of ten Congressmen with its own members, extracted pledges of support from the four other Representatives, and elected John B. Gordon to the United States Senate.[4] In all of its political activity, the Alliance operated under the banner of the Democratic party, and individuals elected with Alliance support were always identified as being Democratic/Alliance candidates.

The organization's involvement in Georgia politics differed remarkably from its record in other Southern states.[5] In Alabama, for example, Alliancemen bolted the Democrats and operated as a separate political party until 1897. As a result, the Alabama Alliance continued to be a force in the state's politics until the turn of the century; while Georgia's Alliance, superimposed on the Democratic party, died with the outbreak of Populism in 1892.

The Georgia Alliance was used by planters to further their hegemony in the state. With its power behind them, they ruthlessly eliminated opponents from state office and replaced them with men whose social and economic ties linked them to the planter elite. Politicians strongly identified with the New South movement were ousted from office, and others—such as John B. Gordon—who had ties with both planters and industrialists survived only by pledging their support to the Alliance and hence to planters. All in all, the triumph of the Alliance in the state elections of 1890 represented the final dissolution of the planter-New South coalition that had governed the state since 1877. Through the Alliance, planters extended their control to all offices in the state government and in the Democratic party.

The assumption of control of the Alliance, the Democratic party, and the state government by planters did not produce any drastic changes in Georgia's economy. Yeoman farmers, sharecroppers, and tenant farmers who looked to the Alliancemen in the General Assembly to provide them with some kind of relief were sorely disappointed. None of the major demands of the Alliance were enacted into law, despite their total domination of the Assembly. Legislative proposals that might have provided some relief for the economic distress of small farmers and sharecroppers were consistently opposed by Alliance leaders. The failure of the Assembly was

---

[4]James C. Bonner, "The Alliance Legislature of 1890," in James C. Bonner and Lucien E. Roberts, eds., *Studies in Georgia History and Government* (Athens: University of Georgia Press, 1940) 164-66.

[5]Rogers, *One-Gallused Rebellion,* 168-69, 215-37. Of particular interest is Rogers's description of the various Alabama county conventions and the political opposition that forced Reuben Kolb and the Alliance out of the Democratic party.

duplicated in Congress where Alliance-elected members quickly forgot their promises and joined the Democratic caucus. Only Thomas E. Watson, a Democrat but not an Allianceman, championed the Alliance demands in Congress, but his efforts were not supported by the other Georgia Representatives.[6] To planters, the Alliance was merely a vehicle for eliminating the influence of Atlanta businessmen.[7]

Under the Alliance legislators, the Prussian Road approach to industry was strengthened. Alliancemen/planters were not opposed to industrialization per se, and the General Assembly of 1890-91 continued the policies of previous legislatures in encouraging the development of local industries. The key to the planters' approach to industrialization was to make it easy for small industries to locate in areas outside the large cities, and this policy resulted in the creation of a new coalition of planters and businessmen. Unlike the alliance of 1877, which recognized the Atlanta business community as the commercial leaders of the state, the coalition of 1890 represented a union of planters and businessmen from the developing areas and smaller towns. The first evidence of the operation of the new alliance came with the election of William Y. Atkinson, a prominent lawyer from LaGrange, as governor in 1894. In 1896, Augustus O. Bacon achieved his revenge on Grady and the Atlanta ring by securing a seat in the United States Senate, the position that Grady had failed to gain in 1888. Both Atkinson and Bacon, ardent opponents of the Atlanta faction, had been denied high state and national office before 1890, and their opposition to Grady and Joseph E. Brown was the major reason for their failure.[8]

The coalition of planters and midstate businessmen, first formed in 1890, dominated the state's politics until the 1960s, when Lester Garfield Maddox became the first Atlanta politician to gain the governor's office. In 1917, the passage of the Neill Primary Act—which created the county unit system as the means of selecting Democratic candidates—formalized the 1890 coalition, and, as a result, Atlanta's importance as a political center declined.[9] The continuous growth of Georgia's cities and towns

---

[6]Wynne, "The Alliance Legislature," 84-112. For an account of Watson's activities, see C. Vann Woodward, *Tom Watson, Agrarian Rebel* (New York: Macmillan, 1938).

[7]Minutes of the Alliance Caucus, 1890-1891, Henry L. Graves Papers, Southern Historical Collection, University of North Carolina Library, Chapel Hill.

[8]Steelman, "Augustus Octavius Bacon," 155-57. Muriel Shipp, "The Public Life of William Yates Atkinson" (Master's thesis, University of Georgia, 1955) 46-74.

[9]Joseph L. Bernd, *Grass Roots Politics in Georgia: The County Unit System and the Importance of the Individual Voting Community in Bifactional Elections, 1942-1954* (Atlanta: Emory University Research Committee, 1960) 1-10. Rigdon, *County Unit System,* 17-41.

throughout the postwar period was not sufficient to offset the concentration of people in the Black Belt counties. As the interests of planters in both the old and the new sections of the Black Belt became more and more closely aligned, the friction between these two sections decreased, and the fusion of interests strengthened the planters' power.

Throughout the years between 1860 and 1890, planters had aggressively pursued a policy of social, economic, and political domination of the state. Despite occasional setbacks during the Republican period and the early 1870s, they were generally successful in their efforts. Essential to the hegemony of planters was the creation of constitutional devices that ensured their political power and that allowed them to control the direction and speed of industrial development. In the Constitutions of 1861, 1865, 1868, and 1877, Black Belt planters were guaranteed a deciding voice in state government through a system of proportional representation based on county population.

Even the Republicans incorporated this feature in the Constitution of 1868 because they were dependent on the votes of freedmen to maintain their control of the state, and most freedmen lived in the rural counties of the Black Belt. Joseph E. Brown predicted the restoration of planter power in 1868 when he urged Rufus B. Bullock to form an alliance with planters because they "possess most of the intelligence and wealth of the State which will always control tenants and laborers."[10] Brown's assessment was correct, and so completely did planters dominate the votes of black sharecroppers, tenants, and laborers that even during the height of the Populist uprising in the 1890s, few of them were willing to disfranchise Negroes. To do so would have seriously weakened planter hegemony and allowed a Populist takeover of Georgia politics. Only when the Populist threat was over and white Georgians had united under the Democratic party's banner did planters approve disenfranchisement.[11]

Planter attitudes toward industrialization were also incorporated into the constitution of the state. With the exception of the Constitution of 1868, all the constitutions written from 1861 to 1877 included provisions allowing planters to direct industrial development. Unlike Alabama, which possessed deposits of coal and iron ore, Georgia had no concentration of natural resources that demanded large capital investment to exploit. Even the highly publicized mining operations of Joseph E. Brown, widely touted as proof of Georgia's industrial potential, were incapable of supporting the sustained development of heavy industries—a necessary first step for modern industrialization. When the combined mining properties of the

---

[10]Joseph E. Brown to Rufus B. Bullock, 8 December 1868, HT.

[11]Kousser, *Shaping of Southern Politics,* 41-42, 62, 78, 214-23.

Brown family were offered for sale in 1887, there were no buyers, although the asking price was only $1.2 million.[12]

Industrialization in Georgia was best fitted to the labor-intensive, rather than the capital-intensive, mode. This was the pattern of development planters encouraged, and they included provisions in the Constitution of 1877 that promoted the growth of small, local corporations. In taking the power of incorporation out of the hands of the General Assembly and putting it into the office of the Secretary of State, planters diverted capital from large corporations by making it much easier to invest in small industries in rural locales.

The creation of hundreds of small industries discouraged the rise of an independent entrepreneurial class in Georgia. By providing businessmen with the opportunity to invest their money locally, planters were able to perpetuate the antebellum pattern of an industrial class bound to the planter elites through social, economic, and political ties. Planters were not, on the whole, anti-industrial in their feelings, but they did favor the development of industries that were tied to agriculture. Throughout the postwar period, they actively worked to promote local industries and often were among the principal investors in them. "Take the cotton mills to the cotton fields" was a cry frequently heard in proplanter newspapers, and it accurately summed up planter attitudes toward industrialization.[13] It was better to have a thousand mills scattered throughout the countryside, where they could be subject to planter influence and control, than to have a hundred large mills concentrated in urban areas, where they would be free from planter domination. The proliferation of small factories was essential to the Prussian Road idea.

The development of small factories in rural areas also strengthened the power of planters in other ways. Faced with a possible labor shortage if industrial development was confined to a few urban centers, they sought to prevent the flight of workers to cities by building factories in the countryside. Industrial labor in Georgia came from the ranks of yeoman farmers, sharecroppers, and tenant farmers; and factories in rural areas could be manned by workers who combined their agricultural activities with factory labor during slack seasons. The absence of highly technical industries or the need for skilled workers allowed for the frequent interchange of farm and factory labor. As Wilbur J. Cash noted, individuals who worked in a local cotton mill often did so with the specific intention of returning to farming as soon as they had accumulated small amounts of cash. The very nature of the Prussian Road pattern of industrial development—small textile mills in small rural towns—encouraged the movement of labor from

---

[12]Parks, *Brown*, 574-75.

[13]Cash, *Mind*, 175-89. Gaston, *New South Creed*, 78-79. Atlanta *Constitution*, 27 August 1889.

factory to farm and back again. With such ease of movement, Georgia, and much of the rest of the South, did not have a permanent factory class.[14]

The constant movement of laborers from factory to farm weakened the potential political and economic strength of industrialists. Factory workers retained their identification with the values of their relatives on the farms. The election returns for the 1870s and the 1880s illustrate this continuity of values: in virtually every election during those decades, the majority of urban votes were cast for the same candidates as those supported by planters in the old Black Belt. This occurrence can be explained in several ways. First, the retention of rural values by urban workers meant that they tended to see candidates in the same light as did their rural brothers, and the two groups voted for the same people. Second, the interests of factory owners and planters—often the same people—coincided, and factory laborers were not subjected to economic pressure that might have forced them to vote differently. Third, the Democratic party was firmly in the hands of planters, and its advocacy of white supremacy appealed to factory workers who were mostly white. Finally, the absence of a viable second party based on different economic or ideological principles tended to prevent factory workers from leaving the Democratic party. The abortive Republican and Independent efforts of the 1870s and 1880s were not noticeably different from their Democratic adversaries, except for their identification with Negroes; because of this, they failed to win many converts among workers.

The restoration of planter hegemony after the Civil War was not, however, an easy task. The Republican party, the Independent movement, and the Norwood candidacy presented problems for the planters; and the opposition of the postwar merchant class added to them. It was not until 1877 that planter authority was completely restored. The Constitution of 1877, with its proplanter provisions, became the basis for their continued domination. Indeed, that document marked the culmination of ongoing attempts by planters to firmly establish their control of the state. Built on their previous successes, it included many provisions of the Constitutions of 1861 and 1865. So strong were the constitutional safeguards constructed by planters from 1861 to 1877 that even the power of the federal government and four years of Republican occupation of the governor's office could not destroy them.

Just as the Republicans in the late 1860s, the Independents in the 1870s, and the New South men of the 1880s had discovered, so, too, would the Populists in the 1890s find out that Georgia's planters were too firmly entrenched to be displaced. As long as agriculture remained the dominant force in the state's economy and as long as planters controlled the land, protest was possible, but successful change was improbable. Georgia in 1892 was, with slight modifications, as much of a planter republic as it had been in 1861.

---

[14]Cash, *Mind*, 165-69.

BIBLIOGRAPHY

MANUSCRIPT COLLECTIONS

Elijah E. Brown Collection. Atlanta Historical Society.

Howell Cobb Collection. University of Georgia.

Alfred H. Colquitt. Incoming Correspondence. Georgia Department of Archives and History. Atlanta.

Alfred H. Colquitt Scrapbooks. University of Georgia.

John S. Dobbins Collection. Atlanta Historical Society.

John S. Dobbins Collection. Emory University.

Henry Pattillo Farrow Collection. University of Georgia.

William H. and Rebecca L. Felton Collection. University of Georgia.

Hugh H. Gordon Letterbooks. Georgia Department of Archives and History. Atlanta.

John B. Gordon Collection. University of Georgia.

John B. Gordon Letterbooks. Georgia Department of Archives and History. Atlanta.

Henry W. Grady Collection. Emory University.

Henry L. Graves Papers. Southern Historical Collection. University of North Carolina.

James Pinkney Hambleton Collection. Emory University.

Felix Hargrett Typescripts. University of Georgia.

Henry McCay Papers. Atlanta Historical Society.

Cora Brown McLeod Collection. University of Georgia.

William McNaught Papers. Atlanta Historical Society.

John W. Pattillo Collection. Southern Technical Institute.

Alexander H. Stephens Collection. Emory University.

Leander Newton Trammell Collection. Emory University.

Bureau of Refugees, Freedmen, and Abandoned Land, 1865-1869. Records of the Assistant Commissioner for the State of Georgia. Record Group 105, M-798. National Archives, Washington, DC.

GOVERNMENT DOCUMENTS (1850-1900)

Acts of the General Assembly of Georgia, 1860-1900. Various State Printers.

Annual Report of the Comptroller General of Georgia, 1860-1900. Various State Printers.

Annual Report of the Secretary of War, 1868. Washington: Government Printing Office, 1868.

Bureau of the Census Reports, 1850-1900. Washington: Government Printing Office.

Candler, Allen D., ed. *The Confederate Records of the State of Georgia*. 6 vols. Atlanta: C. P. Byrd, state printer, 1909-1911.

Georgia Laws, 1865-1900. Various State Printers.

House of Representatives: Miscellaneous Documents. 40th Congress, 3rd Session, No. 52. Washington: Government Printing Office, 1869.

Journal of the Georgia House of Representatives, 1860-1900. Various State Printers.

Journal of the Proceedings of the Convention of the People of Georgia Held in Milledgeville in October and November, 1865. Milledgeville: R. G. Orme and Son, 1865.

Journal of the Georgia Senate, 1860-1900. Various State Printers.

Public Laws Passed by the General Assembly of the State of Georgia at the Session of 1870. Atlanta: New Era Printing Establishment, 1870.

Supplemental Report, 1887, Georgia Department of Agriculture. Atlanta: Constitution Book and Job Office, 1887.

Transactions of the Georgia State Agricultural Society from August, 1876, to February, 1878. Atlanta: James P. Harrington and Company, 1878.

GEORGIA NEWSPAPERS (1860-1900)

Acworth *News and Farmer*.

Albany *News*.

Americus *Recorder*.

Athens *Banner*.

Atlanta *Constitution*.

Atlanta *Intelligencer*.

Atlanta *Journal*.

Atlanta *New Era*.

Atlanta *Post-Appeal*.

Augusta *Chronicle and Sentinel*.

Augusta *Daily Constitutionalist*.

Bulloch (County) *Times*.

Calhoun *Times*.

Carroll (County) *Times*.

Columbus *Daily Sun*.

Columbus *Enquirer*.

Columbus *Enquirer-Sun*.

Columbus *Times*.

Dawson *Journal*.

Eastman *Times-Journal.*
Greensboro *Herald.*
Greenville *Meriwether Vindicator.*
Griffin *Star.*
Henry County Weekly.
LaGrange *Reporter.*
Lexington *Oglethorpe Echo.*
Macon *Telegraph.*
Marietta *Journal.*
Middle Georgia Progress.
Milledgeville *Federal Union (Southern Federal Union).*
Milledgeville *Southern Recorder.*
Quitman *Banner.*
Rome *Weekly Courier.*
Savannah *News.*
Savannah *Republican.*
Sparta *Ishmaelite.*
Statesboro *Eagle.*

BOOKS

Argersinger, Peter H. *Populism and Politics: William Alfred Peffer and the People's Party.* Lexington: University Press of Kentucky, 1974.

Arnett, Alex Mathews. *The Populist Movement in Georgia: A View of the Agrarian Crusade in the Light of Solid South Politics.* New York: Columbia University Press, 1922.

Avery, Isaac W. *History of the State of Georgia, 1850-1881.* New York: Brown and Derby, 1881.

Barney, William L. *The Road to Secession: A New Perspective on the Old South.* New York: Praeger Publishers, 1972.

Bartley, Numan V. *The Creation of Modern Georgia.* Athens: University of Georgia Press, 1983.

Bell, Daniel, ed. *The New American Right.* New York: Criterion Books, 1955.

Bently, George R. *A History of the Freedman's Bureau.* Reprint. New York: Octagon Books, 1970.

Bernd, Joseph L. *Grass Roots Politics in Georgia: The County Unit System and the Importance of the Individual Voting Community in Bifactional Elections, 1942-1954.* Atlanta: Emory University Research Committee, 1960.

Billings, Dwight B., Jr. *Planters and the Making of a "New South": Class, Politics, and Development in North Carolina, 1865-1900.* Chapel Hill: University of North Carolina Press, 1979.

Bonner, James C. *The Georgia Story.* Oklahoma City: Harlow Publishing Company, 1958.

_____, ed. *The Journal of a Milledgeville Girl, 1861-1867*. Athens: University of Georgia Press, 1964.

Bonner, James C., and Lucien E. Roberts, eds. *Studies in Georgia History and Government*. Athens: University of Georgia Press, 1940.

Boorstin, Daniel J. *The Americans: The Democratic Experience*. New York: Random House, 1973.

Brooks, Robert P. *The Agrarian Revolution in Georgia, 1865-1912*. Madison: University of Wisconsin, 1914.

_____. *History of Georgia*. Boston: Atkinson, Mentzer and Company, 1913.

Bryan, T. Conn. *Confederate Georgia*. Athens: University of Georgia Press, 1953.

Buck, Solon J. *The Agrarian Crusade: A Chronicle of Farmers in Politics*. New Haven: Yale University Press, 1920.

Burnham, Walter Dean. *Presidential Ballots, 1836-1892*. Baltimore: Johns Hopkins Press, 1955.

Cash, Wilbur J. *The Mind of the South*. New York: Vintage Books, 1941.

Channing, Steven A. *Crisis of Fear: Secession in South Carolina*. New York: W. W. Norton, 1974.

Clark, Thomas D. *Pills, Petticoats and Plows: The Southern Country Store*. Indianapolis: Bobbs-Merrill, 1944.

Cole, Arthur C. *The Whig Party in the South*. Washington DC: American Historical Association, 1914.

Coleman, Kenneth, ed. *A History of Georgia*. Athens: University of Georgia Press, 1977.

Conway, Alan. *The Reconstruction of Georgia*. Minneapolis: University of Minnesota Press, 1966.

Cooper, William J. *The Conservative Regime: South Carolina, 1877-1890*. Baltimore: Johns Hopkins Press, 1968.

Coulter, E. Merton. *Georgia: A Short History*. Chapel Hill: University of North Carolina Press, 1960.

_____. *James Monroe Smith: Georgia Planter, before Death and After*. Athens: University of Georgia Press, 1961.

_____. *Negro Legislators in Georgia during the Reconstruction Period*. Athens: University of Georgia Press, 1968.

Cruden, Robert. *The Negro in Reconstruction*. Englewood Cliffs NJ: Prentice-Hall, 1969.

Daniel, Pete. *The Shadow of Slavery: Peonage in the South, 1901-1969*. Urbana: University of Illinois Press, 1972.

DeCanio, Stephen J. *Agriculture in the Postbellum South: The Economics of Production and Supply*. Cambridge: MIT Press, 1974.

Degler, Carl N. *The Age of the Economic Revolution, 1876-1900*. Atlanta: Scott, Foresman and Company, 1967.

_____. *The Other South: Southern Dissenters in the Nineteenth Century*. New York: Harper and Row, 1974.

Donald, David, and James G. Randall. *The Civil War and Reconstruction.* Boston: D. C. Heath and Company, 1974.

Dumond, Dwight Lowell. *The Secession Movement, 1860-1861.* New York: Macmillan, 1931.

Durden, Robert. *The Climax of Populism: The Election of 1896.* Lexington: University Press of Kentucky, 1965.

Eaton, Clement. *The Mind of the Old South.* Baton Rouge: Louisiana State University Press, 1968.

_____. *The Waning of the Old South Civilization.* Athens: University of Georgia Press, 1968.

Escott, Paul D. *After Secession: Jefferson Davis and the Failure of Confederate Nationalism.* Baton Rouge: Louisiana State University Press, 1978.

Evans, Lawton B. *A History of Georgia.* New York: American Book Company, 1911.

Felton, Rebecca L. *My Memoirs of Georgia Politics.* Atlanta: Index Printing Company, 1911.

Flippin, Percy Scott. *Herschel V. Johnson of Georgia: State Rights Unionist.* Richmond: Dietz Printing Company, 1931.

Fogel, Robert W. *Railroads and American Economic Growth: Essays in Econometric History.* Baltimore: Johns Hopkins Press, 1964.

Gaston, Paul M. *The New South Creed: A Study in Southern Mythmaking.* New York: Alfred A. Knopf, 1970.

Genovese, Eugene D. *In Red and Black: Marxian Explorations in Southern and Afro-American History.* New York: Vintage Books, 1971.

_____. *The Political Economy of Slavery: Studies in the Economy and Society of the Slave South.* New York: Random House, 1965.

_____. *Roll, Jordan, Roll: The World the Slaves Made.* New York: Vintage Books, 1976.

_____. *The World the Slaveholders Made: Two Essays in Interpretation.* New York: Random House, 1969.

Gerteis, Louis S. *From Contraband to Freedom: Federal Policy toward Southern Blacks, 1861-1865.* Westport CT: Greenwood Press, 1973.

Ginger, Ray. *Age of Excess: The United States from 1877 to 1914.* New York: Macmillan, 1965.

Goldman, Eric F. *Rendezvous with Destiny.* New York: Vintage Books, 1956.

Goodwyn, Lawrence. *Democratic Promise: The Populist Movement in America.* New York: Oxford University Press, 1976.

Gosnell, Cullen B. *Government and Politics of Georgia.* New York: Thomas Nelson and Sons, 1936.

Grossman, Lawrence. *The Democratic Party and the Negro: Northern and National Politics, 1868-1892.* Urbana: University of Illinois Press, 1976.

Hackney, Sheldon. *Populism to Progressivism in Alabama.* Princeton: Princeton University Press, 1969.

Hahn, Steven. *The Roots of Southern Populism: Yeoman Farmers and the Transformation of the Georgia Upcountry, 1850-1890.* New York: Oxford University Press, 1983.

Hair, William Ivy. *Bourbonism and Agrarian Protest: Louisiana Politics, 1877-1900.* Baton Rouge: Louisiana State University Press, 1969.

Hart, Roger L. *Redeemers, Bourbons and Populists: Tennessee, 1870-1896.* Baton Rouge: Louisiana State University Press, 1975.

Hays, Samuel P. *The Response to Industrialism: 1885-1914.* Chicago: University of Chicago Press, 1957.

Heath, Milton S. *Constructive Liberalism: The Role of the State in Economic Development in Georgia to 1860.* Cambridge: Harvard University Press, 1954.

Hesseltine, William B. *Confederate Leaders in the New South.* Baton Rouge: Louisiana State University Press, 1950.

Hicks, John D. *The Populist Revolt: A History of the Farmers' Alliance and the People's Party.* Minneapolis: University of Minnesota Press, 1931.

Higgs, Robert. *Competition and Coercion: Blacks in the American Economy, 1865-1914.* Cambridge: Cambridge University Press, 1977.

————————. *The Transformation of the American Economy, 1865-1914: An Essay in Interpretation.* New York: John Wiley and Sons, 1971.

Hill, Benjamin H., Jr. *Senator Benjamin H. Hill of Georgia, His Life, Speeches and Writings.* Atlanta: T. H. P. Bloodworth, 1893.

Hill, Louise Biles. *Joseph E. Brown and the Confederacy.* Westport CT: Greenwood Press, 1939.

Hirshson, Stanley P. *Farewell to the Bloody Shirt: Northern Republicans and the Southern Negro, 1877-1913.* Bloomington: Indiana University Press, 1962.

Hofstadter, Richard. *The Age of Reform from Bryan to FDR.* New York: Alfred A. Knopf, 1955.

Horn, Stanley F. *Invisible Empire: The Story of the Ku Klux Klan, 1866-1871.* Reprint. New York: Haskell House Publishers, 1973.

Johnson, Michael P. *Toward A Patriarchal Republic: The Secession of Georgia.* Baton Rouge: Louisiana State University Press, 1977.

Key, V. O., Jr. *Southern Politics in State and Nation.* New York: Alfred A. Knopf, 1949.

Killion, Ronald, and Charles Waller, eds. *Slavery Time When I Was Chillun Down on Marster's Plantation.* Savannah: Beehive Press, 1973.

Kolchin, Peter. *First Freedom: The Responses of Alabama's Blacks to Emancipation and Reconstruction.* Westport CT: Greenwood Press, 1972.

Kolko, Gabriel. *The Triumph of Conservatism.* New York: Vintage Books, 1967.

Kousser, J. Morgan. *The Shaping of Southern Politics: Suffrage Restrictions and the Establishment of the One-Party South, 1880-1910.* New Haven: Yale University Press, 1974.

Lane, Mills B., ed. *The New South: Writings and Speeches of Henry Grady.* Savannah: Beehive Press, 1971.

Lee, Susan Previant. *The Westward Movement of the Cotton Economy, 1840-1860: Perceived Interests and Economic Realities.* New York: Arno Press, 1977.

Loewen, James W. *The Mississippi Chinese: Between Black and White.* Cambridge: Harvard University Press, 1971.

Luraghi, Raimondo. *The Rise and Fall of the Plantation South.* n.p.: New Viewpoints, 1978.

Mandle, Jay R. *The Roots of Black Poverty: The Southern Plantation Economy after the Civil War.* Durham: Duke University Press, 1978.

Mantell, Martin E. *Johnson, Grant and the Politics of Reconstruction.* New York: Columbia University Press, 1973.

McFeely, William S. *Yankee Stepfather: General O. O. Howard and the Freedmen.* New Haven: Yale University Press, 1968.

McMath, Robert C., Jr. *Populist Vanguard: A History of the Southern Farmers' Alliance.* Chapel Hill: University of North Carolina Press, 1975.

McWhiney, Grady. *Southerners and Other Americans.* New York: Basic Books, 1973.

Meier, August. *Negro Thought in America, 1880-1915.* Ann Arbor: University of Michigan Press, 1963.

Mitchell, Broadus. *The Rise of Cotton Mills in the South.* Reprint. New York: DeCapo Press, 1968.

Mitchell, Frances Letcher. *Georgia, Land and People.* Spartanburg SC: The Reprint Company, 1974.

Montgomery, Horace. *Cracker Parties.* Baton Rouge: Louisiana State University Press, 1950.

Moore, Barrington, Jr. *Social Origins of Dictatorship and Democracy: Lord and Peasant in the Making of the Modern World.* Boston: Beacon Press, 1966.

Myers, Robert Manson, ed. *The Children of Pride: A True Story of Georgia and the Civil War.* New Haven: Yale University Press, 1972.

Myrdal, Gunnar. *An American Dilemma: The Negro Problem and Modern Democracy.* 2 vols. New York: Harper and Brothers, 1944.

Nathans, Elizabeth Studley. *Losing the Peace: Georgia Republicans and Reconstruction, 1865-1871.* Baton Rouge: Louisiana State University Press, 1969.

Nixon, Raymond B. *Henry W. Grady, Spokesman of the New South.* New York: Russell and Russell, 1969.

Nugent, Walter T. K. *The Tolerant Populists: Kansas Populism and Nativism.* Chicago: University of Chicago Press, 1963.

Nye, Russell B. *William Lloyd Garrison and the Humanitarian Reformers.* Boston: Little, Brown and Company, 1955.

Osterweis, Rollin G. *The Myth of the Lost Cause, 1865-1900.* Hamden CT: Archon Books, 1973.

Parks, Joseph H. *Joseph E. Brown of Georgia.* Baton Rouge: Louisiana State University Press, 1977.

Parsons, Stanley B. *The Populist Context: Rural versus Urban on a Great Plains Frontier.* Westport CT: Greenwood Press, 1973.

Pearce, Haywood J., Jr. *Benjamin H. Hill: Secession and Reconstruction.* Chicago: University of Chicago Press, 1928.

Phillips, Ulrich Bonnell. *Georgia and State Rights: A Study of the Political History of Georgia from the Revolution to the Civil War, with Particular Regard to Federal Relations.* Yellow Springs OH: Antioch Press, 1968. ROSE edition: Macon GA: Mercer University Press, 1984.

——————————. *The Life of Robert Toombs.* Reprint. New York: Burt Franklin Press, 1968.

Polakoff, Keith Ian. *The Politics of Inertia: The Election of 1876 and the End of Reconstruction.* Baton Rouge: Louisiana State University Press, 1973.

Pollack, Norman. *The Populist Response to Industrial America.* Cambridge: Harvard University Press, 1962.

Potter, David M. *Lincoln and His Party in the Secession Crisis.* New Haven: Yale University Press, 1962.

Pressly, Thomas J. *Americans Interpret Their Civil War.* Princeton: Princeton University Press, 1954.

Pressly, Thomas J., and William H. Scofield, eds. *Farm Real Estate Values in the United States by Counties, 1850-1959.* Seattle: University of Washington Press, 1965.

Rabinowitz, Howard N., ed. *Southern Black Leaders of the Reconstruction Era.* Urbana: University of Illinois Press, 1982.

Rable, George C. *But There Was No Peace: The Role of Violence in the Politics of Reconstruction.* Athens: University of Georgia Press, 1984.

Range, Willard. *A Century of Georgia Agriculture, 1850-1950.* Athens: University of Georgia Press, 1954.

Ransom, Roger L., and Richard Sutch. *One Kind of Freedom: The Economic Consequences of Emancipation.* Cambridge: Cambridge University Press, 1977.

Rawick, George P., ed. *The American Slave: A Composite Autobiography.* Vol. 13, Georgia Narratives. Westport CT: Greenwood Press, 1972.

Rigdon, Louis T. II, *Georgia's County Unit System.* Decatur GA: Selective Books, 1961.

Roark, James L. *Masters without Slaves: Southern Planters in the Civil War and Reconstruction.* New York: W. W. Norton, 1977.

Roberts, Derrell C. *Joseph E. Brown and the Politics of Reconstruction.* Tuscaloosa: University of Alabama Press, 1973.

Rogers, William Warren. *The One-Gallused Rebellion: Agrarianism in Alabama, 1865-1896.* Baton Rouge: Louisiana State University Press, 1970.

Roper, John Herbert. *U. B. Phillips: A Southern Mind.* Macon: Mercer University Press, 1984.

Rose, Willie Lee. *Rehearsal for Reconstruction: The Port Royal Experiment.* New York: Vintage Books, 1964.

Saye, Albert Berry. *A Constitutional History of Georgia, 1732-1945.* Athens: University of Georgia Press, 1948.

Sefton, James E. *The United States Army and Reconstruction, 1865-1877.* Baton Rouge: Louisiana State University Press, 1967.

Shadgett, Olive Hall. *The Republican Party in Georgia from Reconstruction through 1900.* Athens: University of Georgia Press, 1964.

Shannon, David A. *The Farmer's Last Frontier: Agriculture, 1860-1897.* New York: Farrar and Rinehart, 1945.

Sharkey, Robert P. *Money, Class, and Party: An Economic Study of the Civil War and Reconstruction.* Baltimore: Johns Hopkins Press, 1959.

Shryock, Richard H. *Georgia and the Union in 1850.* Durham: Duke University Press, 1926.

Shugg, Roger W. *Origins of the Class Struggle in Louisiana: A Social History of White Farmers and Laborers during Slavery and After, 1840-1875.* Baton Rouge: Louisiana State University Press, 1939.

Small, Samuel W., ed. *A Stenographic Report of the Proceedings of the Constitutional Convention Held in Atlanta, Georgia, 1877.* Atlanta: The Constitution Publishing Company, 1877.

Smith, Howard R. *Economic History of the United States.* New York: Ronald Press, 1955.

Stampp, Kenneth M. *The Era of Reconstruction, 1865-1877.* New York: Vintage Books, 1965.

Starobin, Robert S. *Industrial Slavery in the Old South.* London: Oxford University Press, 1970.

Stovall, Pleasant A. *Robert Toombs, Statesman, Speaker, Soldier, Sage.* New York: Cassell Publishing Company, 1892.

Takaki, Ronald T. *A Pro-Slavery Crusade: The Agitation to Reopen the African Slave Trade.* New York: Free Press, 1971.

Talmadge, John E. *Rebecca Latimer Felton: Nine Stormy Decades.* Athens: University of Georgia Press, 1960.

Tang, Anthony M. *Economic Development in the Southern Piedmont, 1860-1950: Its Impact on Agriculture.* Chapel Hill: University of North Carolina Press, 1958.

Tankersly, Allen P. *John B. Gordon: A Study in Gallantry.* Atlanta: Whitehall Press, 1955.

Taylor, William R. *Cavalier and Yankee: The Old South and American National Character.* Garden City NY: Doubleday, 1963.

Temin, Peter. *Causal Factors in American Economic Growth in the Nineteenth Century.* London: Macmillan, 1975.

Thomas, Emory M. *The Confederacy as a Revolutionary Experience.* Englewood Cliffs NJ: Prentice-Hall, 1971.

Thompson, C. Mildred. *Reconstruction in Georgia: Economic, Social, Political, 1865-1872.* Reprint. Savannah: Beehive Press, 1972.

Thompson, William Y. *Robert Toombs of Georgia.* Baton Rouge: Louisiana State University Press, 1966.

Trelease, Allen W. *White Terror: The Ku Klux Klan Conspiracy and Southern Reconstruction.* New York: Harper and Row, 1971.

von Abele, Rudolph. *Alexander H. Stephens: A Biography.* New York: Alfred A. Knopf, 1946.

Wiener, Jonathan M. *Social Origins of the New South: Alabama, 1860-1885.* Baton Rouge: Louisiana State University Press, 1978.

Woodman, Harold D. *King Cotton and His Retainers: Financing and Marketing the Cotton Crop of the South, 1800-1925.* Lexington: University of Kentucky Press, 1968.

—————, ed. *The Legacy of the American Civil War.* New York: John Wiley and Sons, 1973.

Woodward, C. Vann. *The Burden of Southern History.* Baton Rouge: Louisiana State University Press, 1968.

—————. *Origins of the New South, 1877-1913.* Baton Rouge: Louisiana State University Press, 1951.

—————. *Reunion and Reaction: The Compromise of 1877 and the End of Reconstruction.* Boston: Little, Brown and Company, 1951.

—————. *The Strange Career of Jim Crow.* London: Oxford University Press, 1966.

—————. *Tom Watson, Agrarian Rebel.* New York: Macmillan, 1938.

Wooster, Ralph A. *The People in Power: Courthouse and Statehouse in the Lower South 1850-1860.* Knoxville: University of Tennessee Press, 1969.

—————. *The Secession Conventions of the South.* Princeton: Princeton University Press, 1962.

Wright, Gavin. *The Political Economy of the Cotton South: Households, Markets, and Wealth in the Nineteenth Century.* New York: W. W. Norton, 1978.

PERIODICALS

Abbot, Martin. "Free Land, Free Labor, and the Freedmen's Bureau." *Agricultural History* 30 (1956): 150-56.

Alexander, Thomas B. "Persistent Whiggery in the Confederate South, 1860-1877." *Journal of Southern History* 27 (1961): 305-29.

Almand, Bond. "The Convention of 1877: The Making and Adoption of a New Constitution." *Georgia Bar Journal* 7 (1945): 419-31.

Anderson, Ralph V. "Slaves as Fixed Capital: Slave Labor and Southern Economic Development." *Journal of American History* 64 (1977): 24-46.

Anderson, William. "The Resignation of John B. Gordon from the United States Senate in 1880." *Georgia Historical Quarterly* 52 (1968): 438-42.

Bacote, Clarence A. "Negro Proscriptions, Protests, and Proposed Solutions, 1880-1910." *Journal of Southern History* 25 (1958): 471-98.

—————. "Some Aspects of Negro Life in Georgia, 1880-1908." *Journal of Negro History* 43 (1958): 186-213.

Blocker, Jack S., Jr. "The Politics of Reform: Populists, Prohibition, and Woman Suffrage, 1891-1892." *The Historian* 34 (1972): 614-32.

Bonner, James C. "Profile of a Late Ante-Bellum Community." *American Historical Review* 49 (1944): 663-80.

Brandon, William P. "Calling the Georgia Constitutional Convention of 1877." *Georgia Historical Quarterly* 17 (1933): 189-204.

Bull, Jacqueline P. "The General Merchant in the Economic History of the New South." *Journal of Southern History* 18 (1952): 37-59.

Clark, Thomas D. "The Furnishing and Supply System in Southern Agriculture since 1865." *Journal of Southern History* 12 (1946): 24-44.

Cochran, Thomas C. "Did the Civil War Retard Industrialization?" *Mississippi Valley Historical Review* 48 (1961): 197-210.

Cohen, William. "Negro Involuntary Servitude in the South, 1865-1940: A Preliminary Analysis." *Journal of Southern History* 42 (1976): 31-60.

Coleman, Kenneth. "The Georgia Gubernatorial Election of 1880." *Georgia Historical Quarterly* 25 (1941): 89-119.

Coulter, E. Merton. "Henry M. Turner: Georgia Negro Preacher-Politician during the Reconstruction Era." *Georgia Historical Quarterly* 47 (1964): 371-410.

_____. "The New South: Benjamin H. Hill's Speech before the Alumni Society of the University of Georgia, 1871." *Georgia Historical Quarterly* 57 (1973): 179-99.

Cox, LaWanda. "The Promise of Land for the Freedmen." *Mississippi Valley Historical Review* 45 (1958): 413-39.

Davis, Ronald F. "The U.S. Army and the Origins of Sharecropping in the Natchez District—A Case Study." *Journal of Negro History* 62(1977): 60-80.

DeCanio, Stephen J. "Productivity and Income Distribution in the Post-Bellum South." *Journal of Economic History* 34 (1974): 422-46.

DeSantis, Vincent P. "Negro Dissatisfaction with Republican Policy in the South, 1882-1884." *Journal of Negro History* 36 (1953): 148-59.

_____. "President Arthur and the Independent Movements in the South in 1882." *Journal of Southern History* 19 (1953): 346-63.

_____. "The Republican Party and the Southern Negro, 1877-1897." *Journal of Negro History* 45 (1960): 71-87.

Doster, James F. "The Georgia Railroad and Banking Company in the Reconstruction Era." *Georgia Historical Quarterly* 48 (1964): 1-32.

FitzSimons, Theodore B., Jr. "The Camilla Riot." *Georgia Historical Quarterly* 35 (1951): 116-25.

Floyd, Josephine Bone. "Rebecca Latimer Felton, Political Independent." *Georgia Historical Quarterly* 30 (1946): 14-34.

Foust, James D., and Dale E. Swan. "Productivity and Profitability of Antebellum Slave Labor: A Micro Approach." *Agricultural History* 44 (1970): 46-57.

Hackney, Sheldon. "Origins of the New South in Retrospect." *Journal of Southern History* 38 (1972): 191-216.

Harris, Carl V. "Right or Left Fork? The Section-Party Alignments of Southern Democrats in Congress, 1873-1897." *Journal of Southern History* 42 (1976): 471-506.

Higgs, Robert. "Patterns of Farm Rental in the Georgia Cotton Belt, 1880-1900." *Journal of Economic History* 34 (1974): 468-82.

Hopkins, Richard J. "Occupational and Geographic Mobility in Atlanta, 1870-1896." *Journal of Southern History* 24 (1968): 200-13.

Johnson, Michael P. "A New Look at the Popular Vote for Delegates to the Georgia Secession Convention." *Georgia Historical Quarterly* 56 (1972): 259-75.

Linden, Fabian. "Economic Democracy in the Slave South: An Appraisal of Some Recent Views." *Journal of Negro History* 31 (1946): 140-89.

Loewenberg, Bert James. "Efforts of the South to Encourage Immigration, 1865-1900." *South Atlantic Quarterly* 33 (1934): 377-84.

Mancini, Matthew H. "Race, Economics, and the Abandonment of Convict Leasing." *Journal of Negro History* 63 (1978): 339-52.

Matthews, John M. "Negro Republicans in the Reconstruction of Georgia." *Georgia Historical Quarterly* 60 (1976): 145-64.

McDaniel, Ruth Currie. "Black Power in Georgia: William A. Pledger and the Takeover of the Republican Party." *Georgia Historical Quarterly* 62 (1978): 225-39.

McKelvey, Blake. "Penal Slavery and Southern Reconstruction." *Journal of Negro History* 20 (1935): 153-79.

McKinney, Gordon B. "Southern Mountain Republicans and the Negro, 1865-1900." *Journal of Southern History* 41 (1975): 493-516.

Mitchell, Edward M. "H. I. Kimball: His Career and Defense." *Atlanta Historical Bulletin* 3 (1938): 249-83.

Range, Willard. "Hannibal I. Kimball." *Georgia Historical Quarterly* 29 (1945): 47-70.

Ransom, Roger L., and Richard Sutch. "Debt Peonage in the Cotton South after the Civil War." *Journal of Economic History* 32 (1972): 641-69.

_____. "The 'Lock-In' Mechanism and Overproduction of Cotton in the Post-Bellum South." *Agricultural History* 49 (1975): 405-25.

Reid, Joseph D., Jr. "Sharecropping in History and Theory." *Agricultural History* 49 (1975): 426-40.

Rensi, Ray C. "The Gospel according to Sam Jones." *Georgia Historical Quarterly* 60 (1976): 251-63.

Ringold, May Spencer. "Robert Newman Gourdin and the '1860 Association.' " *Georgia Historical Quarterly* 55 (1971): 501-509.

Roberts, Derrell C. "Joseph E. Brown and the Convict Lease System." *Georgia Historical Quarterly* 44 (1960): 399-410.

_____. "Joseph E. Brown and His Georgia Mines." *Georgia Historical Quarterly* 52 (1968): 285-92.

Rogers, William W. "The Negro Alliance in Alabama." *Journal of Negro History* 45 (1960): 38-44.

Russ, William A., Jr. "Radical Disfranchisement in Georgia, 1867-1871." *Georgia Historical Quarterly* 19 (1935): 175-201.

Scroggs, Jack B. "Southern Reconstruction: A Radical View." *Journal of Southern History* 24 (1958): 407-29.

Shugg, Roger W. "Survival of the Plantation System in Louisiana." *Journal of Southern History* 3 (1937): 311-25.

Talmadge, John E. "The Death Blow to Independentism in Georgia." *Georgia Historical Quarterly* 39 (1955): 37-47.

Taylor, A. Elizabeth. "The Origin and Development of the Convict Lease System in Georgia." *Georgia Historical Quarterly* 26 (1942): 113-28.

Thompson, William Y. "Robert Toombs and the Georgia Railroads." *Georgia Historical Quarterly* 40 (1956): 56-64.

Ward, Judson C., Jr. "The New Departure Democrats of Georgia: An Interpretation." *Georgia Historical Quarterly* 41 (1957): 227-36.

_____. "The Republican Party in Bourbon Georgia, 1872-1900." *Journal of Southern History* 9 (1943): 196-209.

Weiss, Thomas. "The Participation of Planters in Manufacturing in the Antebellum South." *Agricultural History* 48 (1974): 277-97.

Wiener, Jonathan M. "Planter-Merchant Conflict in Reconstruction Alabama." *Past and Present* 68 (1975): 73-94.

_____. "Planter Persistence and Social Change: Alabama, 1850-1870." *Journal of Interdisciplinary History* 7 (1976): 235-60.

Wilson, Richard L. "Sam Jones: An Apostle of the New South." *Georgia Historical Quarterly* 57 (1973): 459-74.

Wooster, Ralph A. "The Secession of the Lower South: An Examination of Changing Interpretations." *Civil War History* 7 (1961): 117-27.

Wright, Gavin. "Cotton Competition and the Post-Bellum Recovery of the American South." *Journal of Economic History* 34 (1974): 610-35.

_____. " 'Economic Democracy' and the Concentration of Agricultural Wealth in the Cotton South, 1850-1860." *Agricultural History* 44 (1970): 63-93.

Wright, Gavin, and Howard Konreuther. "Cotton, Corn and Risk in the Nineteenth Century." *Journal of Economic History* 35 (1975): 526-51.

Wynne, Lewis N. "The Farmers' Alliance: Georgia's Experiment in Agrarian Politics." *Atlanta Historical Bulletin* 17 (1972): 21-30.

Zeichner, Oscar. "The Legal Status of the Agricultural Laborer in the South." *Political Science Quarterly* 55 (1940): 412-28.

THESES AND DISSERTATIONS

‣ Adams, Olin B. "The Negro and the Agrarian Movement in Georgia, 1874-1890." Ph.D. diss., Florida State University, 1973.

Bacote, Clarence A. "The Negro in Georgia Politics, 1880-1908." Ph.D. diss., University of Chicago, 1955.

Coleman, Kenneth. "The Constitutional Convention of 1877." Master's thesis, University of Georgia, 1940.

Cooper, Fleeta. "The Triumvirate of Colquitt, Gordon, and Brown." Master's thesis, Emory University, 1931.

Crutcher, III, Luke Fain. "Disunity and Dissolution: The Georgia Parties and the Crisis of the Union, 1859-1861." Ph.D. diss., University of California, Los Angeles, 1974.

DeBats, Donald Arthur. "Elites and Masses: Political Structure, Communication and Behavior in Antebellum Georgia." Ph.D. diss., University of Wisconsin, 1973.

Doster, Helen Ophelia. "The Administration of Henry D. McDaniel as Governor of Georgia, 1883-1886." Master's thesis, University of Georgia, 1962.

Hunter, Joan Conerly. "Rebecca Latimer Felton." Master's thesis, University of Georgia, 1944.

Irons, George V. "The Secession Movement in Georgia, 1850-1861." Ph.D. diss., Duke University, 1936.

Jones, George L. "The Political Career of Henry Pattillo Farrow, Georgia Republican, 1865-1904." Master's thesis, University of Georgia, 1966.

——————. "William H. Felton and the Independent Democratic Movement in Georgia, 1870-1890." Ph.D. diss., University of Georgia, 1971.

Jones, Warren Lee. "Alexander H. Stephens, Governor of Georgia, 1882-1883." Master's thesis, University of Georgia, 1942.

Roberts, Derrell C. "Joseph E. Brown and the New South." Ph.D. diss., University of Georgia, 1958.

Shadgett, Olive Hall. "A History of the Republican Party in Georgia from Reconstruction through 1900." Ph.D. diss., University of Georgia, 1962.

Shipp, Muriel. "The Public Life of William Yates Atkinson." Master's thesis, University of Georgia, 1955.

Steelman, Lala Carr. "The Georgia Constitutional Convention of 1877." Master's thesis, University of North Carolina, 1946.

——————. "The Public Career of Augustus Octavius Bacon." Ph.D. diss., University of North Carolina, 1950.

Taylor, A. Elizabeth. "The Convict Lease System in Georgia, 1866-1908." Master's thesis, University of North Carolina, 1940.

Towery, James Gaston. "The Georgia Gubernatorial Campaign of 1886." Master's thesis, Emory University, 1945.

Ward, Judson Clements, Jr. "Georgia under the Bourbon Democrats, 1872-1890." Ph.D. diss., University of North Carolina, 1947.

Wingo, Horace Calvin. "Race Relations in Georgia, 1872-1908." Ph.D. diss., University of Georgia, 1969.

Wynne, Lewis N. "The Alliance Legislature of 1890." Master's thesis, University of Georgia, 1970.

Young, Edward Barham. "The Negro in Georgia Politics, 1867-1877." Master's thesis, Emory University, 1955.

INDEX